A COMPACT DICTIONARY

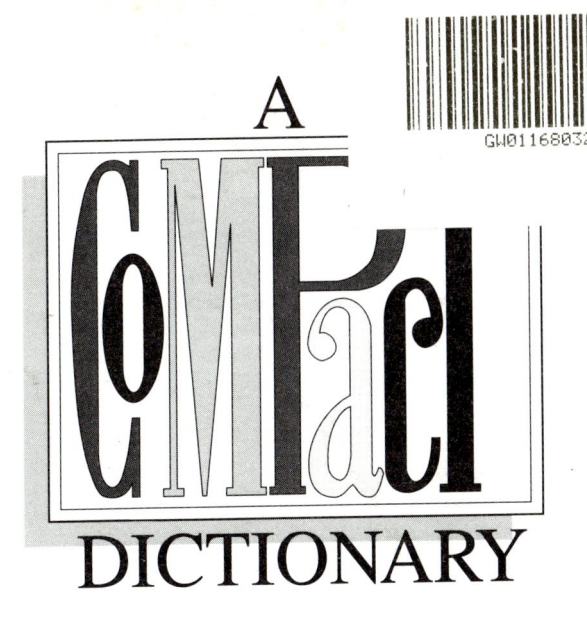

Edited by **Iseabail Macleod**
and **Patrick McLaughlin**
with **Alasdair Anderson**

BROUGHAM PRIMARY SCHOOL
BROUGHAM TERRACE
HARTLEPOOL CLEVELAND
TS24 8EY
TEL 273663

Schofield & Sims Ltd. Huddersfield

© **1991 Schofield & Sims Ltd.**

All rights reserved.
No part of this publication may be reproduced,
stored in a retrieval system, or transmitted
in any form, or by any means, electronic,
mechanical, photocopying, recording or otherwise,
without the prior permission of Schofield & Sims Ltd.

0 7217 0653 3

First printed 1991

Designed by Graphic Art Concepts, Leeds
Printed in Great Britain by The Bath Press, Avon

Introduction

This dictionary moves a step further than the *Concise Junior Dictionary* in providing 9 to 13-year-olds with a bridge towards adult dictionaries. Its main aim is to include as much information as possible in its limited space and give special prominence to areas, such as leisure, which are known to interest children of this age group. Numerous new words, such as aerobics, fax, hatchback, reggae, VDU, which may not be found in other dictionaries for this age group, are included, among them computer terms (which may be more familiar to today's children than to many adults).

Great efforts have been made to keep the information as clear as possible, both in wording and typography. This inevitably takes up a great deal of space, and so certain types of information have been deliberately omitted to allow for a wide vocabulary. Words omitted include obvious derivative words, such as nouns and adverbs formed from adjectives, verbs from nouns, etc., for example **loudness**, **loudly** from **loud**.

As in the *Concise Junior Dictionary*, pronouns, conjunctions and prepositions have been left out, on the grounds that they are already known to this age group and are unlikely to be looked up.

Pronunciation is only indicated (in a simple respelling system) where it might otherwise cause difficulty. Most problems with pronunciation are with stress, and in all pronunciation keys the stressed syllable is printed in bold type. The dictionary always notes where a word has two pronunciations, for example differing stress on a noun and a verb:

record *noun* [**re**cord] ....
       verb [ri**cord**] ....

A companion book of exercises, **Compact Dictionary Exercises**, is available. It is based on the dictionary entries and aims to develop skills in the use of the dictionary, the discrimination of similar words, the use of words in sentences and in building up vocabulary.

Compact Dictionary Exercises   0 7217 0654 1

A

abacus a wire frame with beads for counting.

abandon 1 to leave, often for ever. 2 to give up.

abate to grow less.

abattoir a place where animals are brought to be killed for meat.

abbess a woman who is head of an abbey.

abbey a place where monks or nuns live; a church which belongs to it or used to belong to it.

abbot a man who is head of an abbey.

abbreviation a shortened word, for example **Dr** (Doctor), **Rd** (Road).

abdomen the lower part of the body containing the stomach etc.

abduct to take (someone) away against their will, usually by force.

abeyance: in abeyance not in use.

abhor to hate very much.

abide 1 (*old-fashioned*) to stay. 2 to put up with. 3 **abide by** to follow, keep to (a rule etc.).

ability being able to do things.

abject pitiful, wretched, worthless.

able 1 having the power to do something. 2 clever, talented.

abnormal unusual, strange.

aboard on(to) a ship or aircraft.

abode a dwelling-place, home.

abolish to get rid of (something).

abominable very unpleasant, hateful.

aborigines the original inhabitants of a country, especially Australia.

abortion the loss of an unborn child, often by deliberate act.

abound to have plenty of (something).

abrasion a small cut or scrape.

abreast one beside the other, in line.

abridged of a book, shortened.

abroad in or to another country.

abruptly very quickly, suddenly.

abscess a kind of boil or collection of pus in the body.

abseil [absyle] to climb down from a high place using a rope.

absence being absent.

absent not here, not present.

absolutely quite, completely.

absorb 1 to soak up. 2 to take up all the attention of.

abstain to hold off (from doing something).

abstemious careful, not taking too much in eating and drinking usually.

abstinence going without something you like.

abstract *adjective* existing only in the mind.
noun a summary of a document.

abstruse difficult to understand.

absurd silly, without any sense.

abundance a great amount of something, plenty.

abundant plentiful.

abuse *noun* [rhymes with 'loose']
1 a wrong use of something. 2 very insulting language.
verb [rhymes with 'fuse'] 1 to use wrongly. 2 to use insulting language to.

abysmal very bad.

abyss a bottomless pit.

academy 1 a college or school. 2 a society concerned with higher studies.

accelerate to increase speed.

accent 1 the way people speak a language. 2 the stress or emphasis on a word or syllable.

accept to take something which is offered or given.

access the way into something.

accessible within reach.

accessory an item of clothing, for example, which is additional to the main outfit.

accident something bad that happens by chance.

acclaim to praise publicly.

acclimatise to become used to a new climate, your surroundings etc.

accommodate 1 to find room for. 2 to change to suit other people or conditions.

accommodation somewhere to live or stay.

accompaniment something which accompanies, especially music which supports a soloist.

accompanist someone who accompanies a singer or another musician.

accompany 1 to go with. 2 to play a musical instrument along with.

accomplice someone who helps another especially in crime.

accomplish to finish, achieve.

accord agreement, harmony.

accordion a hand-held musical instrument operated by bellows and keys or buttons.

account *noun* 1 a bill showing money to be paid. 2 a story, description. *verb* **account for** to explain how something happened.

accountant a person who looks after money, for example for a business.

accumulate to gather more and more.

accurate exactly right.

accursed under a curse, hateful.

accuse to say that someone has done something wrong.

accustomed to used to.

ace 1 the playing card in each suit which has one spot, usually the highest card. 2 an expert, a person who is very good at something.

ache a pain in some part of the body.

achieve to manage to do something, usually with effort.

acid a strong liquid that can burn things.

acknowledge 1 to admit that something is true or really exists. 2 to write to say that you have received something.

acne a skin disorder which produces pimples.

acorn the seed of the oak tree.

acoustic 1 of sound or hearing. 2 of a guitar etc., not amplified by electricity.

acoustics 1 the study of sounds. 2 the quality of sound in a particular place.

acquaintance a person you know (slightly).

acquire to gain possession of, to get.

acquit to declare (someone) to be innocent of a crime.

acre a unit of area used in measuring land, equal to 4840 square yards (about 4000 square metres).

acrid smelling and tasting very bitter.

acrimony bitterness, especially of speech.

acrobat someone who does leaping and balancing tricks, for example in a circus.

acronym a word formed from the initial letters of other words, for example UNO for United Nations Organisation.

act *verb* 1 to do something. 2 to perform on stage. *noun* a part of a play.

action doing something; something done.

active lively.

actor a man who performs in a play, film or on television.

actress a woman who performs in a play, film or on television.

actual real and clear.

acumen quickness of mind and judgement.

acupuncture a type of healing using needles applied to parts of the body.

acute 1 sharp; severe. 2 (of an angle) less than 90 degrees. 3 **acute accent** a sign ′ put over a vowel to change its sound.

adage an old saying or proverb.

adamant very hard, stubborn.

adapt to make suitable for a new or different purpose.

add 1 to put together with something else. 2 to find the total of two or more numbers.

adder a small poisonous snake found in Britain.

addict someone who depends very much on something (for example a drug).

additive something added in small quantities, to food, for example.

address *noun* the house, street and town where you live.
verb 1 to write to, to speak to. 2 to write an address on (a parcel or envelope).

adept very skilful, very good (at something).

adequate just enough and no more.

adhere to stick (to something).

adhesive *adjective* sticky.
noun a sticky substance for sticking things together.

adjacent next to, right beside.

adjective a word which describes something.

adjoin to lie alongside.

adjourn to put off till later.

adjudicate to judge, act as a judge, especially in a competition.

adjust to put in order, to arrange, especially for a special purpose.

administer 1 to manage the affairs of. 2 to give (punishment or medicine).

administration the management of an organisation; the government of a country.

admiral the most important officer in the Navy.

admire to think well of (someone or something).

admission being allowed in (to a place or group); what you pay for this.

admit 1 to agree that something has happened or is true. 2 to allow (somebody or something) to enter.

admonish to tell someone off, to warn.

ado fuss, bother.

adolescence the time of being an adolescent.

adolescent someone half-way between being a child and an adult.

adopt to take (someone else's child) into your family and care for it as if it was your own.

adore to love very much.

adorn to decorate.

adrift floating on water helplessly in a boat or on a raft.

adroit clever, skilful.

adulation very great or too much praise.

adult a grown-up person.

adultery being unfaithful to a husband or wife.

advance to move forward.

advantage something which helps you, especially if it puts you in a better position than others.

advent 1 the arrival, coming. 2 **Advent** the four weeks before Christmas.

adventure an exciting happening.

adverb a word which tells you about a verb, an adjective or another adverb.

adversary an enemy, opponent.

adverse unfavourable, against you.

adversity trouble, misfortune.

advertise to make well-known, for example in a newspaper.

advice what you say to someone to help them.

advise to tell other people what you think they should do.

advocate to speak in favour of (something).

aerate to put bubbles of air or gas into a liquid.

aerial *noun* a wire which sends out or picks up radio or television signals. *adjective* of or in the air.

aerobatics tricks performed by aeroplanes.

aerobics very active exercise aimed at strengthening the body.

aeroplane a flying machine.

aerosol a container of liquid and gas under pressure which is squirted out in the form of a mist.

aesthetic 1 concerning beauty or the appreciation of beauty. 2 pleasing to the eye or ear.

affable good-natured.

affair 1 a thing, event, business. 2 **affairs** business of any kind.

affect to cause (things or people) to change.

affectionate showing love for somebody or something.

affiliated (to) connected with an organisation.

afflict to hurt, cause harm to.

affluent wealthy, rich.

afford to be able to pay for.

affront to annoy, upset, insult.

afraid frightened, full of fear.

aft near or towards the back of a ship or aeroplane.

after behind, following.

aftermath the result of something that has happened.

afternoon the time of the day between morning and early evening.

against 1 on the opposite side to (in a fight or a game). 2 next to and touching someone or something.

agate a kind of stone with coloured bands, used in jewellery.

age 1 how old a person is. 2 a special time in history such as the **Stone Age**.

aged 1 [ayjd] of a certain age. 2 [**ay**jid] very old.

agency 1 the means by which something is done. 2 the (place of) business of an agent or representative.

agenda a list of things to be discussed or done, especially at a meeting.

agent a person who acts for another.

aggravate 1 to make worse. 2 to annoy.

aggression an attack, hostility towards others.

aggressive acting with aggression.

aghast terrified, amazed, shocked.

agile quick-moving, nimble.

agitate to shake, stir; to make anxious, disturb.

ago in the past.

agog very eager, amazed.

agonise to suffer or worry (about something).

agony very great pain.

agree 1 to think the same as someone else. 2 to say that you will do something.

agriculture cultivating the land or rearing animals, farming.

aground (of a boat) caught in sand or rocks in shallow water.

ahead in front.

aid help.

aikido a Japanese form of self-defence, now often used as a sport.

aileron a flap at the back edge of the wing for guiding an aeroplane.

ailment a (slight) illness.

aim 1 to point at, for example with a gun. 2 to try to do something.

air *noun* what you breathe.
verb to make (clothes or a room) fresh by letting air into them.

aircraft an aeroplane.

airport a place where aircraft land and take off.

aisle [like 'I'll'] a passageway in a church or theatre.

ajar partly open.

akimbo (of the arms) with hands on hips and elbows turned out.

alabaster a kind of smooth white stone used for making ornaments, for example.

alacrity quickness.

alarm 1 a warning bell or other sound. 2 a sudden fright.

alas a word used when you are feeling very sad.

albatross a kind of large seabird.

albino a person or animal with no natural colouring.

album 1 a book for keeping a collection of things such as stamps. 2 a long-playing record.

alcohol 1 a colourless liquid found in wine, beer and spirits. 2 a drink containing this liquid.

alcoholic *adjective* containing alcohol.
noun a person who makes him- or herself ill by regularly drinking too much alcohol.

alcove a bend in the wall of a room etc. to produce an extra space.

alderman a city or town councillor next to the mayor in rank.

ale a kind of beer.

alert ready to act, wide awake.

algae very simple small plants found in or near water.

algebra a branch of mathematics in which letters and signs are used to represent numbers.

alias a name you use other than your own.

alibi saying that you were somewhere else when a crime was committed.

alien foreign, strange.

alienate to make (someone) an enemy.

alight *adverb* on fire, burning.
verb to come to land; to come down out of a train or bus, for example.

align to make into a line or lines.

alimony money due to be paid by a husband to a wife after divorce or separation.

alive living, not dead.

alkali a substance that reduces the power of acids.

all everything; everyone.

allay to soothe, relieve.

allege to make a statement without proof.

allegiance loyalty to a government or a sovereign, for example.

allergic made ill by certain foods or things.

alleviate to relieve, lessen.

alley a very narrow street between buildings.

alliance an agreement or union between countries or groups.

alligator a kind of crocodile.

alliteration words starting with the same letter.

allocate to share out.

allow to let someone do something.

allowance money given for a particular purpose, especially regularly.

alloy a mixture of metals.

allude (to) to refer to (something) indirectly.

allure charm, attractiveness.

alluring attractive.

ally someone who helps you, for example in a battle.

almighty having all power.

almond a kind of nut used in cooking.

almost nearly, not quite.

alms [rhymes with 'palms'] (*old-fashioned*) money or goods given to the poor.

aloft high up.

alone by yourself.

aloof not friendly, not willing to talk to others.

aloud in a voice loud enough to be heard.

alphabet the letters of a language in a fixed order, A, B, C and so on.

altar the holy table in church.

alter to make something different in some way, to change.

alternate every other one.

alternative one or the other of two things.

altimeter an instrument for showing height above sea level.

altitude height above sea-level.

alto a singing voice between soprano and tenor.

altogether counting everybody or everything.

altruism unselfishness, fondness for others.

aluminium a very light silvery-coloured metal.

always for ever, at all times.

amalgam a mixture of two or more substances.

amalgamate to join together, combine.

amateur someone who does something for love of it rather than for money, as a hobby rather than as a job.

amazing very surprising.

ambassador someone who represents his or her country in a foreign country.

amber 1 a hard, clear, yellow or brownish substance used to make jewellery, for example. 2 the colour of the traffic light which means prepare to stop or go.

ambidextrous able to use left or right hand equally well.

ambiguous having more than one possible meaning, uncertain.

ambition a strong desire to do well.

ambitious keen to do well at something.

amble to walk in a slow or relaxed way.

ambulance a van to carry sick or injured people.

ambush hiding to make a surprise attack.

amen the ending of a prayer.

amenable able to be persuaded (to do something).

amend to change, to improve.

amethyst a purple precious stone.

amiable friendly, likeable.

amicable friendly.

amid in the middle of.

amiss wrong, not in its proper place.

ammunition things you can throw or shoot from a weapon to hurt others.

amnesia loss of memory.

amnesty a pardon given to a whole group of people.

amoeba [ameeba] a very small creature consisting of a single cell.

amok: run amok to become mad and cause a lot of damage.

amorous showing love for someone.

amount a quantity, a sum, for example of money.

amphibian 1 an animal which can live on land and in water. 2 a vehicle for use on land or water.

ample (more than) enough.

amplifier a machine for increasing loudness, of music, for example.

amputate to cut off (a limb or part of a limb).

amulet an object worn to keep away evil, a charm.

amuse to make (someone) laugh or smile.

anachronism placing something in the wrong period of time.

anaconda a kind of large South American snake that kills by crushing.

anaemia an unhealthy state when your blood has too few red cells.

anaesthetic a drug which causes lack of feeling in a part of the body or unconsciousness.

anagram a word or phrase formed by changing the order of letters in another word or phrase.

analyse to divide (something) into the parts which make it up; to examine in this way.

analysis a detailed examination of something.

anarchy complete lack of control or order.

anatomy the study of the bodies of human beings or animals.

ancestor someone in your family who lived before you.

anchor a heavy metal hook used to stop a ship from moving.

anchovy a kind of small fish of the herring family.

ancient very old, belonging to long ago.

anecdote a little story, especially an amusing or interesting one.

anemone [anemony] 1 kind of small garden or wild flower. 2 a sea anemone.

angel someone who is believed to bring messages from God.

angle the space between two straight lines which meet at a point.

angora 1 a kind of long-haired goat or rabbit. 2 fine wool made from the hair of the angora goat or rabbit.

angry wanting to hurt or harm someone because of something.

anguish great sorrow or mental pain.

animal a living creature that can move.

animated 1 (of a cartoon) given the appearance of motion in a series of pictures shown at speed. 2 lively.

animosity strong dislike towards someone.

aniseed a kind of seed with a strong flavour like liquorice.

ankle the joint between the leg and the foot.

annals historical accounts of events.

annex(e) a building added to another building.

anniversary the same date each year that something happened in the past.

announce to say things to a lot of people.

annoy to make (somebody) upset or angry.

annual *adjective* happening every year. *noun* a book which comes out each year.

anoint to smear with oil for a religious reason.

anonymous of which the name of the author etc. is not known.

anorak a waterproof jacket with a hood.

anorexia an illness causing great loss of appetite.

answer what you say or write when asked a question.

ant a small insect that lives in large groups.

antagonist an opponent, enemy.

Antarctic (of) the area round the South Pole.

antelope an animal like a deer, found in Africa.

antenatal before birth.

antenna 1 the feeler of an insect. 2 an aerial for a television set, for example.

anteroom a room leading into a larger room.

anthem a song of praise, especially a religious song sung by a church choir.

anthology a collection of stories, poems etc.

anthropology the scientific study of mankind.

antibiotic a kind of drug which destroys harmful germs.

anticipate to think about in advance; to do something before someone else; to expect.

anticlimax something dull or disappointing after something exciting.

anticlockwise in the opposite direction to clockwise.

antics strange or playful games or tricks.

antidote a substance which stops a poison or a disease from harming you.

antifreeze a substance added to water to keep it from freezing.

antipathy a deep hatred.

antique *adjective* very old (and valuable because of its age).
noun an object, such as a piece of furniture or jewellery, which is very old and usually valuable.

antiseptic (a substance) which destroys germs.

antler one of the two branched horns of a male deer.

anvil the iron stand on which a blacksmith hammers metal.

anxiety being anxious.

anxious worried.

apart away from others; away from each other.

apartheid (the policy of) keeping people of different races apart, especially in South Africa.

apartment 1 a single room in a house or building. 2 a set of rooms, a flat.

apathy lack of interest.

ape a large monkey.

aperture a narrow opening, especially one which lets light into a camera.

apex the tip or highest point of something.

aphid a kind of small insect which feeds on plants.

apiary a place where bees are kept.

aplomb self-confidence, especially in difficult circumstances.

apologise to say you are sorry for something you may have done or not done.

apology an act of apologising.

apoplectic very upset with anger or rage.

appalled shocked, horrified.

apparatus instruments, tools or equipment.

apparel clothing, dress.

apparent easily seen or understood; seeming to be true, though not necessarily so.

appeal to ask for something needed.

appear 1 to come into view. 2 to seem to be.

appendicitis a disease caused by inflammation of the appendix.

appendix 1 a small tube in the body, attached to the intestines. 2 a part added to the end of a book.

appetite the wish to eat.

applaud to clap your hands together to show pleasure.

apple a round hard fruit.

applicant a person who asks for or applies for something, for example a job.

apply 1 **apply for** to ask for (something), especially in writing.
2 **apply to** to affect, concern. 3 to put on (an ointment etc.).

appoint to give a job to.

appointment a time set aside to see someone.

appreciate 1 to think highly of. 2 to understand. 3 to become more valuable.

apprehensive afraid, nervous.

apprentice a young person who is learning a trade.

approach to come near to.

approbation good opinion, praise.

appropriate suitable, proper.

approve 1 to think well of. 2 to agree to.

approximately very nearly, not exactly.

apricot a round soft yellow fruit with a stone in it.

apron a piece of cloth you put on top of your clothes to keep them clean.

apt 1 suitable, fitting. 2 **apt to** likely to.

aqualung a breathing apparatus used by divers.

aquarium a glass or plastic container to keep fish in.

aquatic growing, living or taking place in water.

aqueduct a bridge which carries water across land.

aquiline of or like an eagle.

arable (of land) suitable or used for growing crops.

arbitrary decided without the use of rules or reason.

arcade a covered passageway, especially one with shops, amusement machines, for example.

arch a curved part of a building or bridge.

archaeology the study of people in the past by looking at buildings and objects left behind.

archaic out of date, old-fashioned.

archangel a chief angel.

archbishop a chief bishop.

archer a person who shoots with a bow and arrow.

archery the art or sport of shooting with bows and arrows.

architect a person who makes the plans for a building.

archives historical records; the place where they are stored.

arctic 1 **Arctic** (of) the area round the North Pole. 2 **arctic** very cold.

ardent feeling very strongly, passionate.

arduous hard, difficult.

area 1 a piece of land or sea. 2 the size of a surface.

arena a place where public contests or performances take place.

argue to discuss with disagreement.

argument a disagreement, a fight with words.

arid dry.

arise 1 to come into being. 2 (*old-fashioned*) to rise.

artistocrat a person of noble family.

arithmetic working in numbers, adding, subtracting, multiplying and dividing.

arm the part of the body between the shoulder and the hand.

armadillo a kind of small American animal whose body is protected by hard plates.

armaments equipment for war.

armour a covering of metal worn by soldiers in battle.

armoury a storage place for weapons.

army a large number of soldiers.

aroma a pleasant smell.

arouse to wake from sleep; to make lively or excited.

arrange 1 to put in the right order. 2 to make plans for.

arrears: in arrears behind with payments.

arrest to make (someone) a prisoner.

arrive to reach the place you are going to.

arrogant too proud, thinking yourself better than others.

arrow 1 the straight sharp piece of wood which is shot from a bow. 2 a sign shaped like an arrow to show direction.

arsenic a kind of poison.

arson the crime of setting fire to property on purpose.

art the making of pictures or sculpture.

artery a tube carrying blood from the heart to other parts of the body.

artichoke one of two kinds of vegetables whose flower-head (**globe artichoke**) or root (**Jerusalem artichoke**) is eaten.

article 1 a thing. 2 a piece of writing in a newspaper or magazine.

articulate able to speak well and clearly.

articulated (of a lorry etc.) having joints that allow the parts to move separately.

artificial not natural; made by people.

artillery large guns; the part of an army that uses them.

artist 1 a person who makes pictures or sculpture. 2 a person who performs on a stage etc.

artistic of artists; having the abilities of an artist.

asbestos a kind of mineral which will not burn.

ascend to climb, go up.

ascent 1 an act of ascending. 2 an upward slope.

ash 1 the grey powder left after a fire. 2 a kind of large tree.

ashamed feeling bad about something you have done or not done.

ashore on land.

aside to one side.

asinine stupid, like an ass.

ask 1 to put a question to. 2 **ask for** to say that you want (something).

askew off the straight.

asleep sleeping.

asp a kind of small poisonous snake.

asparagus a kind of plant whose young shoots are eaten as a vegetable.

aspect look, appearance, view.

aspen a kind of tree whose leaves shake in the slightest wind.

asphalt a tar-like mixture used as a surface on roads, for example.

asphyxiate suffocate, stop the breath of.

aspire to to try to get or do (especially something difficult).

aspirin a kind of medicine which helps to relieve pain, a tablet of this.

ass a donkey.

assassin a person who assassinates.

assassinate to murder, especially for political reasons.

assault a sudden and violent attack.

assembly a large group of people gathered together.

assent *verb* to agree (to). *noun* agreement.

assert to state strongly.

assess to work out the value of (something).

asset 1 something of value that belongs to you. 2 a help.

assiduous hard-working.

assist to help.

associate with 1 to join for a purpose. 2 to connect in thought with.

association 1 a group of people working together for a particular purpose. 2 the act of associating.

assorted various, mixed.

assortment a mixture of different things.

assume 1 to accept as true without proper proof. 2 to take on.

assure to tell (someone) something for certain.

assured confident; certain.

aster a kind of brightly coloured garden flower.

asterisk a star-shaped mark * used to draw attention to something, for example.

asthma a disease which makes breathing difficult.

astonish to surprise very much.

astound to surprise greatly, to shock.

astray wandering away.

astrology the study of how the sun, moon, stars and planets are believed to influence people's lives and characters.

astronaut someone who flies in a spacecraft.

astronomy the scientific study of the sun, moon, planets and stars.

astute wise, clever, especially in business.

asylum 1 a place of safety or refuge. 2 an old name for a centre for the care of the mentally ill.

atheist a person who does not believe in God.

athlete a person who is trained for sports.

athletics sports such as running, jumping etc.

atlas a book of maps.

atmosphere the air round the earth.

atoll a coral island or reef.

atom the smallest possible part of anything.

atomic energy nuclear energy.

atrocious very bad, very wicked.

attach to fix on to something.

attack to start to fight with.

attempt to try.

attend 1 to be present. 2 **attend to** to look after.

attention care given to doing a job or in listening.

attic a room just under the roof of a house.

attire clothes.

attitude thoughts and feelings you have towards someone or something.

attract 1 to win the liking of. 2 to make things come closer.

attractive good-looking; giving pleasure.

attribute to consider as belonging to (someone or something).

aubergine a kind of vegetable with a purple skin.

auburn (of hair) reddish-brown.

auction a sale in which goods are sold to the person who offers the highest price.

audacious bold, daring.

audacity being audacious.

audible loud enough to be heard.

audience people who listen to or watch a play or a concert, for example.

audit to examine (financial accounts).

audition a test to see whether an actor, singer etc. is good enough to perform.

aunt a father's or mother's sister; the wife of an uncle.

au pair a person who lives with a family in a foreign country in return for light duties.

aural concerned with the ear or hearing.

auspicious favourable, promising.

austere 1 living without luxury. 2 severe towards self and others.

author a person who writes books.

authority the power to make people do what you want.

autobiography a writer's own life story.

autograph a person's name written by themselves.

automatic working by itself.

automobile a car.

autonomy the power of self-government.

autumn the season between summer and winter.

auxiliary helping.

available able to be used, seen etc.

avalanche a large amount of snow suddenly rushing down a mountainside.

avarice greed, especially for money.

avenge to punish someone for something they did wrong to you or another person.

avenue a road often with trees along the sides.

average *noun* a number worked out by adding up a number of quantities and dividing the total by the number of quantities.
adjective 1 (of an amount) reached by working out the average. 2 usual, ordinary.

averse not fond of, opposed (to).

avert 1 to stop from happening. 2 to turn (the eyes for example) away (from something).

aviary a place where birds are kept.

aviation the art or practice of flying aircraft.

avid eager.

avoid to keep away from.

await to wait for.

awake not sleeping.

award a prize for something you have done.

aware knowing about something.

awe a feeling of great respect or fear.

awful very bad.

awkward 1 clumsy. 2 difficult to use or deal with.

awl a pointed tool for boring small holes.

axe a sharp-edged piece of metal on a long handle, used for chopping wood.

axle the bar that joins the wheels of a car or cart.

azure sky blue.

B

babble to talk without making much sense.

baboon a kind of large monkey with a long snout and tail.

baby a very young child.

bachelor a man who is not married.

back 1 the part furthest from the front. 2 the part of the body between the neck and the bottom of the spine.

backbone the long row of bones down the middle of your back.

backfire 1 to go wrong. 2 to make an explosive noise in the exhaust of a car.

backing 1 material put at the back of something, for example a picture. 2 support. 3 a musical accompaniment.

backstroke a stroke used in swimming when lying on your back.

bacon salted or smoked meat from the back or sides of a pig.

bacteria disease-producing germs.

bad not good.

badge a special sign you wear to show your school or club, for example.

badger an animal with a black and white face which burrows in the ground.

badminton a game like tennis played indoors.

baffle to confuse, puzzle.

bag a container with an open top.

baggage bags and cases used when travelling.

bagpipes a wind instrument with a bag and several pipes.

bail *noun* 1 a small piece of wood placed on the stumps at cricket. 2 money paid to allow someone out of prison as a promise that they will appear in court later.
verb to empty water from the bottom of a boat.

bait something used in a trap or on a hook to attract an animal or a fish.

baize a kind of thick woollen cloth, usually green, used to cover snooker tables for example.

bake to cook in an oven.

balance *verb* to stay steady.
noun a machine for weighing things.

balcony 1 a raised floor in a theatre or cinema. 2 a platform outside a window.

bald having no hair on the head.

balderdash nonsense.

bale *noun* a large amount of goods or material tied together.
verb to empty water from the bottom of a boat.

balk 1 to hinder, stop (something being done). 2 to refuse to do something.

ball 1 a round object, often used in games. 2 a special event with dancing.

ballad a simple song or poem that tells a story.

ballast heavy material put in a boat or ship to keep it steady in the water.

ballerina a female ballet dancer.

ballet a graceful dance, often one telling a story.

balloon a rubber bag which rises when filled with air or gas.

ballot a kind of secret vote to choose someone or something.

balsa-wood a very light kind of wood.

balustrade a hard rail supported by posts on a balcony for example.

bamboo a kind of grass with stiff, hollow stems.

bamboozle to trick or puzzle (someone).

ban not to allow something.

banal very ordinary, boring.

banana a long sweet fruit with a yellow skin.

band 1 a group of musicians playing together. 2 a strip of material used to hold things together or as a decoration. 3 a group of people.

bandage a strip of material used to wind round a wound to protect it.

bandit a thief, a robber.

bandy(-legged) having legs that curve outward at the knee.

bang 1 a sharp blow. 2 a sudden loud noise.

bangle a bracelet.

banish to send away for a long time, especially out of a country as a punishment.

banister a handrail beside a staircase.

banjo a musical instrument played by plucking the strings.

bank 1 the side of a river. 2 a place where money is looked after. 3 a pile of earth or sand with sloping sides.

bankrupt having no money so that you are unable to pay your debts.

banner a flag hanging from a pole, mast or rope.

banns public announcement that a marriage is going to take place.

banquet a feast; a large public meal.

bantam a small kind of hen.

banter friendly chat of a joking kind.

baptise to christen; to give a name to.

bar 1 a rod of metal or wood. 2 a division in music. 3 a counter where drinks and sometimes food are served.

barb a V-shaped point, for example on a fish-hook.

barbarian an uncivilised, coarse person.

barbecue 1 a frame for cooking meat on out of doors. 2 a party at which food is cooked in this way.

barber a men's hairdresser.

bard a poet.

bare 1 having no clothes or covering on, naked. 2 empty.

bargain something bought cheaply.

barge a boat with a flat bottom, used on a canal or river.

baritone a male voice or instrument between tenor and bass.

bark 1 the noise made by a dog. 2 the hard covering round a tree or branch.

barley a kind of grain used as food and in making beer and whisky.

barn a storehouse on a farm.

barnacle a very small shellfish which grips tightly to rocks, bottoms of ships etc.

barometer an instrument for measuring air pressure as a way of forecasting weather.

baron a lord, a nobleman.

barracks a building where soldiers live.

barrage 1 a constant flow of bullets, shells, words etc. 2 a bar across a river to dam the water.

barrel 1 a large round container, flat at each end. 2 the long tube of a gun out of which the bullets are fired.

barren not able to produce young, crops, fruit etc.

barricade a barrier for defence, especially one put up in a hurry.

barrier something, like a fence or gate, put up to stop you going somewhere.

barrister a lawyer who takes cases to a high court.

barrow a small cart that is pushed.

barter to exchange goods for other goods.

basalt a kind of hard dark rock thrown up by a volcano.

base 1 the bottom part. 2 where someone or something started out from.

basement a room or space under a building, a cellar.

bashful shy.

basic forming a base, necessary.

basil a kind of herb used as a flavouring in cooking.

basin a wide round bowl, usually for food or washing in.

basis something which underlies or supports something else.

bask to lie in the sun or in something warm.

basket a bag or container made of woven cane, straw etc.

basketball a game in which two teams try to throw a ball into a metal hoop.

bass [baiss] the lowest voice or instrument in music.

bassoon a long low-toned woodwind musical instrument.

baste 1 to pour melted fat over (meat) when roasting. 2 to stitch together with long loose stitches.

bat 1 the piece of wood used to strike a ball (in cricket, for example). 2 a small mouse-like animal that flies at night.

batch a number of things together, for example loaves being baked.

bath a water container you can lie or sit in to wash yourself.

bathe 1 to swim or play in water. 2 to wash (a wound, for example).

batman an army officer's servant.

baton 1 a short stick used by the conductor of an orchestra or choir. 2 a short club carried by a policeman, for example.

battalion a division of a regiment of soldiers.

batter *verb* to strike again and again. *noun* a thin mixture of milk, flour and eggs, used in cooking.

battery 1 a closed container which stores electricity. 2 a series of cages in which chickens, for example, are kept.

battle a fight between two large groups of people.

bawl to cry or shout loudly.

bay a place where the shore curves inwards.

bayonet a long knife put at the end of a gun.

bazaar 1 a market in Eastern countries. 2 a sale of goods to help a church or school, for example.

beach land by the sea, usually covered with sand or small stones.

beacon a warning light or fire set up on a high place.

beads small pieces of glass, wood, plastic etc. which are threaded on to a string.

beagle a kind of small hound used for hunting.

beak the hard pointed mouth of a bird.

beaker 1 a drinking mug, often without a handle. 2 a glass for pouring liquids in chemistry.

beam 1 a large heavy piece of wood or metal. 2 a ray of light.

bean a seed of the bean-plant, used for food.

bear *noun* a large hairy animal with very strong teeth and claws.
verb 1 to carry. 2 to put up with.

beard hair growing on a man's face.

bearing 1 the way a person carries him- or herself. 2 the position or direction something lies in.

beast an animal, especially a four-footed one.

beat 1 to hit again and again. 2 to keep time in music with a stick. 3 to do better than (someone) in a game or fight.

beautiful having very good looks, looking lovely.

beauty being beautiful; a very beautiful person or thing.

beaver an animal found in cool lands, near to water or in water.

beckon to call (someone) with a movement of the hand or head.

bed 1 a piece of furniture for sleeping on. 2 a part of a garden where plants are grown. 3 the bottom of the sea or of a river.

bedlam a scene of uproar and confusion.

bedraggled wet, dirty and untidy.

bee an insect with a sting which makes honey.

beech a kind of tree with smooth grey bark.

beef meat from cattle.

beer an alcoholic drink made from barley.

beetle an insect with wings which fold to form a hard back.

beetroot a dark-red vegetable used in salads.

before 1 in front of; earlier than. 2 in past times.

beg to ask someone for money or goods.

beggar someone who lives by begging.

begin to start.

beguile to amuse, to pass (time) pleasantly.

behave to act in a certain way, especially to act well towards others.

behaviour the way you behave.

behind at the back of.

beige a very light brown colour.

being something that is alive.

belch to let wind from the stomach pass noisily through your mouth.

belfry the part of a tower where bells are hung.

belief what you feel to be true.

believe to feel sure that something is true, to trust in something.

bell 1 a piece of rounded metal which rings when you hit it. 2 something which is rung to attract attention, for example a **doorbell**.

belligerent quarrelsome.

bellow to shout loudly, to roar like a bull.

bellows an instrument for blowing air into a fire, organ pipes etc.

belong 1 to be your own. 2 to be part of.

below underneath; lower down.

belt a narrow piece of cloth, leather, plastic etc. worn round the waist.

bench 1 a long wooden seat. 2 a work-table.

bend *noun* a turn, a curve, in a road, for example.
verb to make something turned or curved.

beneath under, below.

benediction a blessing.

benefactor a person who does good to others, especially by giving money.

beneficial helpful.

benefit to do good to.

benevolent kind, generous, doing good.

benign gentle, mild; of an illness, not causing death.

bequeath to leave someone (something) in a will.

bequest something bequeathed.

bereaved having lost someone close to you by death.

bereavement being bereaved.

beret [**be**ray] a soft round cap, sometimes worn by soldiers.

berry a small juicy fruit.

berserk wild, mad.

berth 1 a ship's mooring place. 2 a bed or bunk in a ship, train etc.

beside at the side of, next to.

besides also, too.

besiege to surround (a town, for example) in an effort to capture it.

besotted (with) wildly fond (of someone).

bestial like a beast, savage.

bet *noun* money risked when you guess the result of a sporting event, for example.
verb to place a bet.

betray to give away someone's secret.

betrothed engaged to be married to (someone).

better 1 finer than, nicer than. 2 less ill than you were.

between 1 in the middle of (two things or people). 2 shared by two people.

bevelled having a slanted edge.

beverage a refreshing drink.

beware to be very careful of.

bewildered confused, puzzled.

bewilderment being bewildered.

bewitch to cast a spell over, to control by charm.

beyond farther on than.

bias leaning to one side, for example in an argument.

bib a piece of cloth put under a child's chin when eating to keep clothes clean.

Bible the religious book of the Christians.

Biblical of, from or like the Bible.

bicentenary happening once every two years.

biceps the muscle at the front of the upper arm.

bicker to quarrel, especially about something unimportant.

bicycle a two-wheeled machine you sit on to ride.

bid *noun* 1 an amount of money offered to buy something, especially at an auction. 2 a try.
verb to make a bid.

biennial 1 happening every two years. 2 (of plants) living for two years.

bigamy the crime of going through a marriage ceremony with someone when you are married already.

bike short for bicycle.

bikini a woman's short two-piece bathing suit.

bilateral having two sides; on two sides.

bile a kind of bitter liquid in the body which helps digestion.

bilingual in two languages; able to speak two languages.

bilious 1 suffering from a type of stomach illness. 2 bad-tempered (as a result of 1).

bill 1 a piece of paper that shows the money you owe for something. 2 a bird's beak.

billet to provide (soldiers etc.) with somewhere to stay, usually in a private house.

billiards a ball game played on a table, using a long stick called a cue.

billion a thousand million.

billow a large wave.

bin a large box, especially one for putting rubbish in.

binary system a mathematical system using only two numbers (usually 0 and 1), used in computers.

bind to wrap round with rope or string, for example.

bingo a game of chance using numbered squares.

binoculars a special pair of glasses to let you see far into the distance.

biochemistry a study of the chemical make-up of plants and animals.

biodegradable able to be disposed of safely by being consumed by living organisms.

biography the written life story of a person.

biology the study of living things.

bionic having mechanical or electronic body-parts.

biped a two-footed animal.

biplane an aeroplane with two sets of wings.

birch a tree with a silvery-coloured bark.

bird a feathered animal which has wings and can usually fly.

birthday the day of the year when a person was born.

biscuit a thin dry cake.

bisect to cut in two equal parts.

bishop the priest in charge of a large district such as a city in the Roman Catholic and certain other churches.

bison a large wild ox.

bit 1 a small piece. 2 a piece of metal in a horse's bridle held in the mouth. 3 a unit of information stored in a computer.

bitch a female dog.

bite to cut something with the teeth.

bitter tasting sour, not sweet.

bittern a kind of wading bird.

bivouac to sleep in the open without using a tent.

bizarre very odd, very strange.

black the darkest colour, the opposite of white.

blackberry a wild juicy black fruit used as food.

blackbird a kind of bird, the male of which has black feathers.

blackboard a board used for writing on with chalk.

blackmail getting money etc. from someone by threatening to tell something harmful about them.

blacksmith someone who makes things out of iron (for example horseshoes).

bladder 1 the part of the body in which urine collects. 2 a bag of rubber, leather etc. which can be filled with air or liquid.

blade the part of a knife or sword used for cutting.

blame to find fault with, to say who has done wrong.

blank empty, with nothing written on it.

blanket a warm, usually woollen bed-covering.

blare to make a loud sound like a trumpet.

blast *noun* a sudden rush of wind; a loud noise.
verb to break something up by explosions.

blatant very obvious, clearly seen.

blaze to burn with bright flames.

blazer a jacket, often with a badge on its top pocket.

bleach *verb* to make something lighter or whiter in colour.
noun a substance which does this.

bleak cold and dismal.

bleat the sound made by sheep and lambs.

bleed to lose blood.

blemish a fault, mark, flaw.

blend to mix together.

bless 1 to ask God to help somebody. 2 to wish happiness to.

blessing 1 something you are glad about. 2 asking or receiving God's help.

blight 1 a disease of plants. 2 a bad influence, especially on an area.

blind *adjective* not able to see.
verb to make blind.
noun a covering for a window.

blindfold a covering for the eyes to stop someone seeing.

blink to close and open both eyes quickly.

blip a small pulse of light on a radar screen.

bliss joy, great happiness.

blister a swelling on the skin with liquid inside it.

blithe happy, cheerful.

blitz a sudden violent attack (especially from the air).

blizzard a strong wind with heavy snow.

bloated swollen up.

block *noun* 1 a thick piece of something (for example wood or stone). 2 a large building with a lot of flats or offices.
verb to be in the way of.

blockade to surround an area (with soldiers or ships) to stop people and goods from going in or out.

blond(e) fair in colour.

blood the red liquid which moves round your body.

bloodshed murder, killing.

bloom *noun* a blossom, flower.
verb (of a plant) to come into flower.

blossom the flowers of plants and trees.

blot a dirty mark, especially an ink stain.

blotch a large uneven spot.

blouse a light garment worn by women and girls on the top part of the body.

blow *verb* 1 to shoot air out of the mouth. 2 (of air) to move quickly.
noun a hit made with the hand or a weapon.

blubber the fat of whales etc.

bludgeon to strike (someone) with a short heavy stick, for example.

blue the colour of the sky without clouds.

bluebell a wild spring flower with small blue bell-shaped flowers.

bluff to deceive an opponent by pretending you are in a strong position.

blunder a stupid mistake.

blunt 1 not able to cut, not sharp. 2 too straightforward in manner.

blur something not seen clearly.

blurt (out) to say (something) quickly, especially something you shouldn't say.

blush when your face goes red because you are ashamed, excited or shy.

BMX bicycle moto-cross, the sport of riding bicycles over rough country.

boa (constrictor) a very large South American snake that kills by crushing.

boar 1 a male pig. 2 a wild pig (usually wild boar).

board *noun* a flat piece of wood.
verb to go on to (a ship, train or aeroplane, for example).

boast to speak too proudly about yourself or something that belongs to you.

boat a small ship.

bob to move up and down (in water).

bobbin a small cylinder on which thread is wound.

bobsleigh two short sledges joined together.

bodice a close-fitting part of a woman's dress etc. above the waist.

body 1 the whole of a person or animal which can be seen. 2 the main part of anything, for example the person or animal without the head, legs and arms.

bodyguard a person or group whose job it is to keep someone safe from attack.

bog wet earth, a swamp.

bogus false, not real.

boil *verb* 1 to heat water till it turns to steam. 2 to cook in hot water.
noun a painful swelling on the body.

boisterous rough, noisy and lively.

bold brave, not afraid, willing to do daring things.

bollard a short post used for tying up a ship's ropes or for controlling traffic.

bolt *noun* 1 a fastener on a door. 2 a metal screw.
verb to rush away.

bomb a shell which explodes.

bombard to attack with heavy guns.

bondage slavery.

bone one of the hard parts of the body which make up the skeleton.

bonfire a large fire built in the open air.

bonnet 1 the cover of a motor-car engine. 2 a kind of hat.

bonus an extra payment over and above what is due.

book *noun* a number of pages bound together.
verb to arrange for (a seat at the cinema, for example) to be kept for you.

boom a loud hollow noise.

boomerang a curved weapon used by the natives of Australia, which can be made to return to the thrower.

boon something asked as a favour.

boost a favour, something good.

booster a device for increasing the power of a machine or rocket.

boot 1 footwear which comes above the ankles. 2 a covered place for luggage in a car.

booth 1 a small enclosed space for telephoning, voting etc. 2 a covered stall at a market etc.

booty plunder, loot.

border 1 the edge of something. 2 the line where two countries meet.

bore 1 to make a hole. 2 to make (someone) fed up by talking in a dull way.

bored feeling dull, for example because you have nothing to do.

boredom feeling bored.

born when a person or animal becomes alive; when something begins.

borrow to use something belonging to someone else with their permission.

borzoi a Russian wolfhound.

bosom the breast.

botany the study of plants.

botch to do (something) badly, spoil (something).

bother *noun* trouble.
verb to annoy.

bottle a glass or plastic container for liquids, usually with a narrow neck.

bottom 1 the underneath part of something. 2 the part of your body you sit on.

bough a tree branch.

boulder a large stone or rock.

boulevard a broad street, lined with trees usually.

bounce to (make something) spring up and down.

bound 1 forced to do something. 2 tied together.

boundary 1 the outside edge, for example of a cricket field. 2 the line where one piece of land touches another.

bounteous generous, giving freely.

bouquet a special bunch of flowers.

bout 1 a period of time doing or suffering from something. 2 (part of) a contest in wrestling, boxing.

boutique a small shop or part of a shop for selling fashionable clothes and accessories.

bovine of or like a cow or ox: slow, stupid.

bow [rhymes with 'low'] 1 a ribbon with loops on it. 2 a weapon used to fire arrows.

bow [rhymes with 'now'] *noun* the front part of a boat.
verb to bend forward from the waist to show respect.

bowels the part of the body in which solid waste matter collects.

bowl *noun* 1 a deep round dish. 2 the ball used in the game of bowls.
verb to send the ball to the person batting (at cricket, for example).

bowler (hat) a kind of hat with a hard round top and a brim.

bowling alley 1 long channel for rolling the ball in the game of skittles. 2 the building where skittles are played.

bowls a game in which a large heavy ball is rolled along the grass or other surface.

box *noun* a container, usually with a lid, often made of wood, cardboard or metal.
verb to fight with the fists.

boy a man child, a young male.

boycott to refuse to buy from someone or to attend something as a protest.

bra short for **brassière**.

brace a device that clasps or holds something tight.

bracelet a decoration worn on the wrist or arm.

braces straps over the shoulders to hold up trousers.

bracken a kind of large fern (especially a lot of them).

bracket a support for a shelf etc.

brackets curved lines like this ( ) you sometimes put round words or figures.

brag to boast a lot.

braggart a boastful person.

braid 1 a kind of woven material used for decoration. 2 a plait.

braille a writing system for the blind using raised dots.

brain the part of the head used for thinking etc.

braise to cook (meat etc.) slowly with liquid in a closed container.

brake the part on a vehicle which makes it go slower or stop.

bramble a prickly bush on which blackberries grow.

bran the crushed outer skin of grain (often used as a breakfast food).

branch the part of the tree on which the leaves grow.

brand the name of a particular kind of goods made by one company.

brandish to shake or wave about.

brandy a kind of strong alcoholic drink made from wine.

brash rash, cheeky, having little consideration for others.

brass a yellowish metal made by mixing copper and zinc.

brassière women's undergarment to support the breasts.

bravado false courage, bold showing-off.

brave *adjective* not afraid, ready to face up to danger or pain.
noun a North American Indian warrior.

brawl a rough quarrel or fight.

brawny strong, having strong muscles.

bray to make a noise like a donkey.

brazen 1 made of brass. 2 impudent, bold.

brazier a container for holding lighted coals.

bread food made from flour, yeast and water baked together.

breadth width, the measurement across something.

break *verb* to cause something to fall to pieces.
noun a short rest from what you are doing.

breakdown 1 (of an engine etc.) a failure to work. 2 (of a person) a collapse, in health for example.

breakfast the first meal of the day.

breakwater a wall built out into the sea to protect the shore.

breast 1 the front upper part of the body. 2 one of the two parts of a woman's body which can produce milk to feed a baby.

breath air taken in and let out of your mouth and lungs.

breathalyser an instrument for measuring the amount of alcohol in the blood.

breathe to take air in and let it out of your lungs.

breed *noun* the family or kind of an animal.
verb to have and bring up young ones.

breeze a gentle wind.

brevity the use of few words in speech or writing.

brew to make beer, tea etc.

briar 1 a prickly bush, especially of the wild rose. 2 a kind of wood from a root used to make tobacco pipes.

bribe to give (someone) money so that they will help you dishonestly.

bric-a-brac bits and pieces of old furniture, ornaments etc.

brick a baked clay block used for building.

bride a woman who is just married or about to be married.

bridegroom a man who is just married or about to be married.

bridesmaid a girl or young woman who attends a bride at her wedding.

bridge 1 something built to let you cross over a river, a road, or a railway. 2 where the captain stands on a ship. 3 a kind of card game.

bridle leather straps put on a horse's head to control it.

brief short.

briefs short underpants.

brigade 1 a subdivision of an army. 2 a band of workers etc.

brigadier an army officer commanding a brigade.

brigand a member of a robber band.

bright 1 shining. 2 clever.

brilliant 1 very bright, shining. 2 very clever.

brim 1 the top edge of a container such as a basin. 2 the part of a hat which sticks out at the edge.

brimful full to the brim.

brine salt water.

bring to take with you.

brink the edge of a steep place.

brisk quick, lively.

bristles short and stiff hairs like those on a brush.

brittle hard yet easily broken.

broad very wide.

broadcast a radio or television programme.

brocade a kind of cloth with a raised pattern.

broccoli a kind of vegetable with green flowers.

broil to cook by grilling.

broken in pieces.

bronchitis an illness of the chest causing coughing and shortness of breath.

bronze a metal made by mixing copper and tin.

brooch [broach] an ornament which can be pinned to the clothing.

brood *noun* a number of young birds hatched together.
verb to think deeply and to worry when there is no need to do so.

brook a small stream.

broom 1 a stiff brush with a long handle. 2 a kind of bush with yellow flowers.

broth 1 a thin soup. 2 **Scotch broth** a thick soup made by boiling meat, vegetables etc. together.

brother a boy or man who has the same parents as someone else.

brow 1 the forehead. 2 the top of a hill.

browbeat to bully, threaten.

brown the colour of earth or of chocolate.

Brownie (Guide) a junior Girl Guide.

browse 1 to look through books and papers in a relaxed way. 2 to nibble on grass, to graze.

bruise a mark on the skin where it has been hit.

brush 1 a tool used for sweeping, scrubbing and painting. 2 a fox's tail.

brusque sharp in speech or manner to others, off-hand.

Brussels sprouts a vegetable, like very small cabbages growing on a long stalk.

brutal cruel, savage.

brute 1 a beast, an animal. 2 a cruel person.

bubble *noun* a hollow ball of liquid filled with air or gas.
verb to give off bubbles like water when it boils.

buccaneer a pirate.

buck a male deer or rabbit.

bucket a container with a handle, often used for carrying liquids, a pail.

buckle a fastener for a belt or shoe, for example.

bud a leaf or flower before it opens.

budge to move slightly.

budgerigar a small brightly-coloured bird often kept as a pet.

budget a plan for spending money.

buffalo a large wild ox.

buffer something which softens a blow or breaks the force of something else.

buffet *noun* [**boof**ay] a meal where you serve yourself.
verb [**buff**it] to knock, strike repeatedly.

buffoon someone who acts the fool.

bug *noun* 1 a small insect. 2 a germ or virus.
verb to put a device in (a room etc.) so that people's conversations can be heard.

bugle a musical wind instrument like a small trumpet.

build to put up; to make into something.

building a structure (usually large) with walls and a roof.

bulb 1 a flower root shaped like an onion. 2 the part of an electric light that shines.

bulge to swell outwards.

bulk 1 the size, volume of something. 2 the large part (of something).

bulky large (for its weight).

bull a male animal of cattle, elephants, whales etc.

bulldozer a large machine for moving earth to make it flat.

bullet a piece of metal shot from a gun.

bulletin a short official message; a news report.

bullion gold or silver bars before they are made into coins etc.

bullock a bull which cannot breed, have offspring.

bully someone who ill-treats those weaker than himself or herself.

bulrush a tall reed-like water plant.

bumble-bee a kind of large bee with a loud hum.

bump 1 a sudden knock. 2 a swelling on the body where it has been hit.

bumper a metal rail at the front and back of a vehicle.

bumptious full of yourself, conceited.

bun 1 a small round cake. 2 hair wound into a round bunch at the back of the head.

bunch several things tied together.

bundle many things tied or held together.

bungalow a house with all its rooms on one floor.

bungle to ruin (something) by clumsiness or stupidity.

bunion a painful swelling on the big toes.

bunk a bed sometimes fixed to a wall like a shelf, often with another above, for example on a ship.

bunker 1 a container for keeping coal, for example. 2 a sand-filled hollow on a golf course.

buoy [boy] a fixed floating object which is fastened to the sea-bed to warn ships of danger.

buoyant 1 able to float. 2 able to recover well from disappointments etc., cheerful in spite of difficulties.

burden something heavy that is carried, a load.

bureau [**byoo**roe] 1 a writing desk with drawers. 2 an office.

burger short for hamburger or beefburger.

burglar a person who enters houses and shops to steal.

burial the burying of a dead body.

burly large and well-built.

burn *verb* to be or to set on fire. *noun* a place where something has been burned, especially a sore place on the skin caused by heat.

burp to bring up wind through the mouth.

burrow an underground tunnel dug by an animal such as a rabbit.

burst 1 to blow into pieces. 2 to break open.

bury to put (something) in a hole in the ground and cover it over.

bus a large motor vehicle which carries passengers who pay.

bush a small tree.

business work, trade.

busker a street-musician or entertainer.

bust 1 a sculpture of a person's head and shoulders. 2 a woman's breasts.

bustle to move about looking busy.

busy having no time to spare, doing a lot of things.

butcher someone who sells meat.

butler the head male servant in a household.

butt *noun* the thick or bottom end of something, for example of a gun. *verb* to hit with the head or horns.

butter a fatty food made from cream.

buttercup a bright-yellow wild flower.

butterfly an insect with large, usually brightly-coloured, wings.

button a fastening for clothing which fits into a hole.

buttress a support for a wall.

buxom plump and cheerful.

buy to get something by giving money.

buzz a low sound made by some insects when flying.

buzzard a kind of large bird of prey.

bye-law a local law or regulation.

byte a group of numbers in a computer.

C

cab 1 a place for the driver of a lorry or train. 2 a taxi.

cabbage a large, usually green, broad-leaved vegetable.

cabin 1 a room on a boat or aeroplane. 2 a small wooden house.

cabinet 1 a piece of furniture with drawers or shelves. 2 **Cabinet** the group of ministers who run the government.

cable 1 wires that carry electricity or telephone calls. 2 a strong rope often made of wires twisted together.

cackle to make a noise like a hen after it lays an egg.

cactus a prickly desert plant with thick stems.

cadaverous looking like a corpse, very thin and pale.

caddie a person who carries a golfer's clubs.

cadet a young person being trained in the army etc.

café a place for eating, usually snacks or simple meals.

cafeteria a self-service café.

caffeine a substance found in tea and coffee which can make you more active.

cage a box or room made of wires or bars in which animals or birds are kept.

cagoule a long waterproof jacket with a hood.

cajole to coax, to get (someone) to do something by flattery.

cake a sweet baked food made of flour, eggs, sugar etc.

calamity a disaster.

calculate 1 to count. 2 to think out exactly.

calculator a small machine, book etc. used to count very large or complicated numbers.

calendar a sheet or book showing the days and months of the year.

calf 1 a young animal, usually a young cow or bull. 2 the soft back part of the leg between knee and ankle.

call 1 to shout to. 2 to visit. 3 to give a name to. 4 to telephone.

calligraphy (the art of) good handwriting.

callipers 1 an instrument with two legs used for measuring. 2 metal supports for weak legs.

callous having no feelings, hard-hearted.

calm quiet and still, peaceful.

calorie a measurement of heat or of the energy value of food.

calypso a West Indian song, usually made up on the spot.

camber a slight rise in the top surface, of a road for example.

camel a humped animal used for carrying people and goods in the desert.

camera a machine for taking photographs.

camouflage a form of colouring or shape which makes something seem part of its background.

camp *noun* a group of tents together. *verb* to live in a tent.

campaign a series of battles, a part of a war; a series of efforts, for example in support of something.

campanology the study of bell-ringing.

can a small sealed container made of tin.

canal a man-made waterway.

canapé [**kan**apay] a light piece of bread or biscuit spread with something savoury.

canary a yellow songbird sometimes kept as a pet.

cancel to stop something happening; to cross out (writing).

cancer a very serious illness caused by a growth in the body.

candid truthful, open, saying what you think.

candidate 1 a person who wants to be elected or to be chosen for a job. 2 a person sitting an examination.

candle a stick of wax with a wick which is burned to give light.

candy (sweets made of) sugar and water boiled together; sweets; a sweet.

cane the hollow stalk of some plants, for example bamboo; a stick made of this.

canine belonging to the dog family.

canister a rounded, usually metal, container.

cannabis a kind of drug made from the Indian hemp plant.

cannibal 1 a person who eats human flesh. 2 an animal that eats its own kind.

cannon a heavy gun which fires shells.

canoe a light boat moved by using a paddle.

canon a clergyman who serves in a cathedral usually.

canopy a light covering hung overhead.

cant 1 meaningless insincere talk. 2 the language used by a group of people often so that they are not understood by others.

cantankerous bad-tempered.

cantata a musical piece for voices.

canteen 1 a place where people eat together (in a factory or school, for example). 2 a box with a set of cutlery.

canter a slow gallop.

cantilever a large beam for supporting a balcony, the end of a bridge etc.

canvas strong cloth used to make tents, sails etc.

canvass to visit people to try to get votes, support, money etc.

canyon a deep narrow river valley.

cap 1 a kind of head covering. 2 a lid or cover.

capable able to do.

capacious able to hold a lot, roomy.

capacity 1 the amount something will hold. 2 an ability. 3 the position you hold.

cape 1 a cloak to cover a person's shoulders and arms. 2 a piece of land jutting out into the sea.

caper *verb* to leap about in a silly manner.
noun 1 capering. 2 a foolish or dishonest activity.

capital 1 the chief city or town. 2 a large letter such as A, B, Y or Z.

capitulate to surrender.

capricious changeable in mood or character.

capsize to overturn.

capsule 1 a small pill containing powdered medicine. 2 the cabin of a spaceship.

captain 1 the person who controls an aeroplane or ship. 2 an officer in the army or navy. 3 the leader of a team or group.

caption 1 the heading of an article or chapter in a book. 2 the words above or below a picture in a book, for example.

captivate to win over by charm.

captive a prisoner.

capture to take prisoner, to catch.

car a motor vehicle to carry people.

carafe a wide-necked bottle for water or wine at table.

caramel a chewy sweet.

carat 1 a unit of weight for precious stones. 2 a measure of the fineness of gold.

caravan a house on wheels.

carbohydrate a substance found in certain foods, such as bread, potatoes, rice, which helps to give you energy.

carbon paper coloured paper used for taking copies, for example of letters.

carcass a dead body, especially of an animal.

card 1 a piece of stiff thick paper. 2 a piece of card with a message and often a picture (sent for example on someone's birthday). 3 one of a set of cards used for playing games.

cardboard a kind of thick stiff paper.

cardigan a knitted woollen jacket.

cardinal *noun* high ranking priest of the Roman Catholic Church. *adjective* of great importance.

care *verb* to be concerned (about) someone. *noun* the act of looking after someone or something.

career *noun* your job or profession; a course or progress through life and work. *verb* to run or dash wildly.

caress to stroke lovingly.

caretaker a person who looks after a building such as a school.

cargo goods carried on a ship or aeroplane.

caricature an exaggerated and comic drawing of someone.

carnage great slaughter.

carnation a sweet-smelling garden flower (usually pink, white or red).

carnival a large procession, usually in fancy-dress.

carnivorous flesh-eating.

carol a Christmas hymn.

carousel a merry-go-round.

carp *noun* a kind of fresh-water fish. *verb* to pick on small faults or errors.

carpenter someone who makes things out of wood.

carpet a thick soft covering for a floor.

carriage 1 a part of a train where people sit. 2 a vehicle pulled by horses.

carrion the dead body of an animal being eaten by another.

carrot a long orange root vegetable.

carry to take from one place to another.

cart a vehicle for carrying goods, often pulled by a horse.

cartilage a piece of flesh between the bony parts of a joint.

carton a box made of cardboard.

cartoon 1 a drawing in a book or newspaper, usually to make you laugh. 2 a short film made out of drawings.

cartridge 1 a case containing the explosive material of a bullet or shell. 2 a container of recording tape, for example.

carve 1 to shape wood or stone with cutting tools. 2 to cut meat into slices.

cascade a (small) waterfall.

case 1 a kind of box to keep or carry things in. 2 a suitcase.

casement a window opening outwards.

cash money in notes and coins.

cashier a person who looks after cash in a shop, bank etc.

cashmere a kind of wool made from soft goat's hair.

casino a gambling place.

cask a barrel often used to store liquids.

casket a small box or chest.

casserole a covered dish in which food is cooked and served; the meal cooked in such a dish.

cassette a recording tape in a holder.

cassock a clergyman's long gown.

cast *verb* to throw. *noun* 1 the people taking part in a play or film. 2 something shaped in a mould.

castaway a person who is shipwrecked.

castle a large stone building with towers and strong walls.

casual 1 easy-going, unplanned. 2 (of clothes) informal, worn for leisure time.

casualty a person who has been injured.

cataclysm a terrible happening.

catalogue a list of things in a special order.

catamaran a boat with two or more hulls.

catapult a forked stick with a piece of elastic attached, used for firing small stones.

cataract a waterfall.

catarrh a discharge of thick liquid from the nose, especially when you have a cold etc.

catastrophe a great disaster.

catch 1 to take hold of. 2 to get (an illness).

catechism the beliefs of a church written down in the form of questions and answers.

category a class or kind of things or people.

cater to provide food etc.

caterpillar a worm-like creature with legs, which will turn into a moth or butterfly.

cathedral a very important church.

catkin a kind of fluffy flower which grows on some trees, for example the willow.

cattle cows, bulls, calves and oxen.

cauldron a large round pot with a hooped handle.

cauliflower a vegetable with a hard white flower.

cause to make something happen.

caution being cautious.

cautious taking great care.

cavalcade a parade, especially of horses or vehicles.

cavalry soldiers who ride on horseback.

cave a hollow place in rocks or in the earth.

cavern a large underground cave.

caviare the eggs of the sturgeon fish which are thought very good to eat.

cavity a hollow, a hole, in a tooth, for example.

caw the cry of a rook or a crow.

cease to stop doing something.

cedar a kind of sweet-smelling evergreen tree.

cede to grant or give up (to another).

ceiling the inside of the roof of a room.

celebrate to remember something in a special way, especially by having a party or feast.

celebrity 1 a famous person. 2 fame.

celery a vegetable with long, whitish-green stalks.

celestial of the sky, heavenly.

celibate unmarried, especially because you have made a religious promise.

cell a room in which a prisoner is kept.

cellar a store-room under a building.

cello a musical instrument like a large violin.

Celsius a temperature scale of 100 degrees, formerly called **centigrade.**

cement a stone dust which sets hard when mixed with water.

cemetery a place where people are buried.

cenotaph a monument to a person or people buried somewhere else.

censor a person appointed to examine books, films etc. and remove anything which might be harmful.

censure to blame (someone) strongly for something.

census an official counting of the population.

cent a coin which is a hundredth part of a dollar, for example.

centaur a fabled monster, half man, half horse.

centenary the hundredth anniversary of something.

centigrade a temperature scale of 100 degrees, now called **Celsius**.

centimetre a measure of length equal to a hundredth part of a metre.

centipede a small crawling creature with a large number of legs.

central 1 in the centre. 2 important.

centre 1 the middle of something. 2 a place where people come together to do things.

century 1 a hundred years. 2 a hundred runs at cricket.

ceramic to do with pottery.

cereal 1 a crop such as wheat, rice or oats used for food. 2 a kind of food made from grain and usually eaten for breakfast.

ceremony a special service held to celebrate something.

certain 1 sure. 2 some, but not all.

certificate a piece of paper which says something important about someone or something.

certify to make an official statement about something.

chafe to make sore or wear away by rubbing.

chaff husks of grain.

chaffinch a kind of small bird.

chagrin annoyance, upset.

chain *noun* a number of rings joined together.
verb to fix with a chain.

chair a piece of furniture for one person to sit on.

chairman, chairperson a person who is in charge of a meeting.

chalet [sha*lay*] 1 a wooden cottage in Swiss style. 2 a small holiday house or hut.

chalice a wide cup for wine, especially one used for a communion service in church.

chalk 1 a soft white rock which crumbles. 2 a white or coloured stick used for writing on a blackboard.

challenge *verb* to offer to fight someone.
noun a test of ability.

chamber 1 (long ago) a room. 2 a place where elected officials meet. 3 the place where bullets are put in a gun.

chameleon a kind of small lizard that can change its colours to match its surroundings.

champ *verb* to chew noisily.
noun (informal) a champion.

champagne a kind of sparkling French wine.

champion the winner over all the others in a competition.

chance 1 an unexpected happening. 2 a time when you can do something you want to do.

chancellor 1 a high official, for example the **Chancellor of the Exchequer**, the minister in charge of the country's finances. 2 the official head of a university.

chandelier a group of lights hanging from the ceiling, arranged in branches.

change *verb* to make or become different.
noun money you get back when you pay more than is needed.

changeling a child supposed to have been substituted for another by fairies.

channel a narrow strip of water.

chant *noun* a kind of religious singing.
verb to sing in this way; to repeat something in rhythm.

chaos total confusion.

chapel 1 a small church or part of a church. 2 a room in a larger building for religious worship.

chaplain a clergyman attached to an organisation such as the Army, a school etc.

chapter a part of a story or book.

char to make black by burning.

character 1 what someone is like as a person. 2 a person in a play or story.

charades [shar**ahds**] a word-guessing game using mime.

charcoal a black substance made by burning wood slowly, used as fuel and for drawing.

charge *verb* to rush at.
noun 1 the price asked for something. 2 **in charge** in control of something.

chariot (long ago) a horse-drawn cart used in battle.

charity giving money to people who need it.

charm 1 a magical spell. 2 a small ornament which is supposed to bring good luck.

charming pleasing to other people.

chart 1 a map used by sailors. 2 a piece of paper with information, often a drawing or a sketch.

charter *noun* a document which gives rights to a person or group.
verb to hire (an aircraft, bus etc.).

chary careful, cautious.

chase to run after.

chasm a gorge, a deep opening in the earth.

chaste pure, modest.

chat to talk in a friendly way.

chatter to speak quickly, especially about things that don't matter.

chauffeur a person whose job it is to drive a motor car for someone.

chauvinist someone with ridiculously strong feelings about the superiority of their country, sex etc.

cheap low in price, not costing a lot.

cheat to act unfairly, to make others believe what is not true.

check *verb* to make sure that everything is in order.
noun a pattern of squares.

checkmate a position (in chess) where defeat is unavoidable.

cheek 1 one of the sides of the face between the nose and the ears. 2 rudeness.

cheer to shout loudly for joy.

cheerful full of fun, looking happy.

cheese a solid food made from milk.

cheetah a swift spotted animal which hunts prey.

chef a head cook in a hotel or restaurant.

chemical of or made by chemistry.

chemist 1 a person who sells medicines. 2 a person who studies chemistry.

chemistry a study of the substances things are made of.

cheque an order written to a bank to pay someone money.

cherish to care for deeply, to look after well.

cherry a small red fruit with a stone in it.

cherub a child-like angel.

chess a game played by two people on a squared board.

chest 1 a large strong box. 2 the upper front part of the body.

chestnut the hard brown seed of the chestnut-tree.

chew to keep biting food in your mouth

chic [sheek] stylish, up to date, fashionable.

chicken a (young) bird kept for its eggs and meat.

chicory a kind of plant of which the leaves are used in salads and the roots are ground to make a drink.

chief 1 the person in charge. 2 the most important.

chilblains painful itching on hands and feet caused by cold.

child a young boy or girl.

chill 1 coldness. 2 a slight cold which causes shivering.

chilli the pod of a kind of pepper from which a hot-tasting powder is made.

chilly (of weather) quite cold.

chime the noise made by bells.

chimney a pipe to take smoke away.

chimpanzee a kind of monkey without a tail.

chin the part of the face below the bottom lip.

china fine pottery, especially cups and saucers and plates.

chink a narrow opening or slit.

chinos [**chee**nos] trousers made from khaki-coloured cotton.

chip 1 a tiny piece broken from something larger. 2 a piece of potato fried in deep fat.

chipmunk a kind of North American animal like a squirrel.

chipolata a small sausage.

chiropodist a person who is skilled at looking after your feet.

chirp a noise made by young birds.

chirpy cheerful, lively.

chisel a sharp steel tool used for cutting wood, stone or metal.

chivalrous well-mannered, helpful to others.

chivalry 1 the honour-code amongst knights long ago. 2 being chivalrous.

chocolate a sweet food made from cocoa.

choice the act of choosing; something you choose.

choir a group of people singing together.

choke 1 to be unable to breathe because of something in the throat. 2 to block up.

cholera a very serious infectious disease.

cholesterol a substance in the blood, which can be harmful.

choose to pick out what is wanted from a large number.

chop *verb* to cut into small pieces; to cut with a heavy blow. *noun* a small slice of meat attached to a bone.

chopsticks small sticks used by the Chinese and Japanese for eating with.

choral of or belonging to a choir.

chord a group of musical notes sounded at the same time.

chorus 1 part of a song or poem which is repeated after each verse. 2 a group of people singing together.

christening when a baby is given its name in a Christian church.

Christian a believer in Jesus Christ.

Christmas a festival on and around 25 December to celebrate the birth of Christ.

chronic (especially of an illness) lasting for a long time.

chronicle a record of events.

chronological arranged in the order in which things happened.

chrysalis the stage in the life of certain insects when the body is wrapped in a hard covering.

chubby plump, fat.

chuckle to laugh quietly.

chum a close friend.

chunk a thick piece cut off from something larger.

church a building in which God is worshipped by Christians.

churn a machine for making butter.

chute a sloping channel or slide.

cider an alcoholic drink made from apples.

cigar dried tobacco leaves rolled tightly together and used for smoking.

cigarette cut-up tobacco leaves rolled in a paper tube for smoking.

cinder a piece of coal which has been partly burned.

cinema a place where films are shown.

cinnamon a sweet-smelling spice made from the bark of a tree.

circle something round, a ring.

circuit 1 a movement round something, for example a racecourse. 2 the path of an electric current.

circuitous roundabout, not direct.

circular round like a ring.

circulate to move or spread around.

circumference the outside edge of a circle.

circumstances the events, the state of affairs connected with something.

circus a travelling show of animals, actors and clowns.

cistern a container for water, especially for a toilet.

citadel a stronghold in a city.

citizen an inhabitant of a city.

citrus fruit fruit such as oranges, lemons, grapefruit.

city a large town, in Britain one with a cathedral.

civil 1 of the ordinary people, not the armed forces. 2 polite.

civilise to bring into a more advanced state of society; to make better-mannered.

claim to say that something belongs to you.

clamber to climb with difficulty on your hands and knees.

clammy cold and wet.

clamour noise and shouting.

clamp to grip together.

clang the sound made by a large bell.

clap *verb* to slap the hands together quickly.
noun the sound made by thunder.

claret red wine from Bordeaux in France.

clarify to make clear.

clarinet a musical instrument played by blowing.

clarity clearness.

clash to bump together noisily; not to go together well.

clasp *verb* to grip or hold tightly.
noun a fastening.

class 1 people who are taught together. 2 a group of people or things of the same kind.

classic *adjective* the best of its kind.
noun 1 a classic book, play, film etc.
2 **classics** Latin and Greek (language and literature).

classical of or like a classic or the classics.

classify to sort (things) into groups.

clatter a loud rattling noise.

claw the sharp hard nails of a bird or an animal.

clay sticky earth from which bricks and pottery may be made.

clean not dirty or dusty.

cleanse to clean (especially a wound etc.).

clear *adjective* easy to see, hear or understand.
verb to put away, to tidy.

cleaver a chopping tool, used by butchers for example.

clef a sign showing the pitch in written music.

cleft a narrow split, crack, opening.

clench to close (your teeth or fingers) tightly.

clergy ministers of the Christian church.

clerk [clark] a person who attends to papers, accounts etc. in an office.

clever 1 quick at learning and understanding things. 2 skilful.

click a small sharp metallic noise.

client a person who pays for help or advice from a professional person, for example a lawyer.

cliff high, steep land often overlooking the sea.

climate the sort of weather a place usually has.

climax the highest, most important or exciting part, of a story for example.

climb to go up a steep place.

cling to hold on tightly.

clinic a place where doctors and nurses give help to people.

clip *noun* a fastener. *verb* to cut with a pair of shears or scissors.

clipper (long ago) a kind of slim, fast sailing ship.

cloak a sleeveless covering for the body and arms.

clock a machine for telling the time.

clockwise moving round in the same direction as the hands of a clock.

clockwork machinery which is worked by winding a spring.

clog *verb* to block, choke (pipes etc.). *noun* a shoe with a wooden sole; a wooden shoe.

close [rhymes with 'dose'] near.

close [rhymes with 'doze'] to shut.

cloth 1 material for making clothes or curtains, for example. 2 a piece of cloth for cleaning something.

clothe to put clothes on.

clothes things you wear to cover your body.

cloud a mass of rainy mist floating in the sky.

clover a small flowering plant with leaves in three parts.

clown a person who acts foolishly to make people laugh.

cloying sickly sweet.

club 1 a heavy stick. 2 a stick used to play golf. 3 a group of people who meet together for a special purpose.

clue something which helps you to find the answer to a puzzle or a question.

clump a cluster of trees, plants etc.

clumsy awkward in the way you move or do things.

cluster a bunch or a group of things.

clutch to hold or grasp tightly.

clutter untidiness, disorder.

coach 1 a passenger vehicle such as a bus or a railway carriage. 2 a person who gives special training (for example to a football team).

coal a kind of black rock dug out of the ground and burned to make heat.

coalition a banding together of political parties etc.

coarse rough, not fine.

coast the strip of land next to the sea.

coat 1 an outer garment with sleeves. 2 the hair of an animal.

coax to try to persuade (someone) to do something.

cobbler a person who mends shoes.

cobra a kind of hooded poisonous snake.

cobweb a net made by a spider to trap insects.

cocaine a drug which can be very harmful.

cock a male bird.

cockatoo a kind of parrot with a crest.

cockle a kind of shellfish you can eat.

cockpit the space for the pilot of an aircraft, for example.

cockroach a kind of dark-brown insect like a large beetle.

cocoa a powder made from cocoa beans, used to make chocolate; a drink made from this powder.

coconut the very hard hairy fruit of a kind of palm tree, filled with milky juice.

cocoon the silky case which covers the young of some insects at the chrysalis stage.

cod a large sea-fish used as food.

coddle to treat very gently and carefully.

code 1 writing with a hidden meaning. 2 a set of rules, for example the **Highway Code**.

coerce to force (someone) to do something.

coffee a drink made from the roasted and crushed seeds of the coffee tree.

coffin a box in which a dead body is put.

cog a toothlike projection on the rim of a wheel.

coil to gather rope, wire or piping in rings (one on top of the other).

coin a piece of metal used as money.

coincidence something happening accidentally at the same time as something else.

coke 1 baked coal from which gas has been taken. 2 **Coke** trade name for a kind of fizzy drink.

colander a kitchen instrument with holes in it for draining off liquid.

cold *adjective* not hot.
noun an illness which makes your nose run.

collaborate to work with someone.

collage a picture made from bits of paper and odds and ends pasted together.

collapse to fall or break down.

collar 1 a leather or metal band put round the neck of an animal. 2 the part of your clothes which fits round the neck.

colleague a person who works with you.

collect to gather together.

collection 1 a number of things gathered in a set. 2 money gathered from a group of people, for example in a church.

college a place where students are taught.

collide to come together with great force.

collie a kind of sheepdog.

colliery a coal-mine.

collision colliding.

colon a punctuation mark like this : used to show a break in a sentence or at the beginning of a list.

colonel [**ker**nel] a senior officer in the army.

colony a settlement of people.

colossal very big.

colour what makes things look green, red etc.

colt 1 a young male horse. 2 **Colt** trade name for a kind of hand gun.

column 1 a post, usually of stone or wood, used to support a part of a building. 2 a strip of printing in a book or newspaper. 3 a line of troops.

coma a very deep unnatural sleep.

comb a thin piece of metal or plastic etc. with many teeth, used to keep hair in order.

combat fighting, a fight.

combine to join or mix together.

combustion burning, setting alight.

comedian a person who tells funny stories in public to make people laugh.

comedy a play or film that makes you laugh.

comely attractive, good-looking.

comet a star-like body with a long fiery tail which appears in the sky.

comfort *noun* a pleasant easy feeling.
verb to show kindness to someone in pain or trouble.

comfortable giving or having comfort.

comic *adjective* which makes you laugh, funny.
noun a magazine or paper for young people, with stories told in pictures.

comma a punctuation mark shaped like this , used to separate words or parts of sentences.

command to order.

commando a soldier specially trained for dangerous duties.

commemorate to officially remember or honour (a person or event).

commence to begin.

commend 1 to praise (someone or something). 2 to recommend (someone) as suitable.

comment something said, an opinion.

commentary a detailed description of something, especially of an event on radio or TV.

commentator a person who gives a commentary.

commerce to do with buying and selling.

commercial *adjective* to do with buying and selling.
noun an advertisement on television etc.

commit 1 to do (something). 2 to hand over. 3 **commit yourself** to promise to do something.

committee a group of people who meet for some special purpose.

common ordinary, usual; found in many places.

commonplace ordinary.

commotion a disturbance, a row.

communal belonging to a number of people.

communicate to make meaning known to someone else, by speech or writing, for example.

communion a special service in a Christian church which celebrates the Last Supper.

community the people of an area as a group.

commuter someone who travels some distance to work every day.

compact *adjective* closely packed, small and neat.
noun 1 an agreement. 2 a container for face-powder.

compact disk a small plastic disk on which large amounts of sound or information can be stored.

companion someone who is with you, often a friend.

company 1 people you are with. 2 a group of people doing business, a firm.

compare to see if things are alike.

compartment a separate section, for example of a railway carriage or a refrigerator.

compass an instrument which helps you to find your direction.

compasses an instrument for drawing circles.

compassion pity.

compatible able to get on with someone else, for example; able to be used along with something else.

compel to force.

compensate to make up (for something).

compete to try to do better than others.

competition a contest to find the best.

competitor a person taking part in a competition.

compile to gather material from books or articles.

complacent self-satisfied.

complain to find fault, to grumble.

complaint an act of complaining.

complement what completes or fills up.

complete *adjective* whole, with nothing missing.
verb to finish altogether.

complicated having a lot of parts; difficult to understand, not simple.

compliment something nice someone says to praise you.

comply (with) to agree (to).

component a part of something larger.

compose 1 to put together; to make up (a piece of music, for example). 2 to make calm and quiet

composer a person who makes up music.

composition something composed, for example a piece of music or writing.

composure calmness.

compound (something) composed of many parts.

comprehend to understand.

comprehensive including everything.

compress to push or press together.

comprise to include, contain; to make up.

compromise to settle a disagreement by each giving up something.

compulsion force.

computer a machine that stores information and can work out answers quickly.

comrade a friend, companion.

concave hollow and curving inwards.

conceal to hide (from).

concede to admit; to give (a right, points in a game, for example).

conceited thinking too much of yourself, too proud.

conceive 1 to become pregnant. 2 to imagine, think.

concentrate to think hard about something.

concept an idea.

concern to be connected with.

concerned worried.

concert music played in front of an audience.

concerto a musical piece for solo instrument and orchestra.

concise giving a lot of information in a few words, brief and to the point.

conclude 1 to come to or bring to an end. 2 to decide.

conclusion the finish, the end.

concoction a mixture, especially of drink or food.

concrete *adjective* solid, that can be touched or felt.
noun a building material made of cement, gravel etc.

concur to agree (with).

concussion injury to the brain, caused by a blow on the head.

condemn 1 to declare to be wrong or bad. 2 to sentence (a criminal) to some punishment.

condense 1 to change from a gas into a liquid. 2 to make (a liquid) stronger and thicker. 3 to say or write something in fewer words.

condition the state of something or someone.

condone to take no notice of someone's offence, to forgive (something wrong).

conduct *noun* [**con**duct] behaviour.
verb [con**duct**] to guide, lead.

conductor 1 a person who is in charge of an orchestra or choir. 2 a person who sells tickets and looks after the passengers on a bus.

cone 1 the fruit of the fir tree. 2 a solid shape that is round at the bottom and pointed at the top, like an ice-cream cornet.

confectioner a person who makes sweets etc.

confectionery sweets, cakes etc.

confer 1 to discuss something with another, others. 2 to give (an honour etc.).

conference a meeting (of a large number of people) for discussion.

confess to tell about things you have done wrong.

confide in to tell secrets to (another person).

confident feeling sure or safe.

confidential that should be kept secret.

confine to keep (by force) in a particular place.

confirm to say or prove that something is right or true.

conflict a struggle, fight.

conform to do what is usual or expected.

confront to face up to.

confuse 1 to throw into disorder. 2 to mix up.

confused not in a clear state of mind; mixed up.

confusion being confused.

congratulate to say to someone that you are pleased about something good that has happened to them.

congregation the people gathered for a religious service.

conifer a cone-bearing tree.

conjuror a magician, someone who can do tricks.

conjunction a word which joins other words or parts of sentences.

connect to join together.

conquer to beat others in a battle.

conquest the act of conquering.

conscience the feeling inside you which tells you if something is right or wrong.

conscientious attentive to your duty, dependable.

conscious awake, knowing what is happening.

consecutive following one after another in order.

consent to agree.

consequence 1 a result, what happens because of something else. 2 importance.

conservation keeping things from harmful change, especially the environment.

consider to think carefully.

considerable fairly large.

considerate thoughtful, kind to others.

consignment a load of goods.

consist to be made up (of).

consistency 1 the degree of thickness of a liquid or semi-liquid. 2 being consistent.

consistent staying the same, especially in views or attitudes.

console to comfort (someone).

consonant a written letter which is not a, e, i, o or u.

conspicuous clearly seen, obvious.

conspiracy a plot to do something wicked.

constable an ordinary policeman or policewoman.

constant always the same, unchanging.

constellation a group of stars.

consternation great upset and surprise.

constituency an area which elects a member of parliament; the voters living in it.

constituent 1 a part of something larger. 2 a voter in a constituency.

constitution 1 the rules by which a country is governed. 2 a person's bodily health.

constrict to hold in, to squeeze.

construct to build.

consul a person who represents their country in an area of another country.

consult to go to a person or to a book etc. for advice or information.

consultant 1 a person who gives specialist advice to others. 2 a senior doctor in a hospital, specialising in some branch of medicine.

consume to eat; to use up.

consumer a person who buys and uses things.

contact *verb* to get in touch with.
noun 1 being in touch with. 2 a person to contact.

contact lens a small piece of plastic worn in the eye to help you to see better.

contagious (of a disease) caught by touching.

contain to have inside, to hold.

container a box, jar, chest or bag in which things may be stored.

contaminate to make impure, diseased or poisonous.

contemplate to think hard about.

contemporary 1 belonging to the same time as someone or something else. 2 belonging to the present time.

contempt scorn, thinking very little of something or someone.

contemptible worthless.

contemptuous feeling or showing contempt.

contend to struggle or fight (with).

content *adjective* [con**tent**] quite pleased, satisfied with things as they are.

contents *noun* [**con**tents] what an object contains.

contest a competition to find the best or the winner.

continent one of the large land masses of the world, such as Europe, Asia or Africa.

continual happening often.

continue to go on with; to go on, to last.

continuous going on all the time.

contorted twisted out of shape.

contour 1 an outline. 2 a line on a map showing height above sea level.

contraband smuggled goods.

contract *noun* [**con**tract] an agreement.
verb [con**tract**] 1 to (cause to) become smaller. 2 to make an agreement. 3 to get (an illness).

contractor a person who agrees to do certain work, especially building work.

contradict to say that what someone else says is wrong or untrue.

contrary *adjective, noun* [**con**trary] (the) opposite.
adjective [con**trary**] awkward, obstinate.

contrast *noun* [**con**trast] the difference between things.
verb [con**trast**] to show the differences between things; to be different.

contribute to give money, help etc. towards something.

contrive to cause something to happen by a clever plan.

control to make (someone or something) act in the way you want; to guide; to keep steady.

controversial causing argument.

conundrum a riddle.

convalescence a time when you slowly recover from illness.

convection the upward movement of heated air.

convenient suitable.

convent the building in which nuns live.

conventional doing the usual things according to custom, not original.

converge 1 (of two lines) to meet at a point. 2 to come together, to join up.

conversation talk between two or more people.

conversion the act of converting or being converted.

convert to change from one thing to another.

convex curved outwards, like the outside of a ball.

convey 1 to carry (goods for example). 2 to pass (information etc.) to others.

convict *verb* [con**vict**] to find (someone) guilty of a crime in a court. *noun* [**con**vict] a criminal in prison.

convince to make (someone) believe something.

convivial jolly, good-natured, enjoying good company.

convoy a line of ships or lorries travelling together.

cook to make food ready to eat by heating it (for example by boiling or frying).

cool not quite cold.

coop *noun* a closed place for hens etc. *verb* to close (someone or something) up inside something.

cooper a person who makes barrels.

cooperate to work together.

cope to manage to do something.

copious in great supply.

copper a kind of reddish-brown metal.

copse a small wood or group of bushes.

copy 1 to do the same as somebody else, to imitate. 2 to make (something) the same as something else.

coral red, pink or white substance formed from the bones etc. of certain tiny sea creatures.

cord a piece of thick string or thin rope.

cordial *adjective* friendly, warm-hearted. *noun* a sweet drink made from fruit juice.

cordon a ring or line of policemen, guards etc.

corduroy a kind of thick ribbed cotton cloth.

core the part in the centre of something (for example of an apple, where the seeds are).

cork 1 a light substance made from the bark of the cork tree. 2 a piece of this or other substance used to close the mouth of a bottle.

cormorant a kind of large black sea-bird with a long neck.

corn 1 the name of certain cereal plants; the seeds of these used as food. 2 maize. 3 a place on the foot.

corner where two roads, lines or walls meet.

coronation the crowning of a king or queen.

corporal a rank in the army below that of sergeant.

corpse a dead body.

correct *adjective* quite right, true. *verb* to make something right.

correspond 1 to exchange letters (with). 2 to be like, to match.

corridor a narrow covered passage which joins rooms or railway compartments.

corrode to (cause to) crumble away like rust.

corrosive corroding.

corrupt bad, wicked.

cosmetics powders, creams etc. to improve the appearance.

cosmic of the universe or outer space.

cosmic rays strong radiation from outer space.

cosmonaut a Russian astronaut.

cost how much you must pay to buy something.

costume clothes worn for a special reason or occasion, for example, on the stage.

cosy *adjective* comfortable and warm. *noun* a cover for a teapot.

cot a baby's bed with high sides.

cottage a small country house.

cotton 1 a kind of light cloth made from a plant grown in warm countries. 2 thread used for sewing.

couch a seat for more than one person, a sofa.

cough to force air from the chest and lungs with a noise.

council a group of people chosen to plan and decide what should be done in a place (for example a town or district).

count *verb* to number in the proper order, to add up.
noun a nobleman in some European countries.

countenance the face.

counter 1 a kind of table over which things are served in a shop, for example. 2 a small disc used in counting and in playing games.

counterfeit (usually of money) false.

counterfoil the part of a cheque, ticket etc. which you keep.

countess a noblewoman, the wife of an earl or a count.

country 1 the whole of a land, such as England or France. 2 the part of a land which is away from towns.

county a division of England, Wales or Ireland or of a state of the USA.

couple two of anything.

coupon a ticket which can be changed for something of value.

courage great bravery.

courgette a small marrow.

courier 1 a messenger. 2 a person who helps tourists on holiday.

course 1 a large stretch of land where certain sports take place. 2 a part of a meal. 3 the direction something takes.

court 1 a piece of land on which certain games are played (for example a **tennis court**). 2 a place where trials are held. 3 the place where a king and queen live and the people who help them.

courteous polite.

courtesy being courteous.

cousin the child of an uncle or aunt.

covenant an agreement, usually written, to do something.

cover to put something over something else.

cow a large female animal kept for its milk and meat.

coward a person who runs away from danger or difficulty.

cowboy man who rides around looking after cattle in America.

cower to huddle down because of fear.

cowl a loose hood worn by monks, for example.

cowslip a kind of small yellow wild flower.

coy shy, pretending to be shy.

crab a kind of shellfish with ten legs; some kinds are used as food.

crack 1 to break, to make a slight break in (something). 2 to make a sharp noise like something hard breaking.

cracker 1 a kind of hard biscuit. 2 a decorated roll of paper which bangs when pulled apart.

crackle to make a noise like dry sticks burning.

cradle a rocking bed for a baby.

craft a job or trade needing skill, especially with the hands.

craftsman a person who is skilled in a craft.

crafty not able to be trusted, cunning.

cram to overfill (something).

cramp *noun* a sudden severe pain in a muscle.
verb to force into a small space; to hinder, keep back.

crampons spikes attached to climbing boots for walking on ice etc.

cranberry a bitter-tasting red berry used in sauces and jams.

crane 1 a tall machine for lifting heavy things. 2 a large water bird with long legs.

cranium the skull.

crash 1 a loud noise made by something breaking. 2 an accident when cars or trains, for example, run into something.

crate a large box for carrying goods, sometimes with spaces for bottles.

crater 1 the mouth of a volcano. 2 a hole in the ground made by a bomb etc.

crawl *verb* 1 to move on the hands and knees. 2 to move slowly.
noun a stroke used in swimming.

crayfish a kind of shellfish like a small lobster, used as food.

crayon a stick of coloured wax etc. for drawing with.

craze a temporary enthusiasm for something.

crazy 1 mad, without sense. 2 likely to do strange or silly things.

creak to make a small sharp noise like a door hinge that needs oiling.

cream 1 the thick liquid found on the top of milk. 2 the colour of cream.

crease 1 the mark made by folding cloth, for example. 2 a mark on a cricket pitch.

create to make something new.

creature any living thing.

crèche a place where very young children are looked after while their parents are at work, for example.

credible able to be believed.

credit 1 good name, honour, approval. 2 buying things to pay for them later. 3 having money in a bank account, for example.

credulous too ready to believe (unlikely things).

creed a statement of beliefs, especially religious beliefs.

creep 1 to move along close to the ground. 2 to move carefully, often to avoid being seen.

creeper a climbing plant.

cremate to burn (a dead body).

crematorium a place where dead bodies are burned.

crescent 1 part of the edge of a circle; the shape of the new moon. 2 a curved street.

cress a kind of small plant often eaten in salads.

crest 1 the top of something, especially the top of a wave. 2 feathers on the top of something.

crestfallen disappointed.

crevasse a deep crack in a glacier.

crevice narrow opening, in ice or rock for example.

crew a team of people who do the work on a ship or an aircraft etc.

crib 1 baby's cot. 2 a wooden container for animal food.

cricket 1 a game played with a ball, bat and stumps. 2 a jumping insect which chirps.

crime breaking the law.

criminal a person who breaks the law.

crimson a deep-red colour.

cringe to shrink away from something through fear.

crinkle to crease, wrinkle.

cripple a person who cannot fully use an arm or a leg.

crisis a time when something serious or dangerous happens.

crisp *adjective* firm and dry.
noun a very thin slice of potato cooked in oil.

crisscross (of lines) to cross in two directions.

critic 1 a person who gives opinions on books, plays etc., for example in a newspaper. 2 a person who criticises.

critical 1 at an important point, in making a decision for example. 2 finding fault.

criticise 1 to find fault with. 2 to give an opinion on (a book for example).

croak a hoarse sound like that of a frog or raven.

crochet [**kroa**shay] a kind of knitting done with one hooked needle.

crockery plates, cups etc.

crocodile a large and dangerous animal found in or near water in some hot countries.

crocus a small yellow, purple or white spring flower.

crook 1 a person who commits a crime, a criminal. 2 a shepherd's stick with a hook at one end.

crooked 1 bent, not straight. 2 dishonest.

crop 1 plants grown for food. 2 the amount of such gathered at one time.

croquet [**kroa**kay] a game played on grass in which wooden balls are hit through hoops.

cross *noun* anything shaped like a × or +.
verb to move from one side to the other.
adjective angry.

crotchet a note in music equal to half a minim.

crouch to bend down low with your legs bent.

crow *noun* a kind of large black bird which has a loud rough call.
verb 1 to make a sound like a cock. 2 to make happy sounds like a baby; to show you are pleased about something you have done.

crowd a large number of people all together in one place.

crown 1 the special head-dress, often made of gold, of a king or queen. 2 the top of an object such as a person's head or a hill.

crucial very important.

crucible a small pot (for melting metals).

crucifix a model of Christ on the Cross, or of the Cross.

crude raw, rough.

cruel very unkind, without pity.

cruise a long journey by boat or aeroplane, usually one made for pleasure.

cruiser a fast-moving warship.

crumb a tiny piece of bread or cake.

crumble to break into little pieces.

crumple to crush (gently) into creases.

crunch to crush noisily with the teeth; to make a noise like this.

crusade (in history) a Christian war against the Muslims; any fight or struggle for a good cause.

crush to press together very tightly, to squash.

crust the hard outside part of anything, especially of bread.

crutch a wood or metal support used by someone with a hurt leg to help them walk.

cry 1 to call out. 2 to have tears in your eyes, to weep.

crypt a room under a church.

crystal 1 a clear ice-like mineral. 2 a very fine kind of glass. 3 the shape into which different substances form as they solidify.

cub 1 a young fox, wolf, lion etc. 2 **Cub (Scout)** a junior Boy Scout.

cube a solid square shape.

cubicle a small compartment of a larger room.

cuckoo a bird which lays its eggs in other birds' nests and makes a sound like its name.

cucumber a long green vegetable often eaten in salads.

cud food chewed for a second time by some animals such as the cow.

cuddle to take into the arms and hug closely.

cudgel a heavy stick.

cue 1 a hint or sign. 2 the stick used in playing billiards and snooker.

cuff *noun* the end of a sleeve.
verb to hit (with the back of the hand).

culprit a person who is guilty of doing wrong, the person to blame.

cultivate to dig or plough (land) so that crops will grow.

culture the beliefs, customs, habits etc. of a country or group; (education in) art, music, writing etc.

cumbersome difficult to handle, hard to hold or support.

cunning clever in a sly way.

cupboard a place with shelves for storing things.

curate an assistant clergyman.

curative that heals, healing.

curator [kew**ray**tor] the head of a museum etc.

curb to hold in check, control.

curd the solid part of sour milk.

curdle to turn sour and thicken.

cure to make someone better from an illness.

curfew an order or signal to remain indoors after a certain time.

curious 1 strange, unusual. 2 wanting to know.

curl *verb* to form into rings or curves. *noun* something of this shape, especially **curls**, hair formed into rings.

curlew a long-billed wading bird.

curling a game played on ice with a large stone.

currant 1 a small dried grape often used in puddings and cakes. 2 a small berry grown on a bush.

currency the money used in a particular country.

current *noun* a flow of water, air, electricity etc.
adjective of the present time.

curry a food with a very hot taste.

curse 1 a bad wish for someone or something. 2 a swear word.

curt short to the point of rudeness, abrupt.

curtail to cut short.

curtain a cloth covering for a window etc.

curtsy a greeting made by women and girls by bending the knee and lowering the body.

curve a rounded line or shape.

cushion a pillow which is often used on a chair.

custard a sweet yellow sauce which is eaten with puddings.

custodian a person who looks after someone or something.

custody 1 imprisonment. 2 care, safe-keeping.

custom what is usually done; what usually happens.

customer a person who buys something in a shop or market.

cut to open or to divide with something sharp.

cutlass a short curved sword.

cutlery knives, forks and spoons.

cutlet a small piece of meat, often with the bone attached.

cycle *noun* 1 a bicycle. 2 events happening again and again in a regular pattern.
verb to make a bicycle move.

cyclic happening in a regular manner or pattern.

cyclone a violent wind which moves in a circle.

cygnet a young swan.

cylinder a long round shape, like a soup tin.

cymbal a musical instrument made by two bronze plates which are banged together.

cynical sneering, mocking.

cypress a kind of evergreen tree.

cyst a kind of blister which forms in the body.

D

dab to touch lightly.

dabble 1 to dip your hands in a liquid. 2 to work at or to do something without much seriousness.

dachshund [**daks**hoond] a breed of dog with a long body and short legs.

daffodil a yellow spring flower grown from a bulb.

dagger a pointed knife with a short blade, sharp on both sides.

dahlia a kind of brightly-coloured garden flower.

daily each day.

dainty neat, small, delicate.

dairy 1 a place where milk, cream, butter and cheese are produced. 2 a shop where milk, butter, eggs and cheese are sold.

daisy a small flower with a yellow centre and white petals.

dale a valley.

dalmation a breed of large spotted dog.

dam a wall built to hold back water.

damage to harm.

damn *verb* to condemn; to curse. *noun* a mild curseword expressing anger.

damp slightly wet.

damsel (*old-fashioned*) a young unmarried woman.

damson a small dark-purple plum.

dance to move on the feet to music.

dandelion a yellow wild flower.

dandruff tiny pieces of dead skin found in the hair.

danger harm; something that can hurt you.

dangerous likely to hurt, harm or kill.

dangle to hang down from something, to swing loosely from something.

dank unpleasantly cold and damp.

dapper neat, smart in appearance.

dappled spotted in different colours.

dare *verb* 1 to be brave enough to do something dangerous. 2 to ask (someone) to do something dangerous. *noun* something you do to prove how brave you are.

dark not light or bright.

darling a name for someone you love very much.

darn to mend a hole in cloth or clothing with crisscrossed threads.

dart *verb* to move very quickly. *noun* a small arrow thrown at a board in a game.

dash *verb* to rush from place to place. *noun* a short line like this — used in writing.

data facts, information.

date 1 the day, month and year when something takes place. 2 the sweet brown fruit of a palm tree.

daub to paint roughly, to smear.

daughter a female child of a parent.

daunting giving difficulties, frightening.

dawdle to do something so slowly that time is wasted.

dawn the very first light of the day, daybreak.

day 1 a period of twenty-four hours. 2 the time between sunrise and sunset.

dazed not knowing where you are, for example after a blow on the head.

dazzle to blind for a moment with bright light.

dead no longer alive.

deadly able to cause death.

deaf not able to hear (well).

deal *verb* 1 to do business with. 2 **deal with** to do what has to be done with. 3 to give out (cards) in a card game. *noun* **a great deal** a lot.

dear 1 much loved by someone. 2 costing a lot of money.

dearth shortage, scarcity, of food for example.

death when you stop living.

debar to exclude (someone) from (an organisation for example).

debase to reduce in value.

debate a discussion about something, especially a public one.

debris rubbish, rubble.

debt what you owe to someone.

debut the first public appearance (of someone), on the stage or in sport for example.

decade a period of ten years.

decaffeinated of coffee, with the stimulating substance caffeine removed or reduced.

decant to pour off (liquid) carefully.

decapitate to cut the head off, especially as a legal punishment.

decathlon an athletic competition with ten events.

decay to rot, become bad.

deceased (a person) who has died.

deceit the act or habit of deceiving.

deceitful acting with deceit.

deceive to fool or trick (someone) by telling them lies.

decent proper, respectable.

deceptive misleading.

decibel a unit used to measure the loudness of sound.

decide to make up your mind about something.

deciduous (of trees) which lose their leaves in autumn.

decimal a way of counting in tens.

decipher 1 to decode. 2 to read and make sense of (badly-written writing).

decision what you have decided.

deck the floor of a boat, an aeroplane or a bus.

declare to state firmly, to say what you intend to do.

decline *verb* 1 to refuse (something). 2 to get worse (in health, for example). *noun* a downward slope.

decode to find out the meaning of a message written in code.

decompose to decay, to rot away.

decorate to make something more attractive, usually with ornaments, colour etc.

decorous showing decorum.

decorum proper behaviour.

decoy a person or thing used to fool a person or animal or lead them into danger.

decrease to make or become smaller.

decree an official order or judgement.

decrepit old, weak and unsteady.

dedicate to devote (yourself) to a special task etc.

deduce to find (something) out by reasoning.

deduction 1 something which has been deduced. 2 an amount taken out of a larger quantity or number.

deed an action, something done.

deem to believe, consider.

deep far down, often in water; far inside.

deer a kind of large fast-running wild animal.

deface to spoil by marking.

defeat to beat in battle or in a game.

defect a fault, flaw.

defective not complete, damaged; not working properly.

defence the act of defending; something which defends.

defend to protect, guard.

defer 1 to put off till a later time. 2 to give in to the wishes of another.

deficient lacking (in something), not perfect.

defile to spoil or damage by marking.

define to explain, make clear.

definite sure, certain.

deflate 1 to let the air out of (a balloon or tyre for example). 2 to take away someone's confidence in themselves.

deflect to turn (something) aside.

defoliate to strip the leaves from.

deformed badly shaped or formed.

defrost to remove frost or ice from (a refrigerator for example).

deft skilfully quick.

defunct dead, no longer used.

defuse 1 to reduce the possibility of trouble in a situation. 2 to take the fuse out of (a bomb for example).

defy to refuse openly to do what you are told; to refuse to obey (an order).

degrade 1 to reduce to a lower rank. 2 to humiliate (someone).

degree 1 a measurement of heat or of an angle. 2 an amount. 3 a certificate or title given by a university or college.

dehydrate to take the water from, to make dry.

dejected sad, upset.

delay 1 to put off doing something for a while. 2 to make late.

delectable delightful, pleasant.

delegate to appoint as a representative.

delete to cross or rub out.

deliberate done on purpose.

delicate very fine; easily broken.

delicious having a very pleasant taste or smell.

delight great pleasure, joy.

delinquent a person who breaks the law.

delirious 1 in a wild state of mind, usually because of fever. 2 wildly excited.

deliver 1 to bring, to carry; to give. 2 to help with the birth of (a baby).

delivery 1 the act of delivering; something delivered. 2 the birth of a baby. 3 a style of speaking.

dell a small (wooded) valley.

delta a branching river mouth.

delude to fool, deceive.

deluge a large flood.

delusion a mistaken belief, impression etc.

demand to ask very firmly for something.

demented insane.

demobilise to put (troops) back into civilian life.

democracy government by elected representatives of the people.

demolish to destroy entirely, to pull down (a building).

demon an evil spirit.

demonstrate to show clearly to other people how something should be done.

demure shy, modest.

den the place where a wild animal eats and sleeps.

denim strong, usually blue, cotton cloth.

denomination 1 the name used of a group or class of things. 2 a particular religious group.

denounce to accuse publicly.

dense 1 very thick, too thick to see through. 2 stupid.

dent a hollow caused by a blow or knock.

dental concerning the teeth.

dentist a person who looks after teeth.

deny to say firmly that something is not true.

deodorant a substance used on the body to remove unpleasant smells.

departure the moment of leaving or going away.

depend to trust somebody or something for help.

dependant someone who depends on another.

dependent depending; unable to do without something, a drug for example.

depict to describe; to make a picture of.

deplorable very bad, regrettable.

deport to send (a person) out of a country.

deportment the way a person stands and walks, behaviour.

depose to remove (someone) from office, especially a ruler.

deposit *verb* 1 to lay down. 2 to put (money) into a bank account.
noun 1 money deposited in a bank or paid as a first payment for something. 2 a layer of rock etc. in or on the earth.

depot [**dep**oh] a warehouse, storage place.

depraved very bad, corrupt.

depreciate to (become) lower in value.

depress to make someone feel sad.

deprive to take (something) away from someone.

depth how deep something is.

deputy a person who is second in command and acts for the person in charge when necessary.

deranged mad, out of your mind.

derelict abandoned, left empty.

deride to make a fool of, laugh at.

derision ridicule, mockery.

derive to get or come from another thing or person.

derogatory tending to insult or give offence to someone.

derrick 1 a machine for lifting heavy weights, a crane. 2 a tall structure over an oil well which holds the drilling machinery.

descend to go down; to come down.

describe to say how something or someone looks.

description saying what something is.

desert *verb* [de**sert**] to leave when you are expected to stay.
noun [**des**ert] a large empty place where hardly anything grows because of heat and lack of water.

deserve to be worthy of, to have earned some reward or punishment.

design a plan or drawing; a pattern.

designate 1 to appoint to an office or position (in advance). 2 to call by a particular name.

desire to want something very much.

desk a kind of table used for writing at.

desolate 1 empty, with no people. 2 lonely, sad, very upset.

despair to lose hope; to give up hope.

despatch 1 to send out (a parcel etc.). 2 to kill.

desperate ready to do almost anything to get what you want, because you have lost hope.

despise to think that (a thing or person) is bad or useless.

dessert the sweet dish eaten at the end of a meal.

destination the place you are going to or to which something has been sent.

destiny what is going to happen, fate.

destitute in great need (of food, clothes etc.), very poor.

destroy to break up completely, to do away with.

destruction the act of destroying or breaking down completely.

detach to take away from the main part of something.

detail a very small part or fact.

detain to keep late, keep back; to keep by force.

detect to find out by searching.

detective a person, usually a policeman, whose job it is to find out who carried out a crime.

detention being detained, as a punishment usually.

deter to prevent (someone) from doing something.

detergent a kind of soap (for washing clothes or dishes, for example).

deteriorate to get worse.

determination firmness of purpose.

determined having made up your mind firmly.

deterrent something that stops you doing something, out of fear usually.

detest to dislike greatly, to hate.

detonate to explode.

detour a roundabout way.

detrimental harmful.

devastate to ruin, cause disaster to (a place).

develop 1 to grow, to change gradually. 2 to bring out the picture in a photographic film.

deviate to turn aside from something, especially from what is considered right.

device a useful object or plan for doing something.

devil an evil spirit or person; the chief evil spirit.

devious (of a person) insincere, not trustworthy; (of a road or route) winding, not direct.

devise to plan, to make up.

devote to give completely (to).

devour to eat greedily.

devout holy.

dew drops of water found on the ground and on plants in the early morning.

dexterity skill, quickness, especially with the fingers.

diabetes a disease in which the sugar level in the blood is too high.

diabetic (of) a person suffering from diabetes.

diabolical devilish, evil.

diagnose to find out what kind of illness someone has.

diagnosis what is diagnosed.

diagonal a line joining two opposite corners of a rectangle.

diagram a drawing to show how something works or is made.

dial the face of an object such as a clock or telephone, with numbers or letters on it.

dialect how people speak in a certain district.

dialogue conversation; the conversation in a story etc.

diameter a straight line passing from side to side through the centre of a circle.

diamond 1 a very hard precious stone, often used in rings. 2 a shape with four sloping sides the same length; a playing card with these shapes.

diarrhoea an illness causing the bowels to empty too easily.

diary a book in which you write what happens each day.

dice a small cube with numbers on it, used in games.

dictate 1 to tell others what to do. 2 to say something for someone else to write down.

dictionary a book like this one with a list of words and their meanings, arranged in alphabetical order.

die to stop living.

diesel a kind of heavy oil used in a **diesel engine**.

diet 1 the sort of food we eat. 2 an eating plan to let you lose weight or be healthier.

difference what makes something different.

different not like something else, not the same.

difficult not easy to do or to understand.

dig to turn soil over.

digest to break down food in your body after you have eaten it.

digit 1 one of the numbers 0 to 9. 2 a finger or toe.

digital (of a clock etc.) giving information by displaying numbers.

dignified serious, stately, impressive in appearance or behaviour.

digress to wander off the point, in speaking etc.

dike 1 a bank built with stones; a (stone) wall. 2 a ditch.

dilapidated broken down, shabby.

dilatory slow at doing things, delaying.

dilemma a tricky problem.

diligent hard-working.

dilute to reduce the strength of (a liquid) by adding water.

dim not bright; not easy to see.

dimensions the size, measurement of length, breadth and height of something.

diminish to make or become less or smaller.

dimple a small hollow, in the cheek or chin, for example.

din a great noise of many things together.

dinghy a small rowing-boat.

dingy dirty, dull and dark.

dinner the main meal of the day.

dinosaur one of the huge reptiles of long ago, now extinct.

dip 1 to place into a liquid for a short time. 2 to slope downwards.

diphtheria a very serious throat disease.

diploma a certificate showing that you have passed examinations in a particular subject, for example.

diplomat a person who helps to represent his or her country in another country.

diplomatic of diplomats, careful in speech and behaviour.

direct *adjective* of the shortest and quickest way.
verb to tell (somebody) which way to go.

directory a book giving lists of addresses, telephone numbers etc.

dirt mud, dust, something not clean.

dirty not clean.

disabled not able to use part of your body properly.

disagree not to agree with.

disappear to go out of sight, to vanish.

disappoint to make (somebody) sorry because they have not got what they hoped for.

disaster a terrible event, happening or accident.

disc, also spelt **disk** 1 a round, flat object. 2 a plastic **disk** for storing information in a computer.

discard to throw away as no longer needed.

discharge 1 to carry out, duties for example. 2 to fire, a gun for example.

disciple a follower of a leader, especially one of Christ's followers.

discipline a strong set of rules to be followed, at school or in the army, for example.

disco a place where people dance to music on records.

discomfort slight pain, lack of ease or comfort.

disconnect to break the connection of things.

discontented unhappy.

discord 1 anger and disagreement between (people). 2 a musical chord which sounds harsh or unpleasant.

discount *verb* [dis**count**] to dismiss as unimportant.
noun [**dis**count] an amount by which the price of something is reduced.

discover to find out about (something); to find for the first time.

discreet careful in words and actions.

discriminate (**against**) to act unjustly against (someone) because of their race or religion for example.

discus a heavy round disk that is thrown in athletic competition.

discuss to talk about (something) with other people.

disdainful looking down on (someone).

disease an illness.

disengage to break off a battle for example.

disfigure to spoil the appearance of.

disgraceful so bad you should be ashamed of it.

disguise to change your appearance by altering your face and clothes.

disgust strong feeling against something.

dish 1 a bowl or plate. 2 food served at a meal.

dishevelled very untidily dressed, with untidy hair.

dishonest not honest or trustworthy.

disinfect to cleanse from infection.

disk *see* **disc**.

dislike not to like.

dislocate 1 to put (a bone) out of its proper place in a joint. 2 to put in disorder.

dislodge to remove from a place or position by force.

dismal dull or sad, not bright.

dismantle to pull down, to take to pieces.

dismiss 1 to send (someone) away. 2 to put out of your mind.

dismount to get down from a horse or bicycle.

disobey to go against someone's orders.

disobedient disobeying.

dispel to drive away.

dispense 1 to give out. 2 to prepare (medicines) for giving out. 3 **dispense with** to do without.

dispenser a machine which gives out things or amounts at a regular rate.

disperse to go or drive off in different directions, to scatter.

display a show.

dispute a quarrel, an angry discussion.

disreputable of bad character.

disrupt to put into disorder, to cause (a meeting) to break up in disorder.

dissect to cut up (an animal for example) for examination.

dissent disagreement, especially when publicly shown.

dissolve to mix completely with a liquid.

dissuade to advise (someone) against doing something.

distance 1 somewhere far away. 2 the space between two points or places.

distemper 1 a disease of dogs. 2 a kind of paint.

distil to purify or strengthen (a liquid) by turning it into gas and back to liquid again.

distillery a place where alcoholic spirit is made.

distinct 1 quite clearly seen or heard. 2 different.

distinguish 1 to make out the differences between things. 2 to be the difference between.

distinguished famous, highly regarded.

distort to twist out of shape.

distract to draw someone's attention away.

distress great trouble, sorrow or unhappiness.

distribute 1 to share out. 2 to bring (goods) to customers.

district a part of a country or a town.

disturb 1 to upset, to worry. 2 to put out of order.

disturbance trouble; an upset.

ditch a long narrow hole dug in the ground, for example to let water flow away.

divan a long low seat with no back or arms that can be used as a bed.

dive to jump head first into water.

diver someone wearing special equipment who works under water.

diverge to move away (from) in different directions.

diverse different, varied.

diversion 1 an alternative route when a road is closed. 2 a pleasant pastime.

divide 1 to share between; to split up. 2 to work out how many times one number goes into another.

divine of God, holy.

divorce a legal ending of a marriage.

divot a small piece of earth and grass cut out by clubs when making a shot in golf.

dizzy unsteady, feeling as though you are spinning round.

docile tame, obedient.

dock 1 the place where boats are loaded and unloaded. 2 the place where a prisoner stands in a court of law.

doctor 1 a person who looks after people's health. 2 a person with a high academic qualification.

document a piece of paper with writing on it, especially one used for an official purpose.

dodge to move quickly from one side to the other; to avoid.

doe a female deer or rabbit.

dog a four-legged animal often kept as a pet.

dole money paid to people who are unemployed.

doleful sad.

doll a toy which looks like a baby or child.

dollar a form of money used in some countries, such as America or Canada.

dolphin a kind of warm-blooded sea animal.

dome a rounded roof of a large building such as a church.

domestic belonging to the home; (of animals) tame, used by people.

dominate to rule over, take control over.

domino an oblong piece of wood or plastic with dots on it, used in the game of **dominoes.**

donate to give money etc. for a purpose.

donkey an animal like a small horse with very long ears.

donor a person who gives, especially one who gives or promises a part of their body to help another.

doodle to scribble, to draw with a pen or pencil without thinking.

doom fate, especially if bad.

door an entrance to a room or a building.

dormant sleeping; not active.

dormitory a large room containing several beds.

dormouse a kind of small mouse-like animal with a long furry tail.

dose the amount of medicine that you should take at one time.

dot a tiny round mark or point.

dotage weak-minded old age.

dote on to love too much.

double twice the amount.

doubt not to be sure, to question.

dough a soft mixture of flour and water etc.

doughy of bread etc. not quite cooked.

dove a kind of pigeon, often white.

dowdy not well dressed, old-fashioned in dress.

down *adverb* lower; below.
noun soft hair or feathers.

dowry money or property given by a bride to her husband on their wedding.

doze to sleep lightly.

dozen 12, twelve.

drab dull, uninteresting.

draft a rough early copy of a piece of writing, a plan etc.

drag to pull something along the ground.

dragon an imaginary, fire-breathing animal in stories.

dragon-fly a long insect with fine wings.

dragoon *noun* (long ago) a heavily-armed horse soldier.
verb to force (someone) into doing something.

drain *verb* to take water away from something.
noun a pipe which takes dirty water from buildings.

drake a male duck.

drama 1 stories that can be acted, plays. 2 an exciting happening.

drastic of changes, rules etc., very strong, severe, violent.

draught a cold stream of air entering a warmer room.

draughts a game played with round pieces on a board with black and white squares.

draw 1 to make a picture, usually with a pen or pencil. 2 to pull. 3 to end a game with equal scores.

drawer a box with handles that fits closely into a piece of furniture.

dreadful very bad, terrible.

dream to see and hear things when you are asleep.

dreary gloomy, dull.

dredge to drag something up, especially mud from the bottom of a river.

dregs the solid material that falls to the bottom of a liquid.

drench to soak through with water.

dress *verb* 1 put on your clothes.
2 to clean and cover (a wound).
noun a woman's or girl's garment like a skirt and blouse together.

dribble 1 to flow in drops at a time.
2 to let saliva fall from the mouth.
3 to move a football using small kicks from side to side.

drift *noun* snow blown into a deep pile.
verb to move aimlessly with the tide or with the wind.

drill *noun* 1 a tool for making holes.
2 strict regular exercises, for example for soldiers.
verb 1 to make a hole. 2 to train (soldiers, for example).

drink to swallow liquids.

drip to fall or let fall in drops.

drive *verb* to make a vehicle, such as a car, or an animal move.
noun a private road up to a house.

drivel nonsense.

drizzle light rain falling gently.

droll funny, amusing.

dromedary a kind of camel with one hump.

drone 1 a low humming sound.
2 a male bee.

droop to hang down loosely.

drop *noun* one tiny spot of liquid.
verb to fall from a height.

dross waste material from melted metal, impurities mixed in with something.

drought [rhymes with 'out'] a long time when no rain falls and there is not enough water.

drown to die in water because you cannot breathe.

drowsy sleepy.

drug 1 a substance used as a medicine. 2 a substance used to make you feel different (for example alcohol).

drum a musical instrument which is played by beating with a stick.

dry not wet or damp.

dual double, divided into two.

dubious doubtful, uncertain.

duchess a noblewoman of high rank; the wife of a duke.

duck *noun* a common water bird. *verb* to bend down quickly, for example so as not to be hit.

duel an arranged fight between two people armed with the same sort of weapons.

duet a song or a piece of music for two people.

duffel thick, coarse woollen cloth often made into coats or jackets.

duke a nobleman of high rank.

dull 1 not shining. 2 not clever. 3 boring, uninteresting.

dumb unable to speak.

dump *noun* a place where things are stored roughly or thrown away. *verb* to put (something) down heavily or carelessly.

dungeon a prison below the ground.

duplicate something made as an exact copy of something else.

durable long-lasting, strong.

duration the time during which something happens.

duress threats used to make someone do something.

during as long as something lasts.

dusk the beginning of darkness just after sunset, the half-dark.

dust tiny specks of dirt.

duster a cloth to remove dust.

duty something that you should do.

duvet [**doov**ay] a bed cover stuffed with feathers or other soft materials, used instead of blankets.

dwarf a person or animal much smaller than usual.

dwell to live in a certain place.

dwindle to grow slowly less or smaller.

dye to make something a certain colour by placing it in a special liquid.

dynamite a kind of powerful explosive material.

dysentery a serious disease of the bowels, causing pain, diarrhoea etc.

dyslexia a condition which makes it difficult for a person to read or write.

dyslexic suffering from dyslexia.

E

each every one by itself.
eager very keen.
eagle a kind of large wild bird which kills small animals for food.
eaglet a young eagle.
ear 1 the part of the head with which we hear. 2 where the seed is found in the corn plant.
earache a pain in the ear.
earl a nobleman.
early 1 before the time fixed. 2 near the beginning.
earn 1 to get money etc. by working. 2 to deserve.
earnest serious(-minded).
earnings what you have earned, pay for work done.
earth 1 the world in which we live. 2 the soil in which things grow.
earthquake when the earth's surface shakes.
earwig a kind of small insect with pincers at the end of its tail.
ease comfort; freedom from pain, worry etc.; rest from work.
easel a wooden frame to support a blackboard or a painting.
east the direction from which the sun rises.
easy simple to do, not difficult to understand.
eat to bite, chew and swallow food.
eaves the lower edge of a roof.
eavesdrop to listen secretly.
ebb (of the tide) to go out; to drain away, to move outward, like the tide.
ebony a kind of very hard black wood; its colour.
eccentric behaving oddly.
echo the same sound which comes back to you in an empty place.
éclair [iklair] a finger-shaped pastry filled with cream.
eclipse the hiding of all or part of the sun by the shadow of the moon between it and the Earth or of the moon by the Earth's shadow.
ecology the study of how plants and animals relate to each other and to their surroundings.
economic 1 of economics. 2 making money, profitable.
economical using money, goods etc. carefully, not wastefully.
economics the study of careful management, especially of money.
ecstasy great joy.
eczema a skin disease.
eddy water, air etc. whirling round.
edge the part next to the outside of something, the rim, the border.
edible fit to eat, eatable.
edict an order from an authority.
edifice a large and stately building.
edit to prepare writing for printing; to prepare a film or tape for broadcasting, for example.
editor 1 the person in charge of a newspaper or magazine. 2 a person who prepares a book or a paper for printing.
education learning and teaching, especially in schools, colleges and universities.
eel a kind of snake-like fish.
eerie very strange, weird.
efface to rub out, to wear away.
effect 1 what happens because of something. 2 **effects** belongings. 3 **effects** imitations on stage of sounds etc.
effeminate like a woman.
effervescent 1 (of a liquid) bubbling, fizzing. 2 (of a person) in high spirits.
efficient able to do something well.
effigy a portrait or statue (of someone).
effluent waste material flowing into a river or the sea.

effort the use of (all) your strength in trying to do something.
effrontery impudence, cheek.
effusive (of speech, for example) gushing out, pouring forth.
e.g. for example.
egg the rounded object from which some creatures (for example fish and birds) are hatched.
egoistic always thinking of yourself, selfish.
egotistic full of your own importance, conceited, selfish.
egret a kind of long-beaked wading bird.
eiderdown a bedcover stuffed with feathers or other soft materials.
either one or the other (of two people or things).
eject to throw out, expel.
elaborate complicated.
eland a kind of large South African antelope.
elapse (of time) to pass by.
elastic (of) a material that will stretch and then go back to its own length.
elated very happy, delighted.
elbow the joint in the middle of the arm.
elder 1 the older one of two persons. 2 a kind of tree with white flowers and black berries.
elderly getting old.
elect to choose by voting.
election choosing someone by a vote.
electric using electricity.
electricity a power which travels through wires and is used for heating, lighting, driving things.
electrocute to kill by electricity.
electron a very small piece of matter with the smallest amount of electricity.
electronics the study and use of electric currents in the making of radios, television apparatus etc.

elegant graceful, refined.
elegy a kind of poem or song expressing sorrow for a dead person.
element 1 a part of something. 2 a kind of substance which cannot be divided up into other substances and from which all others are made. 3 the heating wire in an electric fire etc.
elephant a kind of very large animal with a trunk and two tusks, found in Africa and India.
elevate to lift up to a higher level.
elevator a machine for carrying people or goods to higher levels, a lift.
elf a kind of small fairy.
eligible suitable to be chosen for something.
eliminate to take out, get rid of.
elite [ay**leet**] the best of a kind.
elk a very large kind of deer.
ellipse a complete oval.
elliptical shaped like an ellipse.
elm a kind of large tree.
elocution the art of speaking well.
elongate to lengthen, stretch out.
elope to run away with a lover to get married.
eloquent speaking well and fluently.
elude to avoid, escape from (someone).
elusive hard to catch.
emaciated very thin, usually from hunger.
embankment a bank of earth or stones to hold back water, to support a railway etc.
embark to go on board a ship or aeroplane.
embarrass to make (someone) feel uncomfortable or awkward.
embassy the office or home of an ambassador.
embellish to decorate, to improve with ornaments, for example.
embers glowing coals or pieces of wood in a dying fire.

embezzle to steal money which you have been entrusted to look after.

embitter to cause bitter feelings in.

emblem a symbol, badge.

embrace to put your arms round someone lovingly, to hug.

embroider to sew patterns on cloth.

embryo the young of an animal or plant in the very early stages before it is born.

emend to correct (a piece of writing).

emerald 1 a bright-green precious stone. 2 the colour of this.

emerge to come out, to appear (from).

emergency something very bad which needs to be dealt with right away.

emigrate to leave one country to go to live in another.

eminence 1 being eminent. 2 a high place.

eminent famous, notable.

emit to send out (smoke, light etc.).

emotion something you feel strongly, like anger or love.

emperor a man who is the head of a number of countries.

emphasis greater stress given to certain words etc.; greater importance attached to something.

emphasise to put emphasis on.

emphatic said very strongly, with emphasis.

empire many countries which are all under the same ruler.

employ 1 to give paid work to (someone). 2 to use.

employee a person who is employed.

employer a person who employs other people.

empress a woman who is the head of a number of countries; the wife of an emperor.

empty with nothing at all inside.

emu a kind of large wingless Australian bird.

emulate to try to do as well as or better than (someone else).

enamel 1 a special kind of hard shiny paint. 2 the hard covering on your teeth.

enamoured fond of (someone).

enchant 1 to delight, please greatly. 2 to put a spell on.

enchantment the act of enchanting; being enchanted.

enclose 1 to place inside. 2 to surround by a fence or wall.

encore [onkore] a call for a musical or other piece to be repeated; the repeated performance.

encounter to meet.

encourage to act or speak in a way which helps someone to do something.

encroach (upon) to come on to something a bit at a time, especially something which belongs to someone else.

encumbrance a hindrance, a burden.

encyclopedia a book containing all kinds of information in alphabetical order.

end *noun* the last part of something. *verb* to finish.

endearment a loving word, an expression of affection.

endeavour to try.

endorse 1 to confirm, say you agree with. 2 to write your name on the back of (a cheque etc). 3 to write on (a driving licence) stating that the driver has broken the law.

endurance the ability to endure.

endure 1 to put up with, suffer. 2 to last, continue.

enemy someone you fight against.

energetic having or using energy.

energy power, strength to do things.

enforce to make people obey (a law etc.).

engaged 1 going to be married. 2 being used by someone else.

engine a machine driven by some sort of power which makes things move.

engineer someone who plans or looks after machines, roads, buildings, bridges etc.

engrave to draw or write with a special tool on a hard surface.

engulf to swallow up.

enhance to improve on, to make better.

enigma a puzzling or mysterious person or thing.

enjoy to like doing something very much.

enlighten to help (someone) to understand (about something).

enlist to join the army, navy or air force.

enmity the state of being an enemy, hatred.

enormous very large.

enough as many or as much as needed.

enquire *see* **inquire**.

enrage to make angry.

enrol to put someone's name in a register, list etc.

ensign 1 a flag on a ship. 2 an officer of low rank in the US navy. 3 (long ago) an officer of low rank in the British army.

ensue to happen afterwards, to result from something.

entangle to catch up in strands of thread, hair etc.; to make complicated.

enter to go into or to come into.

enterprise 1 a new project or task; a business. 2 being bold and adventurous.

entertain to put people in a good mood by doing something for them.

entertainment something which is done to give pleasure to people.

enthralling very interesting, exciting or pleasant.

enthusiasm being enthusiastic.

enthusiastic very keen, very interested.

entice to tempt (someone), to persuade (someone) by offering them something pleasant.

entire the whole thing, complete.

entrance the place where you enter, the way in.

entreat to beg very strongly, especially for help.

entry 1 going or coming in. 2 an entrance.

enumerate to count or mention one by one.

enunciate to speak clearly.

envelop [env**el**op] to wrap up or cover completely.

envelope [**env**elope] the cover in which a letter etc. is placed.

envious feeling envy.

environment surroundings and conditions which affect life.

envy to wish you could have what somebody else has.

epic a long story, film etc. about exciting events.

epidemic a quickly-spreading outbreak of a disease.

epilepsy a serious nervous condition which causes fits.

epileptic (a person) suffering from epilepsy.

epilogue the end part of a play, poem etc.

episode 1 an incident in a story. 2 a part of a television or radio serial.

epistle a letter, especially one in the New Testament written by one of Christ's apostles.

epitaph words written on a tomb.

epoch [**ee**pock] a long period of time in history.

equal 1 exactly the same as. 2 just as good as.

equality being equal.

equator an imaginary line round the earth half-way between the North and South Poles.

equerry a male member of the royal household.

equestrian to do with horse-riding.

equilateral having all sides equal.

equilibrium balance.

equip to provide the things needed for something.

equipment the things you need to do something.

equitable fair, just.

equity fairness, justice.

equivalent equal in value, amount, meaning etc.

era a long period of time.

eradicate to root out, to destroy completely.

erase to rub out, to remove all traces of (something).

erect *adjective* perfectly upright. *verb* to build.

ermine white winter fur of the stoat (with a black tip to its tail).

erosion wearing away, especially of the earth's surface by water, wind etc.

err to make a mistake, to go wrong.

errand a short journey to take a message or to fetch something.

erratic unreliable, changeable in behaviour.

erroneous wrong, in error.

error a mistake.

erupt to burst out, especially of lava etc. coming from a volcano.

escalator a moving staircase.

escapade a (harmless) adventure.

escape to get away, to find a way out.

escort *noun* [**es**cort] a person or persons who accompany or guard another.
verb [es**cort**] to act as an escort to (someone or something).

esparto a type of grass used to make paper.

especially very, more than usual.

espionage spying.

essay a piece of writing on a particular subject.

essential needed, (something) which you must have.

establish 1 to set up (a business, organisation etc.). 2 to prove (something).

estate 1 a large piece of land belonging to one person. 2 a number of houses or factories built in one place. 3 everything a person possesses.

esteem to value highly.

estimate to guess the size or price of (something).

estuary a wide river mouth where it flows into the sea.

etc. and so on.

eternal lasting for ever.

eternity 1 the whole of time. 2 a very long time.

ether a colourless liquid which stops you feeling pain.

etiquette rules of polite and correct behaviour.

eucalyptus a kind of large Australian evergreen tree which produces wood, oil and gum.

evacuate 1 to empty (the bowels). 2 to remove (people) from a place which is dangerous.

evade to avoid, dodge.

evaporate to change from liquid to gas form; to disappear.

evasive 1 trying to avoid being seen. 2 trying to avoid telling someone something.

eve the evening or day before a special event.

even 1 flat and smooth. 2 (of a number) that can be divided by two, not odd.

evening the time between afternoon and night.

event 1 a happening, especially an important one. 2 an item on a sports programme.

eventually at last, in the end.

ever always, at all times.

evergreen (a tree or bush) that does not lose its leaves in the winter.

every each one of many.

evict to force (a person) to leave their property by a court order.

evidence 1 proof, facts, which prove something. 2 a statement given in court.

evident easy to see, plain.

evil very bad, very wicked.

evolution 1 gradual growth and development over a long period of time. 2 the belief that people, animals and plants developed from lower forms of life.

ewe [yoo] a female sheep.

exact absolutely correct, quite right.

exaggerate to say more than is really true.

exalt to raise (someone) up to a high position; to praise highly.

examination a test of how good someone or something is, a check.

examine 1 to look at closely. 2 to test the knowledge of.

example 1 one thing taken out of a number of things to show what the rest are like. 2 good behaviour you should copy.

exasperate to make (a person) very annoyed.

excavate to dig out, especially from a mine or deep place.

exceed 1 to do more than you need to. 2 to be greater than something else.

exceedingly very.

excellent very good.

except *preposition* leaving out, not including.
verb to leave out.

exception something which does not follow the normal rule.

exceptional unusual; unusually good.

excerpt a passage taken from a book, for example.

excess too much or too many of something.

exchange *verb* to change for something else.
noun 1 the act of exchanging. 2 a building where telephone lines are connected.

excise a tax to be paid on goods.

excite to give strong and often pleasant feelings.

exclaim to shout out suddenly.

exclude to leave or shut out.

excommunicate to put outside the membership of a Church.

excruciating (of pain) very severe.

excursion a journey for pleasure.

excuse *noun* [rhymes with 'loose'] a reason for not doing what you should have done.
verb [rhymes with 'news'] to forgive.

execute 1 to put to death as a punishment. 2 to carry out, perform.

executive a person in a high position in a business or other organisation.

exemplary deserving to be followed as an example.

exemplify to show by use of an example.

exercise movement such as walking, running etc. to keep you fit.

exertion hard effort.

exhale to breathe out.

exhaust *verb* 1 to tire out. 2 to use up entirely.
noun the part of a motor engine that draws off used gases.

exhibition a display, show, for example of pictures.

exhilarating making you glad and lively.

exile *noun* 1 a person who lives outside his native country. 2 a long spell spent outside your native country. *verb* to force (a person) to leave their native country.

exist to live; to be.

exit the way out of a place.

exodus leaving, going out.

expand to grow larger, to spread out.

expanse a wide stretch of space.

expansion expanding or being expanded; something expanded.

expect to think something will happen.

expedient (what is) in someone's interest, what is useful to do.

expedition a special journey to a place to find out more about it.

expel to send away; to drive out, force to leave.

expenditure spending; the amount spent or used up, especially of money.

expensive costing a lot of money.

experience 1 something that happens to you. 2 what you learn from seeing, hearing, touching etc.

experiment a test done on something to find out more about it.

expert a person who is very good at something or knows a lot about something.

expire 1 to come to an end; to die. 2 to breathe out.

explain to say clearly how something happened or what something is about.

explicit made very clear.

explode to burst or blow up with a loud noise.

exploit *noun* [**ex**ploit] a brave or daring deed.
verb [ex**ploit**] 1 to use (especially a person) for your own purposes. 2 to use in order to get the best out of.

explore to search a place thoroughly to find out more about it.

export to send goods out of a country.

expose to uncover, allow to be seen; to let light into (a photographic film).

express *verb* to state clearly.
adjective (of a bus, train etc.) travelling more quickly than usual.

expulsion expelling; being expelled.

exquisite very delicate and beautiful.

extend to stretch out, to make longer or larger.

extension 1 extending or being extended. 2 a part added to something else, for example a building.

extent the size or amount of something.

exterior (on) the outside of something.

exterminate to destroy completely, to kill off.

external outside.

extinct 1 not in existence any more. 2 (of a volcano) not active.

extinguish to put out (a light or a fire).

extol to praise very highly.

extortion getting money, usually by threats or by violence.

extra 1 in addition to. 2 more than is needed or usual.

extract *verb* [ex**tract**] to remove, take out (teeth, for example).
noun [**ex**tract] a part taken out of something else.

extraordinary very strange, unusual.

extravagant foolishly wasteful.

extreme 1 farthest away. 2 very great indeed.

exuberant full of life and high spirits.

exult to rejoice greatly.

eye 1 the part of the head with which you see. 2 the hole in a needle.

eyrie the nest of a bird of prey.

F

fable a story or legend, often about animals, which teaches you something.

fabric 1 cloth, material. 2 the outside parts of a building (walls, roof etc.).

fabulous 1 astonishingly good, great. 2 like something in a fable.

façade the front face of a building.

face *noun* 1 the front part of the head. 2 the front of an object. *verb* to turn towards (something).

facetious witty, funny in a cheeky way.

facial concerning the face.

facility 1 the ability to do something easily. 2 **facilities** the equipment or the means to do something.

facsimile an exact copy of a piece of writing etc.

fact something that is true.

faction a group within a group.

factor 1 something which leads to a result. 2 a number used in multiplication.

factory a place where goods are made by machinery.

factual real, true.

fad something someone likes or dislikes very much, for example a kind of food; a fashion which lasts only a short time.

faddy having fads, especially about food.

fade 1 to lose colour, become dim. 2 to begin to grow weaker.

fahrenheit a scale for measuring temperature in which water freezes at 32 degrees and boils at 212 degrees.

fail 1 not to do something that you are expected to do. 2 not to pass an exam.

failure lack of success.

faint *adjective* 1 not clear, not easy to see, hear etc. 2 about to faint, weak. *verb* to lose one's senses, become unconscious.

fair *adjective* 1 light in colour, not dark, blonde. 2 reasonable, just. 3 neither good nor bad, quite good. *noun* a travelling open-air entertainment with sideshows etc.; a market.

fairy an imaginary person with magic power.

faith belief in somebody or something.

faithful true; able to be trusted.

fake *verb* to make a false copy of (something), often in order to deceive; to pretend to have (an illness etc.). *noun* an object which or person who is not genuine.

falcon a kind of bird of prey.

fall to drop, come down; to become lower.

fallacious false, not true.

fallible liable to make mistakes or to be wrong.

fallow (of land) ploughed but left without crops.

fallow deer a kind of small light brown deer.

false 1 not true; not real. 2 not able to be trusted.

falsify to change (words, for example in a document) for a bad purpose.

falter to hesitate, stumble.

fame being famous.

familiar well-known to you.

family a group of close relatives, especially a father, mother and their children.

famine being without food for a very long time.

famished very hungry.

famous well known, recognised by many people.

fan 1 an instrument to make air move and keep you cool. 2 a person who takes a great interest in a football team or a pop singer.

fanatic a person who is too enthusiastic about something.

fanciful unreal, imaginary.

fancy *verb* 1 to think that you can see something. 2 to want.
adjective decorated, not plain.

fanfare a short burst of music from a trumpet or trumpets.

fang a long sharp tooth on some animals and snakes.

fantastic 1 strange, unreal, belonging to fantasy. 2 (*informal*) very good, marvellous.

fantasy imaginary, unreal things; a story based on these.

far not near, a long way away.

farce 1 a ridiculous type of play. 2 a mockery.

fare money paid for a journey.

farewell goodbye; taking leave of someone.

far-fetched not easy to believe.

farm land (usually with a house and other buildings) used for growing crops and keeping animals.

farmer a person who owns or looks after a farm.

farther at a greater distance away.

farthing an old-fashioned coin, formerly the lowest value British coin.

fascinate to please (someone) by arousing delight or curiosity.

fashion up-to-date dress and style.

fast *adjective* 1 very quick, at great speed. 2 stopped from moving.
noun a time without food.

fasten to tie or join things together.

fastidious very careful about details, hard to please.

fat *adjective* very big all round, not thin.
noun the greasy part of meat.

fatal causing death.

fate what is going to happen or is likely to happen in the future.

father the male parent.

fathom a unit for measuring the depth of water, equal to six feet (about 1.8 metres).

fatigue 1 great tiredness. 2 weakness in metals caused by overuse.

fault 1 something which is not right and which spoils a thing or person. 2 a mistake, something you do wrong.

fauna the animals of a region or of a period of time.

favour something good you do for someone.

favourite the one that you like better than any of the others.

fawn 1 a young deer. 2 a light brown colour.

fax *noun* a machine for sending written messages etc. by telephone line; they are copied by another machine on arrival.
verb to send (a message etc.) by fax.

fear to be afraid of; to be frightened that something might happen.

feasible able to be done, likely.

feast a large special meal; a banquet.

feat a clever or daring deed.

feather one of the flat light parts which cover a bird's body and wings.

feature 1 a noticeable or outstanding part of something. 2 **features** the parts of the face, such as the eyes, ears, nose. 3 a long special article in a newspaper; a long film.

feckless (of a person) badly organised, weak.

federal 1 of a country in which several states are joined under one main government. 2 (in the the USA) of the central government rather than the State governments.

fee a payment, especially the amount you are paid to do something.

feeble weak, with no strength.

feed to give food to.

feel 1 to know something by touching it. 2 to think.
feeler the part of an insect which it uses to touch or feel.
feelings how you feel about things, sadness, happiness etc.
feign to pretend (to have an injury, for example).
felicity great joy.
feline of or like a cat or the cat family.
fellow a man or a boy, a person.
felon a person who has committed a felony.
felony a very serious crime.
felt a kind of thick woolly cloth.
female a girl or a woman; an animal which can be a mother.
feminine concerning girls or women.
feminism trying to give women the same rights and opportunities as men.
fen low-lying marshy ground, often flooded.
fence *noun* a wood or metal barrier, for example round a field or garden.
verb to fight with swords as a sport.
fend (off) to keep or push (someone or something) off.
ferment *verb* [fer**ment**] (of a liquid) to bubble and change chemically through the action of yeast, for example.
noun [**fer**ment] great excitement.
fern a plant with feathery leaves but no flowers.
ferocious very wild, savage.
ferret a small furry animal used for hunting rabbits.
ferry a boat which carries people and cars across water.
fertile 1 (of land) able to produce crops. 2 able to produce young.
fertilise to make fertile.
fervent very keen, enthusiastic.
fester (of a wound or sore) to become poisoned.

festival a special occasion for large numbers of people to enjoy themselves.
festive like a festival; in a holiday mood, cheerful.
festoon to decorate with flowers, ribbons, for example.
fetch to go and get, to bring back what you were sent for.
fête an outdoor event with stalls, sideshows etc.
fetlock the back part of a horse's leg just above the foot.
fetters chains round the ankles of a prisoner.
fettle: in good *or* **fine fettle** in good condition, health or spirits.
feud a quarrel between people or groups which lasts for a long time.
fever an illness which makes the body hot.
few not many.
fiancé [feeahnsay] a man to whom a woman is engaged to be married.
fiancée [feeahnsay] a woman to whom a man is engaged to be married.
fiasco a disaster, a complete failure.
fib a lie about something unimportant.
fibre thread-like substance usually used to make into something.
fickle changeable in mood, unreliable.
fiction stories; something which is made up.
fictitious made up, imagined, not true.
fiddle a violin.
fidelity loyalty, faithfulness.
fidget to be restless; to wriggle about.
field a piece of land that is usually enclosed by a hedge, fence or wall.
fiend a devil, evil spirit.
fierce violent, wild, cruel.
fiery 1 quick-tempered. 2 flaming with fire.
fifteen 15, a number.
fifty 50, a number.

fig a sweet fruit full of tiny seeds.

fight a struggle or battle between two or more people.

figment something that only exists in the mind.

figure 1 a number used in mathematics. 2 a shape, especially of the human body.

filch to steal.

file 1 an instrument with a rough edge for making things smooth. 2 a line of people one behind the other. 3 a box or folder for keeping papers in an office.

filial of or like a son or daughter.

filigree a kind of very finely worked wire used to make jewellery etc.

filings the small scraps or dust rubbed off by a file.

fill to make full.

filly a young female horse.

film 1 a very thin covering. 2 a roll put into a camera to take photographs. 3 a story etc. shown in a cinema or on television.

filter *noun* 1 something which allows liquid or gas to pass through, leaving behind dirt or other unwanted substances. 2 the part of a camera or telescope which controls the light which enters it. 3 a traffic light which allows one lane of traffic to go while the others are still stopped.

filthy very dirty.

fin one of the thin flat parts of a fish which help it to swim.

final *adjective* at the end, the last.
noun the last match in a competition, which decides the winner.

finale [fin**ah**ly] the last part of a piece of music, a play etc.

finance money matters.

financial concerning money or the use of money.

finch a kind of small seed-eating bird.

find to come across something you have been looking for.

fine *adjective* 1 when the weather is pleasant. 2 very good, excellent; beautiful. 3 very thin.
noun a sum of money paid as a punishment for breaking the law.

finesse great skill and cunning.

finger one of the five long parts of the hand; one of four of these parts apart from the thumb.

finish to complete, to end.

fir a kind of evergreen tree with cones.

fire *noun* things burning.
verb to shoot a gun.

fireman a person whose job it is to prevent or put out fires.

fireproof not able to burn.

firework a container with gunpowder in it which makes a display of coloured flames and sparks when lit.

firm *adjective* without changing; fixed.
noun a group of people running a business.

first 1 at the very beginning. 2 coming before everyone else, for example in a race.

first aid giving help to someone who is injured or ill before a doctor comes.

fish *noun* an animal which lives and breathes in water.
verb to try to catch fish.

fisherman a person who catches fish.

fishmonger a person who sells fish in a shop.

fist the hand and fingers closed tightly together.

fit *adjective* 1 in good health, well and strong. 2 suitable.
verb to be the right size for.

five 5, a number.

fix 1 to put in place firmly. 2 to put right.

fixture 1 anything which is not movable. 2 the date set aside for a sporting event.

fizz bubbles of gas in a liquid.

fizzy with a lot of bubbles.

flabbergasted very surprised, astonished.

flag a piece of cloth with a special pattern and colours, the sign of a country or club etc.

flagon a large container, often for wine, with a handle, spout and lid.

flagrant very obvious or deliberate (in a bad sense).

flail an instrument for threshing corn.

flake a small thin piece of something.

flamboyant brightly coloured; very showy in manner and appearance.

flame the bright blazing part of a fire.

flamingo a kind of tall long-necked wading bird with pink, bright red and black feathers.

flank 1 the side of the body between the ribs and the hip. 2 either side (left or right) of an army etc.

flannel a kind of soft woollen cloth.

flap 1 a piece that hangs down or over something. 2 an up and down movement, of a bird's wings for example.

flare to blaze up suddenly.

flash a beam of light which comes and goes quickly.

flask 1 a narrow-necked bottle. 2 a container for keeping things hot.

flat *adjective* 1 level. 2 below the correct note in music.
noun a set of rooms all on one floor.

flatfish one of several kinds of flat seafish, for example the sole.

flatten to make flat.

flatter to say that (someone) is better than they really are.

flaunt to show clearly or proudly.

flavour the taste of something.

flaw a fault, a weak place.

flax a kind of plant whose fibres can be made into linen.

flaxen (of hair) light yellow.

flea a small jumping insect which bites people and animals.

fleck a tiny piece of something.

fledgeling a young bird which is learning to fly.

flee to go away quickly; to run from trouble or danger.

fleece the wool of a sheep.

fleet a number of ships together.

fleeting quickly passing, very brief.

flesh the soft part of the body which covers the bones.

flex *noun* wire covered with rubber or plastic used to carry electric current.
verb to bend (a muscle, limb etc.).

flexible easily bent.

flick to strike or move (something) very quickly and lightly.

flicker (of a light) to go on and off quickly.

flight 1 flying. 2 escaping.

flimsy thin, weak, easily destroyed.

flinch to draw back from something.

fling to throw something away from you.

flint a kind of very hard stone.

flip to toss (for example, a coin) into the air quickly.

flippant not taking things seriously, joking in manner.

flirt to try to interest a member of the opposite sex in a playful way.

flit to move lightly and in short flights (like a butterfly).

float to stay on the surface of water without sinking.

flock *noun* a number of animals of the same sort together.
verb to gather together.

flog to strike harshly with a stick or whip.

flood when water overflows from rivers and lakes on to roads and fields.

floor the part of a room you walk on.

flop to sit or fall down suddenly and heavily.

flora the plants of a region or of a period of time.

floral having to do with flowers.

florid 1 (of a face) red. 2 too highly ornamented.

florist a person who sells flowers.

flotsam 1 things thrown overboard from a ship. 2 **flotsam and jetsam** unwanted things or people.

flounder *verb* to struggle about in mud or shallow water; to act or speak awkwardly.
noun a kind of small flatfish used as food.

flour wheat or other grain which has been crushed into a powder which is used for baking.

flourish 1 to do well; to be healthy. 2 (of flowers) to grow well. 3 to wave about.

flow to move smoothly along like running water.

flower the part of a plant, usually colourful, which produces the seeds.

flu (short for **influenza**) an illness like a very bad cold which causes shivering and aches all over the body.

fluctuate to rise and fall; to change, vary.

fluent able to speak, write etc. easily, without hesitating.

fluff tiny soft pieces of cloth etc. which can fly about and catch dust.

fluid a substance that flows, a liquid.

flurried flustered, nervously excited.

flurry *noun* a sudden rush, of wind, for example; a small burst of activity or excitement.
verb to fluster, to excite.

flush 1 to become red in the face. 2 to clean out with large quantities of water.

flustered nervous, confused.

flute a high-pitched wood or metal musical instrument played by blowing.

flutter the quick moving of a bird's wings, for example.

fly *verb* to move through the air, especially on wings or in an aircraft.
noun a kind of small insect with wings.

foal a young horse.

foam froth on the top of a liquid.

focus *noun* the point from which light seems to spread; the centre point of something.
verb 1 to direct your sight or attention on something. 2 to adjust (the lens of a camera, telescope etc.) to give a clearer picture.

fodder food for farm animals and horses.

foe an enemy.

fog air which is thick with mist and sometimes smoke.

foible a little weakness or silliness someone has.

foil *verb* to stop (someone or something) succeeding.
noun 1 very thin metal sheet used to cover food, for example. 2 a thin sword used in fencing.

foist to force (something) unwanted on (someone).

fold to bend (paper or clothes, for example) so that one part covers another.

folder a cardboard cover for papers etc.

foliage the leaves of a tree or other plant.

folk people.

folklore stories etc. passed on from person to person over a period of time.

folksong a song passed on from person to person over a period of time.

follow 1 to go after; to come after. 2 to be able to understand (something you heard or read).

folly lack of good sense, stupidity.

fond: to be fond of to like very much.

fondle to caress, stroke.

food what animals and plants take in to make them grow.

fool *noun* a person who behaves in a silly way.
verb 1 to trick (somebody). 2 to behave like a fool.

foolhardy taking silly risks, foolishly brave.

foolish slightly stupid, silly.

foolproof that cannot go wrong.

foot 1 the part of the leg you stand on. 2 a measure of length, equal to twelve inches (about 30.48 centimetres).

football 1 a large ball used in certain outdoor games. 2 a game played by kicking or throwing such a ball.

foothold a place to put your feet when climbing.

footlights the lights set along the front of the stage.

footwear boots and shoes.

forage *noun* food for horses and farm animals.
verb to search for food etc.

forbearance patience, putting up with things.

forbid to tell (somebody) not to do (something).

forbidding (of a person) stern; (of a task etc.) difficult.

force *noun* strength, power.
verb to make (somebody) do something.

ford a place where a river can be crossed on foot.

foreboding a feeling of fear about something which might happen.

forecast to say what is likely to happen.

forefather an ancestor.

forehead the part of the head between the hair and the eyes.

foreign belonging to another country.

foreman the leader of a group of workmen etc.

forest a large area of woodland.

forestall to act quickly to prevent something happening.

forfeit *verb* to lose (a right) because of something you have done.
noun something you give because you lost in a game, for example.

forge *verb* to copy someone's writing, painting or signature, usually for a bad reason.
noun a blacksmith's workshop.

forget 1 not to remember. 2 to leave (something) behind.

forgive to let (someone) off with something, to pardon.

fork 1 a small tool with long thin spikes for eating with. 2 a large tool with long thin spikes for digging and lifting things. 3 where two roads or rivers meet.

forlorn very sad, left alone, without friends.

form *noun* 1 the shape of something. 2 a printed paper with spaces for you to write things in. 3 a class in a school.
verb to make; to take the shape of.

formal strict, done in a precise way, exactly according to the rules.

formality 1 being formal. 2 something done to conform to the rules.

formation 1 the forming of something. 2 an arrangement of troops or aircraft, for example.

former 1 of earlier times, past. 2 **the former** the first of two things or people just mentioned.

formerly in time past, earlier.

formidable (of a person) powerful, frightening; (of a task) difficult, dangerous.

formula a list of figures, letters or words with a special meaning.

formulate to shape or form an idea in words or writing.

forsake to leave (someone), especially if they are in trouble.

fort a strong building to protect people from attack.

forte [*for*tay] *noun* something you are good at.
adjective, adverb (of a piece of music) to be played loudly.

forthwith immediately.

fortification 1 the act of fortifying. 2 a fortress.

fortify to make stronger, especially a building to resist attack.

fortnight a period of two weeks.

fortress a fort, stronghold.

fortuitous happening by chance, lucky.

fortunate lucky, having good fortune.

fortune 1 good or bad luck. 2 a lot of money.

forty 40, a number.

forward towards the front.

fossil the mark or remains of a creature or plant which lived a very long time ago.

foster to look after, to bring up (especially a child who is not your own).

foul *adjective* very dirty or bad.
noun something that is against the rules (for example in a sport).

found to start something such as a hospital, a club or a school.

foundation 1 the act of founding. 2 the solid base on which a building is built.

founder 1 (of a ship) to fill with water and sink. 2 (of a plan etc.) to fail.

foundry a place where metals are melted down and made into objects.

fountain a device for throwing a stream of water into the air.

four 4, a number.

fourteen 14, a number.

fowl a bird, such as a hen, kept for its meat and eggs.

fox a wild animal which looks like a dog with a reddish brown coat and a long thick tail.

fracas [*fra*ka] a noisy quarrel.

fraction 1 a part of a whole number, such as a third or a half. 2 a part of something.

fracture a break, especially in a bone.

fragile easily broken or damaged, delicate.

fragment a small piece from something larger.

fragrant sweet-smelling.

frail weak, delicate.

frame a border placed round a picture etc.

framework the supports around which something is built.

frank *adjective* sincere, open, saying what you think.
verb to mark with a postmark.

frantic very worried or excited.

fraternal of or like a brother.

fraud 1 cheating someone, deceit. 2 a person or thing pretending to be what it is not.

fraudulent dishonest.

fray a battle, fight.

frayed (especially of cloth) worn and ragged at the edges.

freak (something or someone) very odd, abnormal or unusual.

freckle one of the tiny light-brown marks found on the skin of some people.

free 1 able to do as you wish. 2 given away for nothing.

freedom being free.

freeze to make or be very cold and hard, to turn into ice.

freight goods carried in a ship, aircraft, train etc.; the cost of this.

freighter a ship or aircraft for carrying freight.

frenzy wildness, madness, furious excitement.

frequent happening often.

fresco a picture painted on the wet plaster of a wall.

fresh 1 new; newly gathered; not kept too long; (of food) not preserved. 2 not tired. 3 (of water) without salt.

fretful anxious, bad-tempered through worry.

friar a member of a Christian group who, especially long ago, wandered from place to place without possessions and lived by begging.

friction 1 hindrance caused by two things rubbing together. 2 trouble, quarrelling between people or groups.

fridge short for **refrigerator**.

friend somebody you like and trust and enjoy doing things with.

frieze a row of designs or pictures along the top of a wall.

fright sudden fear.

frill a decoration, usually in folds, round the edge.

fringe 1 short hair brushed forward over the forehead. 2 a border of loose threads, used to decorate a rug or a lampshade for example.

frisky lively, jumping with pleasure.

fritter *noun* a small piece of fruit, meat etc. fried in batter. *verb* **fritter away** to allow (something) to be wasted bit by bit.

frivolous not taking things seriously, silly.

frock a dress.

frog a small jumping animal which can live on land and water.

frolic *verb* to jump about playfully. *noun* a piece of lively cheerful sport.

front the part opposite the back, the part at the beginning of something; the part that faces forwards.

frontage the front part of a shop or other building.

frontier the boundary between two countries.

frost 1 white powdery ice seen in very cold weather. 2 very cold, freezing weather.

frostbite an injury, especially to the limbs, caused by great cold.

froth bubbles on top of a liquid, foam.

frown to wrinkle the forehead, to show you are annoyed or puzzled.

frozen very cold; made into ice.

frugal careful with money or goods.

fruit the part of certain plants where the seeds are found; many kinds are used for food, for example strawberries, oranges.

fruitful successful, having good results.

fruition 1 bearing fruit. 2 something happening that you hoped for.

fruitless unsuccessful, useless.

frump a person who wears dull old-fashioned clothes.

frustrate to prevent (someone) doing something.

fry to cook in boiling fat or oil in a pan.

fudge a kind of sweet like a soft toffee.

fuel anything that can be burned to give heat or light.

fugitive a person who is running away from something.

fulcrum the point on which a lever is placed to move something.

fulfil to carry out (a duty, promise etc.).

full unable to hold anything more.

fumble to move the hands awkwardly, often in order to find something.

fume *noun* **fumes** strong-smelling air coming from smoke or gas.
verb 1 to give off fumes. 2 to be very angry.

fun something enjoyable, amusement, lively pleasure.

function *noun* 1 what someone or something does. 2 an important event, gathering etc.
verb to work properly.

fund a collection of money for something special.

fundamental basic, necessary.

funeral the ceremony held when someone dies.

fungus a plant like a mushroom which grows on other plants or on organic material.

funnel 1 the chimney on a ship or an engine. 2 a tube with a wide mouth, used for example to pour liquids into bottles.

funny 1 amusing, making you laugh. 2 strange, odd.

fur the soft hairy covering of some animals.

furious very angry.

furl to roll up and tie (a flag, an umbrella etc.).

furlong a measure of distance equal to an eighth of a mile (about 220 metres).

furnace a covered fire used to melt metals, for example.

furnish 1 to fit out (a room, a building) with furniture etc. 2 to supply with what is needed to do something.

furniture chairs, tables and similar things.

furrow 1 a narrow trench made by a plough. 2 a deep wrinkle on the skin.

furry covered with fur; feeling like fur.

further at a greater distance, beyond.

furtive sly, done to escape notice.

fury great anger, rage.

fuse *noun* 1 a piece of material which is lit to set off an explosion or a firework. 2 a weak part of an electricity plug or system used as a safety device.
verb 1 (of an electric appliance) to stop working because the fuse has melted. 2 to join (metals) together by melting.

fuselage the body of an aircraft.

fuss excited activity, usually about something quite small.

fussy apt to make a fuss; giving too much importance to details.

fusty stuffy, stale-smelling.

futile unnecessary, useless.

future the time yet to come.

fuzz loose fluffy material on the surface of something.

fuzzy blurred, not clearly seen.

G

gabardine (a garment made out of) a kind of smooth hardwearing material.

gabble to talk so fast that you are not understood, to chatter.

gable the triangular upper part of the end wall of a building.

gad (about) to go about in a careless or idle fashion, to wander aimlessly.

gadabout a person who finds it difficult to settle, restlessly moving from place to place in search of pleasure.

gadfly 1 a horse- or cattle-biting fly. 2 a person who is always irritating others.

gadget a small tool or machine which helps you to do something.

gaff a stick with a hook for catching fish.

gag to cover the mouth to prevent a person from speaking.

gaggle a flock (of geese).

gaiety laughter, cheerfulness.

gain to get or win (something).

gainful paid.

gait a way of walking.

gala a special event or sports meeting, for example a swimming gala.

galactic of the galaxy.

galaxy a very large group of stars.

gale a very strong wind.

gall 1 impudence, cheek. 2 bile.

gallant 1 very brave. 2 well-mannered, especially to women. 3 (in poetry, of a ship etc.) grand, stately.

galleon (long ago) a Spanish sailing-ship.

gallery 1 a high platform, often with seats, in a cinema, a theatre or a church. 2 a building or a large room used for showing pictures.

galley 1 a ship's kitchen. 2 (long ago) a kind of low sailing ship with many oars.

gallon a measure of liquid equal to 8 pints (about 4.5 litres).

gallop to move very fast on four legs, like a horse.

galoshes rubber overshoes for wearing in the rain.

gallows a wooden structure on which criminals used to be hanged.

gambit an opening move in chess, or in a conversation, business transaction etc., which aims to be of advantage later.

gamble to play games for money.

gambol to skip or hop about, like a lamb.

game 1 something that you play; a sport. 2 wild animals or birds which are hunted for sport or food.

gamesmanship the art of winning games or other contests by using the rules unfairly.

gammon a kind of ham from the back part of the pig's leg.

gamut the whole range of something, from the highest to the lowest.

gander a male goose.

gang a group of people doing something together.

gangling tall, lanky and awkward.

gangrene a serious medical condition in which part of the body dies because of bad circulation of blood.

gangster a member of a group of criminals.

gangway 1 a pathway between rows of seats. 2 a bridge placed between a ship and a dock.

gannet a kind of large sea-bird.

gaol, jail [jail] a prison.

gap an opening between two things.

gape to open wide; to be wide open.

garage a place where cars etc. are kept or repaired and petrol is sold.

garb (*old-fashioned*) dress, costume.

garbage rubbish, things to be thrown out.

garble to say (something) in a muddled way.

garden ground where flowers, fruit and vegetables are grown.

gargle to wash the throat.

gargoyle a spout on an old building in the form of a strangely-carved figure of a person or animal.

garish over-bright and showy.

garland flowers made into a circle to wear round the neck.

garlic a strong-smelling and strong-tasting plant, related to the onion, used in cooking.

garment a piece of clothing.

garnet a kind of deep red semi-precious stone.

garnish to add something to (food) to improve its look or flavour.

garret a small room on the top floor or in the roof of a building.

garrison troops stationed in a town or castle.

garrulous talking too much.

garter a band used to hold up a sock or stocking.

gas 1 a substance like air which is neither liquid nor solid. 2 a kind of gas which burns, used for heating and cooking.

gash a long deep cut.

gasp to breathe in very quickly, often in surprise.

gastric of the stomach.

gate a kind of door in a wall or fence.

gather 1 to collect together. 2 to pick (flowers or other plants).

gathering an assembly, meeting.

gauche awkward in company.

gaucho a mounted herdsman in South America, especially in Argentina.

gaudy too showy, bright, and glittering.

gauge *verb* to measure; to estimate. *noun* 1 a device for measuring. 2 the distance between the lines of a railway.

gaunt thin, hungry-looking.

gauntlet a heavy glove with a guard for the wrist.

gauze a kind of very thin cloth you can see through.

gawky awkward in movement, ungainly.

gay happy, cheerful.

gaze to look for a long time; to stare steadily.

gazebo a light garden hut or summerhouse open on all sides to provide a view.

gazelle a kind of small deer found in Africa or Asia.

gear 1 a set of wheels with teeth to make an engine turn. 2 what you need to do something, for example to play some sports.

geiger counter a device for detecting and measuring radiation.

gelatine a substance used to make jellies.

gelding a horse that is made unable to produce offspring.

gem a stone, like a diamond or a ruby, which is very valuable.

gene one of the very small parts of the body which pass on characteristics from parents to children.

general *adjective* usual; often done. *noun* an army officer of high rank.

generalise 1 to extend individual examples into a general law or statement. 2 to make a vague general statement.

generate to make, create, bring into existence.

generation 1 the act of generating. 2 a stage in the history of a family. 3 all the people born about the same time.

generator a machine for making electricity etc.

generic 1 general, not specific to a single individual example. 2 of a genus.

generous kind; giving away freely.

genetic concerned with genes or genetics.

genetics the study of how characteristics are passed on through genes.

genial pleasant, good-natured.

genie (in fairy tales) a magical servant who appears and does someone's bidding and grants wishes.

genius a person who is very clever.

genre [**jon**ra] a kind of style, especially of a piece of writing or a painting.

genteel over-refined, showily polite.

gentian a kind of blue flower that grows on mountains.

gentile a non-Jewish person.

gentility being genteel.

gentle soft, not rough; full of care for other people.

gentleman 1 a man who is well-mannered. 2 a polite word for a man.

gentry the people of high social rank (next below the nobility).

genuflect to bend the knee, especially for worship.

genuine real, true.

genus a grouping of living things, for example kinds of plants or animals.

geography knowledge about the earth and its people.

geology knowledge about rocks etc. and how they are made.

geometry the study of the relations of lines, angles, surfaces and solids.

geranium a strongly-smelling plant with red, white or pink flowers.

gerbil a desert animal like a small rat, often kept as a pet.

geriatric concerning the health and care of old people.

germ a very small living thing that often causes illness.

germinate to sprout, begin to grow (from seeds).

gestation the period of carrying or being carried in the womb till birth.

gesticulate to signal excitedly with the hands and arms.

gesture a movement of the body, especially the hands or head, which shows your feelings.

geyser [**gee**zer] 1 a natural hot spring which shoots water into the air. 2 a kind of gas water heater.

ghastly very pale and ill-looking; very bad, horrible.

gherkin a small green cucumber used for pickling.

ghetto a part of a city where a minority group lives in poverty.

ghost the spirit of a dead person, believed to be seen moving about.

ghoul a spirit which eats dead bodies; someone too interested in death.

giant 1 a huge man, for example in a fairy story. 2 anything that is much larger than usual.

gibberish nonsense words.

gibbon a kind of small tailless ape.

giblets parts of the inside of a chicken etc. which can be eaten, for example the liver, heart.

giddy dizzy; when everything seems to be going round and round.

gift something given, a present.

gigantic very big.

giggle to laugh in a foolish way.

gild to cover with gold paint or with a thin layer of gold.

gills the opening in a fish's head by which it breathes.

gimlet a sharp-pointed tool for making holes for screws etc.

gimmick a clever or tricky device to catch attention.

gin a kind of strong colourless alcoholic drink.

ginger 1 a hot flavouring used in cooking. 2 a reddish-brown colour.

gingerbread a kind of ginger-flavoured cake.

gingerly (to move) with great caution.

gipsy see **gypsy**.

giraffe an African wild animal with a very long neck and long legs.

gird to put a belt etc. round.

girder a metal beam used in building.

girdle 1 a belt. 2 a woman's elastic undergarment round the hips and waist.

girl 1 a female child. 2 a young woman.

girth 1 a measurement round something. 2 a band round a horse to keep the saddle on.

gist the main points of a story, message etc.

give to hand over to someone else.

gizzard part of the digestive system of a bird in the lower neck.

glacial 1 of glaciers. 2 extremely cold.

glacier a slow-moving river of ice.

glad happy, pleased, delighted.

gladiator in ancient Rome, a man who fought in an arena as part of a show.

glamorous beautiful, attractive.

glamour exciting beauty or charm, attractiveness.

glance to look at something and then look away quickly.

gland a part of the body that produces certain liquids, some of which go into the bloodstream.

glare *verb* to stare at in anger. *noun* unpleasant brightness.

glass 1 a hard material through which you can usually see. 2 a cup without a handle made of glass.

glasses two pieces of special glass or plastic put in a light frame and worn to help you to see better.

glaze 1 to fit or cover with glass. 2 to give a shiny surface to (pottery for example). 3 (of the eyes) to become glassy.

gleam to shine faintly.

glean 1 to gather grain. 2 to gather (facts etc.) from a document, conversation etc.

glee merriment, joy.

glib speaking smoothly, quickly, but not always truthfully.

glide to move along very smoothly.

glider a kind of aeroplane that glides through the air without an engine.

glimmer a faint light which can hardly be seen.

glimpse a very short look, a glance.

glint to shine in a small way, to sparkle.

glisten to shine (as) from a wet surface.

glitter to throw out bright rays of light, to sparkle.

gloat to look or be pleased in an unpleasant way.

globe 1 an object like a ball. 2 a round ball with a map of the world drawn on it.

globule a small ball or drop of liquid usually.

gloomy 1 dark and dismal. 2 sad and serious.

glorify to make great or glorious, to make (to seem) more splendid.

glorious splendid, giving great glory.

glory great fame given to someone who has done something very important or valuable.

gloss brightness on the surface of something.

glossary a list of words with explanations of their meanings.

glove one of a pair of coverings for the hands with a separate place for each finger.

glow to shine with a soft light, to burn without flame.

glower to look angrily at someone, to scowl.

glucose a form of sugar found in fruits etc.

glue a substance used for sticking things together.

glum looking sad and unhappy.

glut an over-abundance, too much (of something).

glutton a person who eats too much.

gnarled [narled] twisted and knobbly like an old tree.

gnash [nash] to grind the teeth together because you are angry or in trouble.

gnat [nat] a tiny winged insect which bites.

gnaw [naw] to wear away by using the teeth; to eat by scraping away.

gnome [nome] a dwarf or goblin that is supposed to live under the ground.

gnu [noo] a kind of large African antelope.

go to move away, to leave.

goad *noun* 1 a stick used to prod an animal to make it move. 2 something which prods you into action.
verb to make (someone) do something by annoying them.

goal 1 a place you aim at in games such as football and hockey. 2 the score made when the ball goes into goal.

goat a kind of long-haired animal which has horns and gives milk.

gobble to eat greedily and noisily.

goblet a drinking glass or cup with a stem and base, but no handle.

goblin a kind of wicked fairy.

God the being who is above all others and to whom people pray.

goggles large spectacles to protect the eyes, for example when swimming.

gold a kind of yellow precious metal.

golden 1 made of gold. 2 looking like gold.

goldfish a small bright-orange fish often kept in tanks and ponds.

golf a game played on a large stretch of land with special clubs and a small ball.

gondola a long narrow boat used on the canals in Venice.

gondolier a man who operates a gondola.

gong a hanging piece of metal which makes a booming noise when struck.

good 1 right; true. 2 kind. 3 well-behaved.

goodbye something said when leaving people.

goods things which are bought, sold and owned.

goodwill good feelings (towards someone).

goose a kind of bird with webbed feet.

gooseberry a green fruit which grows on a small prickly bush.

gopher a kind of American burrowing animal.

gore *noun* 1 blood. 2 a triangular piece of material on a garment, for example.
verb to injure with the horns or tusks.

gorge *verb* to eat greedily.
noun a narrow valley with steep sides.

gorgeous splendid, magnificent, very beautiful.

gorgon in Greek legend, a female monster whose looks turned people to stone.

gorilla the largest kind of ape.

gorse a kind of prickly bush with yellow flowers.

gory covered in blood.

gosling a young goose.

gospel 1 teachings of Jesus Christ.
2 **Gospel** one of the first four books of the New Testament. 3 something definitely true.

gossamer 1 very light thread left by spiders on grass for example. 2 a very fine material with almost no weight.

gossip *verb* to talk for a long time about unimportant things, often about other people.
noun a person who tells usually hurtful stories about other people.

gouge to scoop out with force.

goulash a kind of spicy meat and vegetable stew.

govern to be in control of, to rule over (a country for example).

government the people who are in charge of a country.

gown a dress.

grab to snatch, to grasp quickly.

grace 1 a short prayer before or after a meal. 2 a beautiful way of moving.

graceful beautiful (in movement).

gracious polite, kind, pleasant.

grade *noun* a level, size, quality.
verb to put into groups (according to size, for example).

gradient a slope.

gradual little by little.

graffiti [gra**fee**tee] writing or drawings on walls.

graft 1 a shoot from one plant put to grow on another. 2 a piece of skin etc. from one part of the body put to grow on another.

grain 1 a tiny piece of sand or soil.
2 the seed of corn, for example.
3 the lines in wood.

gram a small unit of weight.

grammar the rules of a language.

granary a place where grain is stored.

grand very large and fine, splendid.

grandfather the father of your father or mother.

grandiose trying to produce a great effect or impression.

grandmother the mother of your father or mother.

granite a very hard rock often used for buildings and monuments.

grant to give; to allow.

granule a small grain (of something).

grape a small juicy fruit with green or purple skin.

grapefruit a yellow fruit like a large orange.

graph a diagram which shows the relationship between two amounts etc.

graphic 1 very clear, well-described.
2 concerned with drawing or the design of letters.

grapple to try to catch with the hands, like a wrestler, to struggle with.

grasp 1 to hold firmly in the hand.
2 to understand what you have been told.

grass the common green plant used to feed animals and to cover parks and gardens.

grasshopper a kind of insect with strong back legs for jumping.

grate *noun* where the fire burns in a fireplace.
verb 1 to rub something into little pieces using a rough surface. 2 to make a harsh noise.

grateful thankful, feeling gratitude.

grater an instrument with jagged points used to grate cheese, for example.

gratify to please.

grating an arrangement of metal bars used as a door or covering.

gratitude warm feelings towards someone who has been helpful or kind.

gratuitous 1 given or received without payment. 2 not deserved.

grave *noun* a burial place in the ground.
adjective serious.

gravel small pieces of stone.

gravity the force which pulls objects towards the earth.

gravy a brown liquid eaten with meat, often made from the juice of the meat.

graze 1 to rub away the skin. 2 to feed from grass.

grease 1 animal fat. 2 thick oil used to make machinery run smoothly.

great 1 big. 2 important. 3 very good.

greedy always wanting more, never satisfied.

green 1 the colour of grass. 2 an area of grass.

greengage a green kind of plum.

greengrocer a person who sells vegetables and fruit.

greenhouse a building with glass or plastic walls and roof in which plants are grown.

greet to welcome with words and actions.

gregarious fond of company.

grenade a small bomb thrown by hand.

grey a colour half-way between black and white.

greyhound a kind of fast thin long-legged dog.

grid 1 a framework or pattern of crisscrossed bars. 2 a network of power-stations supplying electricity to a large area.

grief sorrow, deep sadness.

grieve to mourn (over or for).

grievous causing great grief; very serious.

griffin a creature in fables with the body of a lion and the head and wings of an eagle.

grill *verb* to cook (meat etc.) using direct heat.
noun 1 a device for grilling, often part of a cooker. 2 food cooked by grilling.

grim stern; severe; fierce.

grime dirt, especially when stuck to a surface.

grin a wide smile.

grind 1 to rub something until it becomes powder. 2 to sharpen (a knife, for example) by rubbing the edge.

grip to grasp tightly.

grisly dreadful, horrible.

gristle the tough part of meat, often found near the bone.

grit 1 very small pieces of stone or sand. 2 courage.

groan to make a low, sad, sound, often when hurt.

grocer a person who sells foods and other goods for the house.

groin the part of the body where the inner part of the thigh joins the rest of the body.

groom *noun* 1 a person who looks after horses. 2 short for **bridegroom.**
verb to brush and clean (a horse).

groove a narrow channel cut into something.

grope to feel for (something) clumsily without seeing it.

gross 1 very fat, bulky and ugly. 2 coarse. 3 (of a sum of money etc.) whole, before anything has been deducted.

grotesque very strange, especially in shape.

grotto a cave.

ground 1 the surface of the earth; land. 2 a place for playing certain outdoor games.

group a number of people, animals or things together.

grouse *noun* a kind of plump game bird found especially on the Scottish moors.
verb to complain, grumble.

grove a small wood, a cluster of trees.

grovel 1 to show a great deal of respect to someone, especially in order to get what you want. 2 to lie or crawl on the ground, as a sign of obedience to someone.

grow 1 to become bigger. 2 to raise (plants).

growl to show anger by snarling, like a dog.

grub an insect, such as a caterpillar, before it has grown wings or legs.

grubby dirty.

grudge *verb* to give (something) unwillingly to someone.
noun a feeling of ill will against someone, often because of something they have done to you.

gruesome horrible.

gruff having a rough coarse voice.

grumble to complain, not loudly but often.

grumpy bad-tempered.

grunt a noise like that made by a pig.

guarantee *noun* a piece of paper promising to do something, especially to replace or repair something if it goes wrong.
verb to give a guarantee, to promise.

guard *verb* to keep safe.
noun 1 a person whose job it is to protect something or someone. 2 a person in charge of a train on its journey.

guardian someone who looks after another person, especially when taking the place of a parent.

guerilla a person who fights secretly against the people in power.

guess to say what you think is correct without really knowing.

guest 1 a visitor to someone's house. 2 a person staying in a hotel etc.

guffaw a loud burst of laughter.

guide *verb* to show the way.
noun 1 a person who does this. 2 **Guide** a Girl Guide, a member of an organisation for girls.

guile deceit, cunning.

guillotine 1 long ago, in France, a machine for beheading people. 2 a machine for cutting paper.

guilt 1 having done wrong. 2 the feeling of having done wrong.

guitar a musical instrument with six strings, played by plucking the strings.

gulf a large bay.

gull a kind of common sea-bird.

gullet the food passage from the throat to the stomach.

gullible easily fooled, over-trustful.

gully a narrow channel made by water.

gulp to swallow greedily and noisily.

gum 1 a substance used to stick things together. 2 the part of the mouth round the roots of the teeth. 3 chewing gum; a chewy sweet.

gun a weapon from which bullets are fired.

gurgle to make a bubbling noise like water leaving a container.

guru [**goo**roo] an Indian religious leader and teacher.

gush to flow out quickly in large amounts.

gust a sudden wind.

gusto great enjoyment, enthusiasm.

gutter a channel for water along the edge of a road or roof, for example.

guy 1 a model of Guy Fawkes, burnt on a bonfire on 5 November. 2 a man.

guy(rope) a rope used to hold a tent in place, for example.

guzzle to eat greedily.

gymnastics exercises for the body.

gymnasium a place for gymnastics.

gypsy, gipsy member of a tribe of wandering people.

gyroscope a wheel which spins inside a frame and keeps balance, used to keep ships steady, for example.

H

habit something you do a lot without thinking about it much, a custom.

habitat the natural home of an animal or plant.

habitual done through habit; usual.

hack to cut roughly.

hackles hairs on the back of the neck of some animals which rise when they are angry or afraid; long feathers on the back of the neck of cocks and other birds.

hacksaw a saw for cutting metal.

haddock a kind of small sea-fish used as food.

hag an ugly old woman.

haggard looking tired, thin and ill.

haggis a Scottish dish made from chopped up heart, lungs and liver of a sheep cooked with oatmeal etc.

haggle to argue hard (over), especially in bargaining.

haiku a short Japanese poem of seventeen syllables.

hail *noun* frozen raindrops.
verb to call to (someone), to greet.

hair thread-like strands which grow on the head and the skins of people and animals.

hairdresser a person who cuts and arranges hair.

halcyon peaceful, gentle, calm.

hale very well, healthy.

half one of two equal parts of a thing.

halibut a kind of large flat sea-fish, used as food.

hall 1 a very large room for meetings etc. 2 an entrance passage. 3 a very large house.

hallmark a sign used to show the quality of gold or silver.

Halloween 31 October, when witches and spirits are believed by some people to be around; in some places children dress up and play special games.

hallucination seeing or hearing something which is not really there.

halo 1 a ring of light round the sun or moon. 2 a circle painted or drawn round the heads of holy people in pictures.

halt to stop.

halter a rope with a head-piece for leading a horse.

halve to divide into two equal parts.

ham salted or smoked meat from a pig's leg.

hamburger a cake of minced meat fried and eaten in a roll.

hamlet a small village.

hammer a hard tool used to drive in nails.

hammock a hanging mattress or bed held up by ropes.

hamper *noun* a large basket with a lid. *verb* to hinder.

hamster a small animal like a large mouse, often kept as a pet.

hand *noun* 1 the part of the arm below the wrist. 2 a pointer on a clock.
verb to pass to someone.

handbag a bag carried in the hand.

handicap something that keeps you back; a disadvantage.

handicapped having something seriously wrong with you (for example, not being able to walk).

handicraft 1 a skill or art using the hands, for example pottery, embroidery. 2 the work produced by this skill.

handily 1 conveniently, suitably. 2 easily.

handiwork 1 work produced using the hands, such as sewing, pottery. 2 something done or brought about by a person.

handkerchief a small piece of cloth for wiping the nose.

handle *verb* to touch with the hand. *noun* the part of something which you hold in your hand.

handlebars the part of a bicycle you hold on to to steer it.

handsome good looking.

handy 1 useful. 2 skilled at doing a number of things.

hang to fasten something at the top, for example with a hook or nail.

hangar a large shed where aircraft are kept.

hanger a piece of wood, plastic or wire specially shaped to hang clothes on.

hang-gliding a sport in which a person flies suspended from a light-framed vehicle with wings and a bar for guidance.

hank a loop or coil of wool, string etc.

hanker to have a strong desire (for).

haphazard without planning or proper arrangement.

happen to take place, to occur.

harangue a loud angry speech to a group of people.

harass to annoy, cause difficulties for.

harbour a place of shelter for boats.

hard 1 difficult to do. 2 tough, firm, not soft.

hardly scarcely, only just.

hardship trouble, distress.

hardware 1 metal goods, tools etc. 2 the machinery which makes up a computer.

hardy strong, able to bear pain, for example; (of a plant) able to live in hard conditions.

hare an animal like a large rabbit.

harem the women's rooms in a Muslim house; the women themselves.

hark 1 to listen. 2 **hark back** to mention something which was being talked about earlier.

harlequin a kind of clown wearing a brightly-coloured costume with a diamond pattern.

harm danger; trouble; damage.

harmonica a mouth organ.

harmonious 1 (of notes in music) in harmony. 2 pleasant, free from ill-feeling.

harmonium a musical instrument, a kind of small organ.

harmony 1 notes in music played pleasantly together. 2 the state of being in agreement, friendship etc.

harness the straps used to control a horse, for example.

harp a large triangular musical instrument which is played by plucking the strings.

harpoon a spear used in catching whales.

harpsichord a musical instrument like a piano except that the strings are plucked rather than struck.

harrow a large heavy spiked implement for loosening earth after ploughing.

harsh rough, severe, unkind.

harvest 1 a crop of food to be gathered in. 2 the time when this is done.

haste speed, quickness, hurry.

hat a head covering, often with a brim.

hatch *verb* 1 to be born from an egg. 2 to make secret plans. *noun* an opening in the deck of a ship, for example.

hatch-back (a car) with a sloping rear that lifts to become a door.

hatchet a small axe.

hate *verb* to dislike very much, to detest. *noun, also* **hatred**, very great dislike.

haughty too proud of yourself and looking down on others.

haul to drag, to pull with effort.

haunch the part of the side of the body between the lower ribs and the thigh.

haunted often visited by a ghost.

have to possess, to own.

haven 1 a harbour. 2 a safe place.

haversack a bag, usually carried by a strap over one shoulder, for holding personal belongings.

havoc great destruction, ruin.

hawk a large bird which hunts small birds or animals for food.

hawthorn a kind of prickly bush with white, pink or red flowers and red berries.

hay dried grass used as animal food.

hazard danger, risk.

haze very light mist or thin cloud.

hazel 1 a kind of small tree with brown nuts which you can eat. 2 a light brown colour.

head 1 the part of the body above the neck. 2 the chief person. 3 the front part or top of something.

headache pain in the head.

headland a strip of land jutting out into the sea or lake.

headlong hastily, without thinking.

headstrong self-willed, obstinate.

heady very excited or exciting; (of wine etc.) making you drunk.

heal to make well again after being hurt or ill, to cure.

health 1 the state of your body or mind. 2 freedom from illness, fitness.

heap things placed one on top of another untidily, a pile.

hear 1 to catch the sound of; to listen to. 2 to get news.

hearing 1 the sense by which you hear things. 2 the distance within which you hear something. 3 the time when a legal case is heard in court.

hearse a car or carriage for carrying a coffin to a funeral.

heart 1 the part of the body which pumps the blood round the body. 2 the centre or most important part of something. 3 a shape with two rounded parts at the top and a sharp point at the bottom. 4 a playing card with red heart shapes on it.

hearth the floor of a fireplace.

heartless without pity, cruel.

hearty 1 strong, healthy. 2 full of life, good-humoured. 3 (of a meal) nourishing.

heat 1 warmth, being hot. 2 one of the races leading to a final.

heath 1 rough open country, moorland. 2 heather.

heather a small plant with purple or white flowers which grows on moorlands.

heave 1 to pull strongly. 2 to lift (something) and then throw it.

heaven the place where God is said to live; perfect happiness.

heavy having great weight, not easily lifted.

heckle to interrupt a public speaker with awkward remarks and questions.

hectare a measure of area equal to 10 000 square metres.

hectic wildly active, exciting; feverish.

hedge small bushes or trees grown in lines to separate fields or gardens.

hedgehog a small animal with prickles on its back which rolls itself into a ball when in danger.

hedgerow a hedge, especially along a country road.

heed to pay attention to.

heel the back part of the foot.

hefty powerful, heavy, bulky.

heifer [**heff**er] a young cow.

height the distance from top to bottom, how tall something is.

heinous (of crimes) very serious, very bad.

heir a man or boy who receives a dead person's property.

heiress a girl or woman who receives a dead person's property.

heirloom a piece of family property handed down from one generation to another.

helicopter an aeroplane which flies by means of a large overhead propeller.

helium a very light gas which does not burn.

hell the place where the Devil is said to live; a place of very great suffering.

helm the wheel or handle by which a ship is steered.

helmet a covering to protect the head.

help to do something for another, to assist.

helpless unable to do something for yourself, needing the help of others.

helter-skelter *noun* a spiral slide at a fair etc.
adverb in disorderly haste.

hem an edge of cloth which has been turned over and stitched.

hemisphere one of the two halves of the world.

hemp a kind of plant from which rope can be made and from which a drug is produced.

hen a female bird, especially the common fowl kept for eggs and meat.

henchman a trusted follower, usually of a bad person.

henna a plant from which a reddish dye is made.

herald 1 (long ago) a messenger of a king or queen. 2 an official who keeps records of coats of arms. 3 a sign of something to come.

herb a plant used as a medicine or for its flavour.

herd a large number of the same kind of animals together.

hereditary passed on by heredity.

heredity the passing on of characteristics from parents to children.

heritage what is passed on from one generation to another.

hermit a person who lives on his own, usually in a lonely place.

hero 1 a man or boy who acts with great bravery. 2 the main man or boy in a story etc.

heroic (behaving) like a hero.

heroine 1 a girl or woman who acts with great bravery. 2 the main girl or woman in a story etc.

heron a kind of wading bird with long legs and neck.

herring a kind of small sea-fish, used for food.

hesitate to stop what you are doing for a moment because you are not sure.

hew to cut or carve out, especially with an axe.

hexagon a flat shape with six sides.

hibernate to sleep through the winter as some animals do.

hiccup a sudden noise in your throat, usually because you have eaten or drunk too quickly.

hide *verb* 1 to keep in a secret place. 2 to go where you cannot be found.
noun 1 the skin of an animal. 2 a place where you can hide to watch birds or animals.

hideous terrible to look at, ugly, frightening.

hierarchy a system of people or groups arranged in order from the highest to the lowest.

hieroglyphics (in ancient Egypt) a system of writing using pictures or symbols.

high 1 tall, well above the ground. 2 great. 3 (of a sound) the opposite of low.

highwayman (long ago) a man who stopped travellers and robbed them.

hijack to seize control of (an aeroplane, ship etc.) by force.

hike a long walk in the country.

hilarious very funny.

hill a high piece of land often with steep sides.

hillock a small hill.

hilt the handle of a sword or dagger.

hind *noun* a female deer. *adjective* back, behind.

hinder to make it difficult for (someone) to do something.

hindrance something which hinders.

hinge a moving joint which allows a door etc. to open and close easily.

hint to say something in a roundabout way; to suggest.

hinterland land lying behind a coast or shore, for example; the inland parts of a country.

hip the place where the legs join the body.

hippopotamus a kind of large African animal which lives near water.

hire to borrow something for a short time and pay for its use.

hiss to push air sharply through the teeth.

historic significant, of great importance in history.

historical 1 belonging to history, dealing with events of the past. 2 based on facts rather than on stories of the past.

history 1 what happened in the past. 2 learning about the past.

hit to strike, give a blow or knock to.

hitch *noun* 1 a small difficulty. 2 a kind of knot. *verb* 1 to fasten by means of a hook, rope etc. 2 to hitch-hike. 3 to move (something) with a jerk.

hitch-hike to beg free lifts on passing cars or lorries.

hive a container in which bees live and make honey.

hoard to gather together and keep to yourself (money, property etc.)

hoar-frost white frost.

hoarse having a rough harsh voice.

hoax a trick, deception.

hobble to walk with a limp.

hobby something you do in your spare time.

hobgoblin a mischievous spirit.

hock 1 a joint in the middle of an animal's back leg. 2 a kind of German white wine.

hockey a game played by two teams with curved sticks and a ball.

hocus-pocus 1 trickery. 2 a form of words meant to deceive or confuse.

hoe a tool used for breaking up the soil and taking out weeds.

hog 1 a male pig. 2 a greedy person.

hoist to raise up, especially using ropes etc.

hold *verb* 1 to keep a grip of. 2 to have inside, to contain. *noun* the storage part of a ship.

hole an opening; a gap.

holiday a time of rest and enjoyment; a time when you are free from work or school.

hollow empty, with nothing inside.

holly a kind of evergreen bush with sharp pointed leaves and red berries.

holocaust great destruction with many deaths, especially by fire.

holster a leather case for a pistol, worn on the belt, for example.

holy connected with God or a god.

homage public display of obedience to a superior.

home the place where you live.

homicide the killing of another human being; a person who does this.

homogeneous all of the same kind.

hone to sharpen using a stone.

honest able to be trusted, truthful.

honesty being honest.

honey a sweet food made by bees.

honeycomb a wax structure in which bees store honey and their eggs.

honeymoon a holiday spent by a newly-married couple.

honeysuckle a climbing plant with sweet-smelling yellow and pink flowers.

honorary having a position or job as an honour without having to do anything or without being paid.

honour 1 great respect. 2 fame.

honourable showing or bringing honour; honest.

hood 1 a covering to protect the head and neck. 2 a folding cover for a baby's pram or for a motor car.

hoodlum a crook, criminal.

hoodwink to fool, cheat.

hoof the hard part of the foot of some animals, for example horses.

hook a bent and pointed piece of metal, plastic, etc. to hold or catch things.

hooligan a wild rough badly-behaved person, a troublemaker, a ruffian.

hoop a ring of wood, metal etc.

hoot 1 the sound made by a car horn etc. 2 the sound made by an owl.

hop to jump up and down on one foot.

hope to wish and believe that something pleasant will happen.

hopeless 1 giving no reason for hope. 2 very bad.

horde a large (disorderly) crowd.

horizon the line where the sky and the earth seem to touch.

horn 1 a piece of hard material which grows out of the head of some animals. 2 a bell-shaped musical instrument you blow through. 3 a device on a car or bus which makes a noise to give a warning.

hornet a large kind of wasp with a painful sting.

hornpipe a lively sailors' dance.

horrendous very bad, terrible.

horrible very unpleasant.

horrid dreadful; causing fear.

horror something very frightening or terrible.

horse a large animal with hooves and a mane, often used to ride on or to pull vehicles.

hose a tube through which water can be directed.

hospitable kindly, welcoming to strangers.

hospital a place where sick people are cared for.

hospitality welcome shown to visitors or guests.

host 1 a man who invites others to his house as guests. 2 a large crowd.

hostage someone kept prisoner to force someone else to do something they don't want to do.

hostel a place where students or young people, for example, can stay.

hostess a woman who invites others to her house as guests.

hostile very unfriendly.

hot very warm.

hot dog a hot sausage in a bread roll.

hotel a building where you can pay to stay the night or buy a meal.

hotfoot in great haste, at speed.

hound a dog which is trained to hunt.

hour a length of time of 60 minutes.

house a building in which people live.

hovel / hydrogen

hovel a poor miserable house.

hover to stay in the air above a place or thing.

hovercraft a vehicle which travels just above the surface of water or land on a cushion of air.

howl a long loud cry like that made by a wolf, for example; a wailing noise.

howler a silly or amusing mistake.

hub the centre part of a wheel.

hubbub a confused noisy disturbance.

huddle to crowd together, especially for warmth or comfort.

hue 1 a shade of a colour. 2 **hue and cry** widespread alarm and chasing after someone.

huff a bad mood.

hug to hold tightly in the arms.

huge very large.

hulk 1 an old ship no longer used. 2 anything large and clumsy.

hulking large and clumsy, overgrown in size.

hull the main part of a ship or aeroplane.

hullabaloo an uproar, a loud disturbance.

hum *noun* a noise like that made by bees.
verb to make the sound of a tune with the lips together.

human connected with people.

humane kind, showing mercy.

humble simple, modest, not proud.

humbug 1 deceit. 2 nonsense. 3 a kind of boiled sweet.

humid moist, damp.

humility being humble.

humour 1 finding or making things funny. 2 a mood.

hump a large lump on the back of a person or an animal.

hunch 1 a hump. 2 an idea that comes from a guess or a feeling.

hundred a number, 100.

hunger a great need, usually for food.

hunk a large piece, of cheese, for example.

hunt 1 to try to catch or kill wild animals. 2 to look very carefully for something.

hurdle 1 a movable frame which is jumped over in athletics and horse-racing. 2 an obstacle or hindrance.

hurl to throw far away.

hurricane a storm with a very strong wind.

hurry to move or do things very quickly; to rush.

hurt to cause pain to, to injure, to damage.

hurtle to rush or dash along.

husband the man to whom a woman is married.

hush to make or become quiet.

husk the outer covering of some seeds and fruits.

husky *adjective* 1 (of a voice) hoarse. 2 big and strong.
noun a kind of large dog used to pull sledges in some Arctic regions.

hustle to hurry or push roughly.

hut a small, often wooden, building.

hutch a box or cage for keeping tame rabbits.

hyacinth a kind of sweet-smelling spring flower grown from a bulb.

hybrid the offspring of two plants or animals of different breeds.

hydrangea a kind of bush with large pink, blue or white flowers.

hydraulic worked by water power.

hydrofoil a kind of ship which skims along the surface of the water at high speed.

hydrogen a light gas which combines with oxygen to form water.

hyena a kind of wolf-like animal which makes a noise like a wild laugh.

hygiene the science of good health, especially by keeping clean.

hymn a religious song of praise or thanks.

hyperbole an exaggerated statement, not meant to be taken literally.

hyphen a punctuation mark like this - used to join words or parts of words together.

hypnosis a state of deep sleep, in which a person's mind may be controlled by that of another.

hypnotist a person who is able to put you to sleep in this way.

hypochondriac a person who is constantly worried about his or her health without good reason.

hypocrite a person who pretends to be good when he or she is not.

hypodermic a fine needle-like instrument for giving injections beneath the skin.

hysteria, hysterics a very wild upset state.

hysterical being in such a state.

I

ibex a kind of wild goat found in mountains in Southern Europe.

ibis a kind of bird with a long curved beak found in warm wet places.

ice 1 frozen water. 2 an ice cream.

iceberg a very large piece of ice floating in the sea.

ice cream a soft sweet creamy frozen food.

icicle a hanging spike of ice.

icing a sweet mixture sometimes spread over cakes and buns.

idea a thought, something in the mind.

ideal just what is needed, the best possible.

identical exactly the same as something else.

identify to point out (someone or something) known to you and say what or who it is.

identity who someone is as a person.

idiot a person who behaves very stupidly.

idle not working; not wanted to work.

idol a thing, such as a statue or image, or a person worshipped as a god, a false god.

idolise to worship, adore.

idyllic (making you) very happy in a calm simple way.

igloo a house made of snow blocks by Eskimos.

ignite to (cause to) start to burn.

ignition the machinery which starts the engine of a car etc.

ignoramus [igno**ray**mus] an ignorant person.

ignorant not wise, knowing nothing or very little.

ignore to pay no attention to, usually on purpose.

iguana a kind of large lizard found in Central and South America; some have spines along the back.

ill 1 not well, in poor health. 2 bad, harmful.

illegal not legal, against the law.

illegible not able to be read.

illegitimate 1 born of parents who were not married. 2 against the rules.

illicit not allowed, unlawful.

illiterate unable to read or write.

illogical against logic, not reasonable or sensible.

ill-treat to treat badly.

illuminate 1 to shine light or lights on, fill with light. 2 to make clearer, explain more clearly.

illusion something you think you see which is not there.

illustrate to explain something by drawing pictures, for example; to add pictures to.

illustration something which illustrates, for example a picture in a book.

illustrious famous, glorious.

image 1 a figure carved in wood or stone, a statue. 2 a shadowy picture, a reflection.

imaginary not real, made up in the mind.

imagine to think up in your mind (often something which does not exist).

imam a religious teacher and leader in a Muslim community.

imitate to do the same as somebody else, to copy.

immature 1 not fully grown or developed. 2 childish in behaviour.

immediate 1 happening at once. 2 nearest.

immediately at once.

immense enormous, very large.

immerse 1 to put completely into liquid. 2 **immerse yourself in (something)** to give all your attention to (something).

immigrant a person who immigrates.

immigrate to come into a country to live there.

imminent about to happen.

immobile not moving.

immobilise to make unable to move.

immoral not moral, wicked.

immortal living forever, never dying.

immune safe, especially from disease.

immunise to make (someone) immune.

imp 1 a little devil. 2 a mischievous child.

impact one thing striking against another; a striking effect.

impair to weaken, spoil.

impale to fix on to a stake etc.; to pierce through.

impart to tell, pass on (information) to others.

impartial fair, neutral, not taking sides.

impassable not able to be travelled over or through.

impassive without emotion, showing no feeling.

impatient unable to wait for something, restless.

impeccable perfect, without a fault.

impecunious having no money.

impede to keep back, get in the way of.

impediment 1 a hindrance. 2 a defect, especially of speech.

impel to push, drive on.

impenetrable 1 not able to be passed through. 2 not able to be understood.

imperative 1 essential, necessary to do. 2 (in grammar) the form of a verb which expresses a command.

imperceptible not able to be noticed.

imperial of an empire or an emperor.

imperious arrogant, over-bearing.

impersonate to act the part of someone else.

impertinent rude, unmannerly, especially towards older people, cheeky.

imperturbable calm, not easily upset or worried.

impetuous hasty, rash, acting without thinking.

impetus a force that drives something forward.

implacable not able to be soothed, unforgiving.

implement a tool, an instrument.

implicate to involve (someone else) in something.

implication 1 the act of implicating. 2 the act of implying.

implore to ask very seriously, to beg for something.

imply to hint, suggest, without actually saying.

impolite rude, unmannerly.

import to bring goods into a country from another country.

important of great value, mattering very much.

impose to force (yourself) on someone.

imposing very grand, impressive.

impossible not able to be done, not possible.

imposter a person who pretends to be someone else.

impoverish to make poor.

impracticable not able to be put into practice.

impractical 1 not able to be done easily or well. 2 (of a person) not good at doing things.

impress 1 to make (someone) notice and admire you. 2 **impress on** to say very firmly to.

impression 1 a (vague) feeling or idea. 2 a mark on something.

impressionable easily led or persuaded.

impressive worthy of admiration.

imprison to put into prison.

improbable unlikely.

impromptu (said or done) without planning, on the spur of the moment.

improve to make (something) better; to get better.

improvise 1 to do or make something without preparation. 2 to perform music which you make up as you go along.

impudent cheeky, rude.

impulse a sudden desire (to do something).

impulsive acting without thinking.

inadvertently not done deliberately, done by accident.

inane silly, stupid.

inanimate not living, showing no signs of life.

inarticulate unable to express yourself clearly and smoothly.

incalculable unable to be counted, too large to be counted.

incandescent burning with a white glow.

incantation a spell or charm, said in a singing kind of voice.

incapable not able to do something.

incendiary that sets on fire deliberately.

incense a substance which gives off a sweet spicy smell when burned.

incentive something that spurs a person into action.

incessant never stopping.

inch a small measure of length (equal to about 2.54 centimetres).

incident a happening, something that takes place.

incinerator a machine for burning material, especially rubbish.

incisive getting straight to the point.

incisor a chisel-shaped tooth at the front of the mouth.

incite to urge on, stir up.

inclement (of the weather) stormy, wet.

inclination a slight preference (for), a tendency.

incline 1 to lean towards, to slope. 2 to be inclined, to have a tendency or liking to do something.

include to put (something) in with other things.

incognito (appearing) in a disguise, using a name which is not your own.

incoherent (of speech) not clear, confused.

income money which is earned or received.

incomparable better than anything, unequalled, that cannot be compared with others.

incompatible not suited to or fitting with each other.

incompetent not good at doing something.

incomprehensible not able to be understood.

incongruous not appropriate, not belonging to a particular group of things.

inconvenient not suitable or helpful at a particular time.

incorrect wrong.

incorrigible very bad, not able to be corrected or improved.

increase to make larger or greater.

incredible impossible or hard to believe.

incredulous unwilling to believe something.

incubate to hatch (eggs) by giving them heat.

indecent not decent, not proper, offensive.

indecisive uncertain; not able to make up your mind.

indeed as a matter of fact, really.

indefatigable not easily tired or defeated.

indelible unable to be rubbed out or removed.

indent to write or print (the first word of a line) in from the margin.

independent able to act on your own.

index 1 a list showing what and where things can be found in a book. 2 **index finger** the finger next to the thumb.

indicate to point out.

indifferent 1 not interested, showing no care (about something). 2 not very good.

indigenous belonging naturally to a particular place.

indigestion stomach pain or discomfort following eating.

indignant angry, annoyed.

indiscreet thoughtless in speech or behaviour, saying things which should not be said.

indistinct not clearly seen or heard.

individual a single person or thing.

indolent lazy.

induce 1 to make (something) happen, especially the birth of a baby. 2 to persuade (someone) to do something.

indulge 1 **indulge in** to take great pleasure in. 2 to give in to the wishes of (someone).

indulgent ready to give people what they want or to overlook their faults.

industrial to do with industry.

industrious hardworking, busy.

industry 1 the making of things to sell, especially in factories. 2 being industrious.

inedible not suitable for eating.

inevitable not able to be avoided, sure to happen.

inexplicable not able to be explained.

inextricable (of a knot or a problem) not able to be unravelled or solved.

infallible never making a mistake.

infamous wicked, very bad.

infant a baby; a very young child.

infantry soldiers who fight on foot.

infatuated having a strong, rather foolish, love (for someone).

infect to pass disease on to (someone).

infection 1 infecting. 2 an infectious disease.

infectious (of an illness) likely to be passed on to someone else.

inferior lower in rank, position or quality, less good.

infernal to do with hell; very bad or annoying.

inferno a very great terrifying fire.

infest (of vermin) to swarm in or about and cause a nuisance.

infiltrate to bring in (troops, for example) gradually and without being noticed.

infinite endless, too big to be measured.

infinitesimal very, very small.

infinity unending distance, space or quantity.

infirm in poor health, weak.

inflame 1 to make hot and red. 2 to stir up (anger for example).

inflammation redness, heat and swelling in a part of the body, causing pain.

inflate to put air into (something) causing it to swell.

inflexible 1 unable to bend or be bent. 2 (of a person) hard, unyielding.

inflict to force (especially something unpleasant) on someone.

influence affecting someone or something.

influential having good influence.

influenza *see* **flu**.

influx a flowing in; a coming (to a place or group) in large numbers.

inform to tell; to give the news.

informal not formal, free and easy, relaxed.

information knowledge, facts, what someone tells you about something.

infringe to break (a rule or law).

infuriate to make very angry.

ingenious very clever, especially at making things; very cleverly made.

ingenuous open-hearted, innocent.

ingot a (brick-shaped) bar of metal, especially of gold.

ingredient one of a number of things which together make up something else, in cooking for example.

inhabit to live in (a certain place).

inhale to breathe in (air, gas, smoke etc.).

inherent existing in (something) as part of its nature.

inherit 1 to receive (something) left to you by someone who has died. 2 to have (qualities) from your parents or ancestors.

inimitable unable to be copied.

initial *noun* the first letter of a name or word.
adjective of or at the beginning.

initiate 1 to start (something) off. 2 to make (someone) a member of a group or society, often with a special ceremony.

initiative the ability to act on your own.

injection the putting of medicine into the body with a special needle.

injure to hurt.

injustice not being just, unfairness.

ink a coloured liquid used for writing, printing or drawing.

inkling a slight idea, a hint.

inland away from the sea.

inlet a small bay.

inmate an occupant (of a house or prison, for example).

inn a place where people can buy a drink or a meal, a small hotel.

innings the time or turn for using the bat in cricket, baseball etc.

innocent not guilty, not at fault.

innocuous harmless.

innovation inventing or bringing in something new.

inoculation an injection given to prevent a disease.

inquest a legal inquiry into the cause of someone's death.

inquire, enquire to ask questions.

inquisitive asking a lot of questions, prying into the affairs of others.

insane not in your right mind, mad.

insatiable not able to be satisfied, greedy.

inscribe to write or mark (a name etc.) on paper, for example.

inscription something inscribed.

insect a small flying or crawling creature with six legs.

inseparable always together, very close.

insert to put into.

inside the part which is surrounded by something else; the part within.

insignificant of no great importance, very small in amount.

insipid dull, uninteresting.

insist 1 to keep on saying something. 2 to demand that something be done.

insolent very cheeky, impudent.

insomnia not being able to sleep.

inspect to look carefully at (something).

inspiration a very good idea.

install 1 to put (something) where it is going to be used. 2 to put (a person) in a particular job or position.

instalment 1 one of several parts of a bill to be paid in sequence. 2 each part of a story to be published or broadcast at different times.

instant *noun* a moment.
adjective made in a moment.

instead of in place of.

instigate to urge or persuade (someone) to do something (usually bad); to start (something) going.

instinct a way of knowing based on feelings.

instinctive done without thinking, natural.

institution a body of people set up for some purpose.

instruct to teach someone how to do something.

instrument 1 a tool. 2 something which is made to give out musical sounds.

insulin a substance in the body which controls the sugar level in the blood; people with diabetes have to be given insulin as their bodies do not produce it.

insult to be rude to (someone) by saying unkind things about them.

insure to arrange to pay regular sums of money so that you will be repaid if something is lost, stolen etc.

insurrection a revolt, rebellion.

intact complete, untouched, undamaged.

integrity honesty, good character.

intellect the ability to think and understand.

intelligent quick to learn, clever.

intelligible able to be understood.

intend to mean to do something.

intense (of feelings etc.) very great, very strong.

intensive care medical treatment with very close supervision for a seriously ill patient.

intention what you intend.

intentional intended, done on purpose.

intercept to stop (someone or something) on their way from one place to another.

interest 1 keen attention, desire to see or hear something. 2 sums of money paid for money lent or deposited in a bank etc.

interfere to get in the way of; to meddle.

interior the inside of something.

interlude a time or event between two others, for example music played between the acts of a play.

intermediate coming between two others in time, place or order.

interminable very long and boring, seeming to have no end.

intermission an interval, especially in a film or play.

internal of or on the inside.

international of, in or for more than one country.

interpret 1 to understand or show your understanding of (something). 2 to translate what someone says into another language.

interrogate to ask questions, especially in an official way.

interrupt to break into what other people are saying or doing.

intersection a place where two lines or roads cross each other.

interval a break, a pause; a space between things.

intervene to come between; to interfere.

interview a meeting at which people ask and answer questions.

intimate *noun* a close friend.
adjective 1 very private or personal. 2 (of a relationship) very close.

intimidate to threaten, bully (someone).

intolerable not tolerable, unbearable.

intolerant not tolerant, not willing or able to accept the opinions or behaviour of others.

intoxicated drunk, wildly excited.

intrepid brave, bold.

intricate complicated, full of detail.

introduce 1 to make people known to each other. 2 to bring in.

intrude 1 to come into a place without being asked. 2 to thrust or force (something) into.

intruder a person who intrudes, especially a burglar.

invade to enter, usually using force.

invalid *noun* [**in**valid] a person weakened by long illness. *adjective* [in**val**id] of a passport, for example, not valid.

invaluable of great value, priceless.

invasion an act of invading, an attack, raid.

invent to think of and make something for the first time.

inventory a list of things, especially goods or possessions.

invertebrate (a creature) not possessing a backbone.

inverted commas quotation marks.

investigate to enquire into, to try to find out about (something, especially a crime).

invincible unbeatable, unable to be defeated.

invisible not visible, not able to be seen.

invitation an act of inviting.

invite to ask somebody to come to your house, or to go out with you.

invoice a list of goods supplied or work done, with their prices.

involuntary unintentional, without meaning to.

involve 1 to cause to become connected (with). 2 **involved** complicated.

iodine a substance sometimes used to kill germs, for example.

iota the tiniest amount.

irascible quick to anger, bad-tempered.

irate very angry.

iris 1 a kind of tall purple or yellow flower. 2 the coloured part of the eye.

irksome annoying.

iron 1 a kind of hard strong metal. 2 a tool for pressing clothes.

ironmonger a person who sells mainly metal articles such as tools, pots and pans.

irrational not rational, not reasonable.

irregular not regular, not usual.

irresponsible not responsible, not trustworthy.

irrigate to supply (lands) with water for growing plants.

irritate 1 to make annoyed or angry. 2 to make sore.

island a piece of land with water all round it.

isolate to put apart from others, to leave (someone or something) on its own.

issue *verb* 1 to come out from. 2 to give out, especially officially. *noun* 1 a subject being discussed or argued about. 2 the copies of a magazine etc. published at a particular time.

isthmus a narrow strip of land connecting two larger pieces of land.

itch a tickling of the skin that makes you want to scratch.

item one thing out of a number of things.

itinerant moving about from place to place.

itinerary a route planned for a journey.

ivory the hard white material elephants' tusks are made from.

ivy a kind of climbing evergreen plant.

J

jab to poke at or to stab with something pointed.

jabber to talk quickly and unclearly.

jack 1 a tool for lifting heavy objects off the ground. 2 the playing card between the ten and the queen. 3 the white marker ball in the game of bowls.

jackal a kind of wild animal that looks like a dog.

jackdaw a kind of small bird of the crow family which often steals bright objects.

jacket a short coat.

jade a kind of green stone used for making ornaments.

jaded tired, weary.

jagged [**jagg**id] having a rough and uneven edge.

jaguar a leopard-like animal from South America.

jail a prison. The word may also be spelt **gaol**.

jam *noun* 1 a food made from fruit and sugar boiled together. 2 a crowding together, for example of traffic.
verb to become fixed or difficult to move.

jamb the side post of a door or window.

jangle to make a harsh ringing sound.

jar 1 a container made of glass etc. with an opening at the top. 2 a movement or sound that makes you shudder.

jargon a special kind of talk used in certain jobs or amongst certain groups of people.

jasmine a sweet-smelling climbing plant with yellow or white flowers.

jaundice a medical condition which makes the skin and the whites of the eyes yellow.

jaunt a short trip for pleasure.

jaunty cheerful and lively.

javelin a light spear, now thrown as a sport.

jaw the bones to which teeth are fixed; the lower part of the face.

jay a noisy bird of the crow family with bright feathers.

jazz a form of modern music with a strong rhythm, originally played by black Americans.

jealous annoyed because you wish you had what others have, envious.

jeans trousers made from a kind of strong, usually blue, cotton.

jeep a small powerful motor car which can be used on very rough ground.

jeer to laugh at or ridicule.

jelly 1 a soft clear food made from fruit juice. 2 any liquid substance in a semi-solid state.

jeopardise to put at risk or in danger.

jerbil *see* **gerbil**.

jerk a sudden push or pull.

jersey a knitted garment worn on the upper part of the body.

jest *verb* to speak or act in a light-hearted way.
noun a joke, something said in fun.

jester (long ago) someone employed to make jokes for a king or nobleman, for example.

jet 1 a thin stream of water, air etc. 2 an engine driven by a stream of air passing through special tubes. 3 a hard black mineral, used to produce jewellery etc.

jetsam things thrown overboard from a ship (and washed ashore). *See also* **flotsam**.

jettison to throw away, especially from a moving ship, aeroplane etc.

jetty a small pier for landing boats.

jewel a valuable stone often used for ornament.

jewellery ornaments that you wear made of precious stones or metal or imitations of these.

jib *noun* 1 a small triangular sail. 2 a beam jutting out from the top of a crane.
verb **jib at** to refuse to do something.

jig a kind of fast lively dance.

jiggle to move or rock (something) from side to side.

jigsaw (puzzle) a kind of puzzle in which many little pieces are put together to make a picture.

jilt to break your promise to marry (someone); to break away from (a lover).

jingle *verb* to make a ringing sound with small metal objects.
noun a short song used in advertising, on television, for example.

jinx a person or thing that is thought to bring bad luck.

job 1 a piece of work. 2 the work you do for a living.

jockey the rider of a racehorse.

jocular funny, fond of joking.

jodhpurs trousers which are loose above the knee and tight below, worn for horse-riding.

joey a young kangaroo.

jog 1 to run at a slow steady pace. 2 to push lightly.

join 1 to fasten together. 2 to become a member of (a club etc).

joiner a person who makes furniture etc. out of wood.

joint 1 the place where two parts fit together. 2 a large piece of meat.

joist one of the parallel supports going from wall to wall on which a floor is laid.

joke something you say to make people laugh.

jolly merry, happy, lively.

jolt a sudden jerk.

joss-stick a stick of incense.

jostle to knock or push against (someone).

jot down to write down notes very quickly.

journal 1 a magazine, especially one on a serious subject. 2 a diary.

journalist a person who writes for a newspaper or magazine.

journey a trip from place to place.

joust (long ago) a sporting contest between knights on horseback, fighting with spears etc.

jovial good-humoured, cheerful.

jowl the part around or under the side of the jaw line, often with loose flesh.

joy great happiness, gladness.

jubilant very happy, rejoicing.

jubilee a celebration of a special anniversary, such as fiftieth (**golden jubilee**).

judge *noun* 1 the person in court who has the final say in matters of law. 2 someone who decides the result of a competition.
verb to decide the value of (something).

judicial concerned with a court of law.

judicious sensible, showing good judgement.

judo a kind of Japanese fighting, now often used as a sport.

jug a container for pouring liquid.

juggler a person who can keep several objects in the air at a time without dropping them.

jugular vein a large vein at the side of the neck.

juice the liquid which comes from fruit and vegetables.

ju-jitsu a Japanese form of unarmed combat which uses an opponent's strength against himself.

juke-box a coin-operated machine for playing music records.

jumble 1 a muddle; many things mixed together in an untidy way. 2 **jumble sale** a sale of old goods to raise money for a charity etc.

jumbo (something which is) very large of its kind.

jump to spring into the air with both feet off the ground.

jumper a knitted garment worn on the top part of the body.

junction a place where two or more railway lines or roads meet or cross.

juncture a particular point or moment.

jungle a thick forest in very hot countries.

junior younger or lower in importance than others.

juniper a kind of evergreen shrub with prickly leaves and dark purple berries.

junk 1 rubbish that is no use to anyone. 2 a Chinese sailing-boat.

junket 1 a kind of sweet dish made with milk. 2 a party, an outing for pleasure.

jury a group of, usually twelve, people appointed to decide in a court case whether a person is guilty or not.

just 1 fair; right. 2 only.

justice 1 being just, fairness. 2 the power of the law.

justify to prove or show to be right.

jut to stick out.

jute a kind of coarse material used to make mats, sacks etc.

juvenile to do with young people; childish.

K

kaleidoscope 1 a toy which produces different coloured shapes and patterns as you turn it. 2 something which changes quickly and often.

kamikaze (pilot) a Japanese airman who deliberately crashed a plane loaded with explosives on an enemy target.

kangaroo a kind of Australian animal with long back legs on which it jumps.

karate a kind of Japanese fighting, now often used as a sport.

kayak a light covered-in canoe, especially one used by Eskimos.

keel the bottom part of a boat on which the rest of the boat is built.

keen 1 anxious to do what should be done, eager. 2 sharp.

keep to hold; to have for oneself.

keepsake something kept to remind you of someone.

kendo a Japanese form of fencing using bamboo sticks, now often used as a sport.

kennel a small house for a dog.

kerb the border or edge of a pavement.

kernel the centre part of a nut, the part you eat.

kestrel a kind of small falcon.

ketchup a thick sauce made from tomatoes, usually.

kettle a container with a handle and spout, used to boil water.

kettledrum a drum shaped like a bowl with a covering of skin.

key 1 a tool to open or close a lock. 2 a part of a musical instrument or a typewriter that you press down.

khaki 1 a dull yellow-brown colour. 2 cloth of this colour, worn especially by soldiers.

kibbutz in Israel, a community of people living and working together.

kick to hit with the foot.

kid 1 a young goat. 2 the leather made from a goat's skin. 3 informal word for a child.

kidnap to seize (a person) and keep them until money is paid for their safe return.

kidney 1 one of two small parts of the inside of the body which remove waste liquid from the blood. 2 the kidney of an animal used as food.

kill to put to death, to cause to die.

kiln a large oven for baking pottery, bricks etc. or for drying hops etc.

kilogram a measure of weight equal to a thousand grams.

kilometre a measure of length equal to a thousand metres.

kilt a kind of pleated skirt usually of tartan cloth sometimes worn by men in Scotland.

kimono a long loose Japanese garment with wide sleeves.

kin family, blood relations; often **next of kin** your closest relations.

kind *noun* a type, a sort. *adjective* good, helpful, gentle.

kindergarten a nursery school or class for very young children.

kindle to set alight; to catch fire.

kindred (people) related by blood.

king a male ruler of a country.

kingdom an area ruled over by a king or queen.

kingfisher a kind of bird with bright feathers which catches fish.

kink 1 a twist or bend in a rope, thread, hair etc. 2 something peculiar, especially in the person's mind.

kiosk 1 a small open stall where newspapers, sweets etc. are sold. 2 a public telephone box.

kipper a herring split open and smoked.

kiss / kraal

kiss to touch with the lips as a sign of love or as a greeting.

kit a set of things you need in order to do something, for example a set of parts which you can make up into something yourself.

kitchen a room used for cooking.

kite 1 a light frame covered with cloth or paper for flying at the end of a long string. 2 a kind of hawk.

kitten a young cat.

kittiwake a kind of seagull.

kleptomaniac (a person) who has an overwhelming urge to steal.

knack an ability to do something cleverly.

knapsack a small pack carried on the back.

knead to work dough with the hands.

knee the joint in the middle of the leg.

kneel to place one or both knees on the ground.

knell [nell] the sound of a bell, especially a funeral bell.

knickers underpants worn by women and girls.

knife a sharp blade with a handle used for cutting.

knight 1 a title given to a man by a king or queen; then 'Sir' is put in front of his name. 2 (long ago) a man who fought battles on horseback.

knit to join loops of wool etc. using long needles or machines.

knob a round handle used on doors and furniture or for tuning a radio or television set; something of this shape.

knock 1 to make a tapping noise, for example at a door. 2 to strike hard.

knoll a small rounded hill.

knot a fastening made by twisting string or rope etc.

know 1 to have something in your mind. 2 to recognise (someone).

knowledge something you know and understand.

knuckle a joint of a finger.

koala (bear) a tree-dwelling marsupial like a small tailless bear, found in Australia.

kosher (of food) that is lawful for a Jew to eat.

kraal in South Africa, a collection of huts surrounded by a fence.

L

label a paper or card for fastening on to a parcel etc. to tell what it is, for example.

laboratory a scientist's workroom; sometimes shortened to **lab**.

laborious needing a lot of hard work or effort.

labour hard work.

laburnum a kind of tree with hanging yellow flowers.

labyrinth a structure with many odd-shaped passages in which it is difficult to find your way, a maze.

lace 1 an open-work pattern made from fine thread. 2 a strong string used to tie a shoe.

lack to be without (something).

lackadaisical lazy, easy-going.

lacklustre dull, unexciting.

laconic brief in speech.

lacquer a hard glossy varnish.

lacrosse a team game in which a small hard ball is caught and thrown in a net at the end of a long stick.

lactic acid an acid found in sour milk.

lad a boy.

ladder a frame with bars for getting up to high places.

ladle a large deep spoon with a long handle, used for serving soup etc.

lady 1 a polite name for a woman. 2 **Lady** a title given to a woman, sometimes because of her husband's or father's title.

ladybird a small kind of beetle, often red with black spots.

lag to move slowly, to fall behind others.

lager a kind of light-coloured beer.

lagoon a stretch of fresh water cut off from the open sea by coral reefs, for example.

lair a wild animal's den.

lake a large stretch of water with land all round it.

lamb a young sheep.

lame not able to walk properly, limping.

lament [la**ment**] to express your sorrow over something.

lamentable [**lament**able] very bad, pitiful.

lamp something made for giving light.

lance a long thin spear.

land *noun* 1 the part of the earth not covered by the sea. 2 a country. *verb* to come to land from air or water.

landlady 1 a woman in charge of a pub, hotel etc. 2 a woman who owns property (and lets it out).

landlord 1 a man in charge of a pub, hotel etc. 2 a man who owns property (and lets it out).

landscape a view of a stretch of land.

lane a narrow road.

language the words used by the people of a particular country.

languid slow-moving, showing no effort, weak.

languish to grow feeble, to droop.

lank (of hair) long and lifeless.

lanky clumsily tall and thin.

lantern a case in which to carry a light.

lap *noun* 1 the space formed on the top of your thighs when you are sitting down. 2 once round a racetrack. *verb* to drink using the tongue, like a dog or cat.

lapel the part of the front of a coat or jacket that is turned back.

lapse 1 slip, a mistake. 2 passing (of time).

lapwing a kind of wild bird with a crested head and a shrill call.

larch a kind of tree which has cones and loses its leaves in winter.

lard melted-down pig fat used in cooking.

larder a cupboard in a house for storing food.

large big, huge.

largesse generous giving.

lark a kind of small singing bird.

larva a grub that later turns into an insect.

larynx the part of the throat containing the vocal chords.

laser a powerful light beam used in science, medicine and industry.

lash *verb* 1 to fasten tightly with rope or string. 2 to whip, hit hard.
noun a small hair on the eyelid.

lassitude weariness, inability to be interested.

lasso [lassoo] a rope with a noose at the end for catching.

last *adjective* coming after all the others.
verb to go on for a period of time.

latch a door catch.

late 1 behind time. 2 near the end of a period of time.

latent hidden, not yet developed.

lateral of, at, from or towards the side.

lathe a machine for turning and shaping wood, metal etc.

lather 1 bubbles made in water when using soap. 2 sweat produced by a horse when working hard.

latitude 1 the degree of distance north or south of the equator. 2 freedom, from rules for example.

latter the second of two.

lattice a window etc. formed out of crisscrossing slabs or wood or metal.

laudable worthy of praise.

laudatory full of praise.

laugh the sound you make when you are amused or happy.

launch *noun* a motor boat.
verb to float a newly-built boat.

launderette a place where you can wash and dry clothes by putting money into the machines there.

laundry 1 a place where clothing is taken to be washed. 2 a pile of clothing ready for washing or ironing.

laurel a kind of evergreen bush with shiny leaves.

lava molten rock for a volcano; the solid rock it forms when cool.

lavatory a toilet.

lavender a kind of bush with pale-purple, sweet-smelling flowers.

lavish (over-)generous, plentiful.

law a rule made by the government that everyone must obey.

lawn an area of short grass in a garden or in a park.

lawyer a person who has studied the law and can advise people about it.

lax not strict, easy-going.

laxative a medicine which makes the bowels empty easily.

lay 1 to put down. 2 to produce (eggs).

lazy not fond of working, liking to do nothing.

lead *noun* 1 [led] a heavy metal. 2 [leed] a strap or chain fixed to a dog's collar in order to control it.
verb [leed] to go in front for others to follow.

leader the person in charge of a group, the head person.

leaf 1 one of the flat green parts of a tree or other plant. 2 a page of a book.

leaflet a printed sheet, often folded, giving information about something.

league 1 a group of persons, nations etc. joining together to help each other. 2 a group of sporting teams who play games against each other to find a winner. 3 (long ago) a measure of length, usually equal to about three miles.

leak a hole or gap through which liquid or gas can escape.

lean *verb* 1 **lean against** to put your weight against. 2 to bend towards. *adjective* thin, not fat.

leap to jump, to spring.

learn to get to know; to become good at doing something.

leash a lead used to control a dog.

least the smallest amount.

leather an animal's skin which has been prepared for making into shoes or handbags, for example.

leave *verb* 1 to go away from. 2 to let (something) stay where it is. *noun* 1 permission, especially to be absent. 2 a holiday time, especially for soldiers etc.

lecture a speech made to a number of people, usually to teach them something.

ledge a narrow shelf.

ledger a book used to keep accounts.

leech a kind of bloodsucking worm.

leek a long white and green vegetable which tastes rather like an onion.

leer to look or smile at in a sly or evil way.

left the same side of the body as the heart, the opposite of right.

leg 1 one of the limbs with which you walk. 2 one of the supports at the corner of a table, for example.

legacy something left to someone in a will.

legal to do with the law.

legend a story from long ago, which may not be true.

legendary of or like a legend; very famous, wonderful.

legible clear enough to be read.

legion 1 a division of the Roman army. 2 a very large number.

legislation (the making of) laws.

legitimate 1 lawful. 2 born when your parents are married to each other.

leisure spare time used for hobbies and enjoying yourself.

lemon a kind of yellow fruit with a sharp taste.

lemonade a sweet fizzy drink flavoured with lemon.

lemur [**lee**mer] a kind of small monkey-like animal with a sharp face and a long tail.

lend to allow somebody to use (something) for a time.

length the distance from one end to the other.

lenient merciful, not severe, mild in punishment.

lens a piece of curved glass or plastic, used to magnify something.

lentil a kind of small brownish seed used in soups, for example.

leopard a large wild animal of the cat family with spotted fur.

leotard a close-fitting single garment worn for gymnastics, dancing etc.

leper a person suffering from leprosy.

leprechaun a kind of Irish fairy thought to bring luck.

leprosy a serious infectious disease which causes the flesh and nerves to waste away.

less smaller, not so big, not so much, not so many.

lesson something to be learned.

let 1 to allow, permit. 2 to allow someone to use (a building) in return for a rent.

lethal causing or likely to cause death.

lethargic lacking in energy or interest.

lethargy being lethargic.

letter 1 a written message sent to somebody. 2 one of the signs we use for writing such as a, b, c.

lettuce a kind of broad-leaved green vegetable used in salads.

leukaemia a very serious illness of the blood.

level 1 the same height all along, flat. 2 equal.

lever a strong metal bar for lifting things.

leveret a young hare.

levity fun, good humour (when you should be serious).

levy *noun* the collecting of a due sum or tax.
verb to demand and collect (a tax etc).

lexicon a dictionary, especially of an old language.

liable 1 likely to happen, for example. 2 responsible (for a payment, for example).

liaison [lee**ay**zon] a connection between people for a particular reason.

liar a person who tells lies.

libel something printed or written which says bad things about someone falsely or unfairly.

liberal 1 having tolerant views. 2 plentiful, abundant. 3 generous, kind-hearted.

liberality generosity, kindness.

liberate to set free.

liberty freedom.

librarian a person with a special training who works in a library.

library a room or building where books are stored.

libretto the text of an opera or other theatrical musical work.

licence a printed paper that gives you permission to do something.

lichen a dry moss-like plant which grows on stones, trees etc.

lick to wet or rub with the tongue.

lid a cover that can be opened or taken off.

lie *verb* 1 to rest in a flat position. 2 to say things that are not true.
noun something which is not true.

lieutenant [lef**ten**ant] a rank in the army or the navy.

life the time when you are alive.

lifeboat a boat kept ready to go to the help of people in danger on the sea.

lift *verb* to raise.
noun 1 a machine which carries people or goods up and down a building. 2 a ride in someone's car etc.

ligament a small band of muscle that holds bones together in the body.

light *noun* brightness, the opposite of darkness.
adjective 1 pale in colour, not dark. 2 having little weight, easy to lift.
verb to make (something) burn, for example a fire or a lamp.

lighthouse a tall building or tower with a powerful light on top to warn ships of danger.

lightning a flash of light you see in the sky during a thunderstorm.

like *verb* to be fond of.
adjective the same as, similar to.

likely what you would expect.

lilac 1 a kind of small tree with sweet-smelling purple or white flowers. 2 a pale-purple colour, like these flowers.

lily a kind of beautiful flower, often white in colour.

limb an arm, a leg or a wing.

lime 1 a kind of greenish fruit like a small lemon. 2 a kind of tree with large pale-green leaves. 3 a white powder made from limestone.

limit *noun* the extreme edge or boundary.
verb to keep within a limit, to restrict.

limp *adjective* not stiff, weak.
noun a lame way of walking.

limpet a kind of small shellfish which clings tightly to rocks etc.

limpid very clear, transparent.

line 1 a long thin mark. 2 a piece of rope or string. 3 people or things standing one behind the other.

lineage [**linn**iage] the line of descendants from your ancestors.

linear 1 of or in a line or lines. 2 of length.

linen a kind of thin cloth used for making sheets or tablecloths, for example.

liner a large passenger ship.

linger to leave slowly, stay behind.

lining cloth used on the inside of clothes etc.

link 1 one of the rings in a chain. 2 a connection.

linseed oil oil made from flax seed.

lintel a beam over a door or window.

lion a kind of large wild animal of the cat family, found in Africa and India.

lip 1 one of the soft round edges of the mouth. 2 the edge of something such as a cup.

lipstick a stick of colouring for the lips.

liqueur [li**cure**] a very strong sweet alcoholic drink, often drunk in small amounts at the end of a meal.

liquid something which flows (for example water or milk).

liquor [**lick**er] 1 (strong) alcoholic drink. 2 liquid from cooked food, for example.

liquorice a kind of chewy black sweet made from a plant root.

lisp to say *th* instead of *s* because of a slight fault in speech.

list *noun* a number of names written down one after the other.
verb 1 to make a list of. 2 (of a ship) to lean to one side.

listen 1 to try to hear. 2 to take notice of what someone is saying.

listless having no energy or enthusiasm.

literacy the ability to read and write.

literal meaning exactly what it says.

literary concerning books or literature.

literate able to read and write.

literature well-written stories and poems.

lithe (especially of the body) able to bend easily.

litmus (paper) a piece of treated paper which reacts differently to acids and alkalis.

litre a measure of liquid.

litter 1 rubbish lying about. 2 a number of animals born together.

little small, tiny, not big.

liturgy the set form of public worship in a Church or religion.

live *verb* [rhymes with 'give'] 1 to stay in a place. 2 to be alive.
adjective [rhymes with 'five'] 1 alive. 2 (of a broadcast etc.) not recorded. 3 carrying electricity (and able to give you an electric shock).

livelihood means of earning money for yourself or your family.

lively full of life, active.

liver 1 a part of the inside of the body which cleans the blood. 2 the liver of an animal used as food.

livid 1 dark bluish grey. 2 very angry.

lizard a kind of animal with four short legs, a long tail and skin like a snake.

llama a kind of woolly South American animal which chews the cud.

load *noun* as much as can be carried at one time.
verb 1 to put goods on to (a ship or vehicle). 2 to put bullets into (a gun).

loaf a large piece of bread which you cut in slices.

loam soil which is good for growing things.

loan something that is lent or borrowed.

loathe to feel hatred for.

loathing hatred.

loathsome hateful, very horrible.

lob a ball sent in a slow high arc, in cricket, football, for example.

lobby an entrance hall.

lobe 1 the rounded hanging part of the ear. 2 a division of the brain or the lungs.

lobster a kind of large shellfish with claws.

local near a particular place, near where you are.

locality a particular place or part of a (larger) district.

locate 1 to find (out) the position of. 2 to put in a certain place.

loch a Scottish lake; a long arm of the sea in Scotland.

lock *verb* to fasten something so that only a key will open it.
noun 1 a fastening for a door etc. with a key. 2 a place in a canal where ships are raised or lowered. 3 a piece of hair.

locker a small cupboard with a lock for keeping clothes, valuables etc.

locket a small flat metal case, worn on a chain round the neck, usually.

locomotive a steam or diesel engine for pulling carriages.

locust an insect like a grasshopper which destroys crops.

lodge *noun* a small cottage near a large country house or estate.
verb 1 to stay in a place by paying rent for it. 2 to become fixed in a position.

loft the space under the roof of a building.

log 1 a part of a tree sawn off for building or for firewood. 2 a ship's diary.

loggerheads: at loggerheads (with) disagreeing or arguing (with someone).

logic the science of good reasoning.

logical according to the rules of logic, reasonable.

loiter to hang about, move around slowly, without doing anything.

loll to lean in a lazy relaxed way.

lollipop a sweet on the end of a stick.

lonely 1 feeling sad and alone; without friends. 2 (of a house etc.) with no others near it.

long *adjective* of great length, not short.
verb to wish for something very much.

longitude the degree of distance east or west of an imaginary line through Greenwich, England.

look 1 to try to see. 2 to appear to be, to seem.

loom *noun* a machine for weaving.
verb to come into sight slowly, often out of mist or darkness.

loop a shape like a ring made in string or rope, for example.

loophole a clever way of avoiding something, a rule or law, for example.

loose not tied or fixed, free to move, slack.

loot stolen goods or money.

lop to cut off (branches from a tree, for example).

lopsided leaning to one side, having one side lower than the other.

loquacious very talkative.

lord a title given to a man by a king or queen.

lorry a large motor vehicle carrying heavy loads.

lose 1 not to be able to find (something), to stop having. 2 to be beaten, not to win.

loss something you have lost.

lotion a liquid for putting on the skin to improve or protect it.

lottery a game of chance in which you buy a ticket which may then be picked out to win a prize.

lotus a beautiful type of water lily found in Eastern countries.

loud making a lot of noise, easily heard.

lounge *noun* a sitting room. *verb* to act lazily.

louring frowning; dark and gloomy.

louse, *plural* **lice** a kind of small insect which feeds on blood.

lousy 1 covered with lice. 2 (slang) very bad, horrible.

lout a very badly-behaved man or boy.

love to like very much.

lovely beautiful.

low *adjective* 1 not high, near to the ground or the bottom of something. 2 quiet, not loud. *verb* (of cattle) to moo.

loyal able to be trusted to defend friends or country.

lozenge 1 a small flat sweet, especially of medicine. 2 a shape with four equal sides and two sharp angles.

lubricate to oil, to make smooth or easier to move with grease or oil.

lucid 1 clear, easy to understand. 2 able to understand clearly.

luck fortune, chance.

lucky having good luck.

lucrative producing gain, profitable.

ludicrous ridiculous, absurd.

lug to drag, pull (something heavy).

luggage bags and suitcases you take with you when travelling.

lugubrious sad and unhappy-looking.

lukewarm 1 neither very hot nor very cold. 2 not very interested or enthusiastic (about something).

lullaby a quiet song to send a baby to sleep.

lumber *noun* 1 timber. 2 useless old pieces of furniture etc. *verb* to move about awkwardly, clumsily.

luminous full of light, shining.

lump 1 a swelling. 2 a piece of something.

lunar of the moon.

lunatic a mad person.

lunch a meal eaten in the middle of the day.

lung one of the two parts of the body with which you breathe.

lunge to move or strike out violently in some direction.

lupin a kind of tall garden flower.

lurch to stagger, move from side to side.

lure to attract, tempt (an animal into a trap, a person away from duty, for example).

lurid (of colour) harshly bright; (of a picture, film etc.) horrifyingly sensational.

lurk to wait in hiding, especially for a bad purpose.

luscious delicious.

lustre brightness, brilliance.

lust very strong desire.

lusty strong, healthy.

lute a kind of stringed musical instrument used especially in ancient times.

luxuriant 1 growing strongly and thick. 2 highly ornamented.

luxury something expensive you like having but you do not need.

lynch (of a crowd) to put (someone) to death as a punishment without a proper trial.

lynx a kind of large animal of the cat family.

lyre a kind of small harp used in ancient times.

lyric the words of a song.

lyrical poetic, very enthusiastic.

M

macabre gruesome, horrible, connected with death.

macaroni a kind of pasta made in long tubes, often cut into short lengths.

macaroon a kind of sweet biscuit made of sugar, almonds, white of egg etc.

macaw a kind of bright-coloured long-tailed parrot of Central and South America.

mace 1 an ornamental rod carried in certain ceremonies as a sign of power, for example in parliament. 2 (long ago) a war club with spikes.

machine something made out of many parts that work together to do a job.

machinery machines; parts of a machine.

mackerel a kind of sea-fish, used as food.

mackintosh a raincoat, a waterproof.

mad 1 insane, crazy; very foolish. 2 very angry.

madam a polite way of speaking or writing to a woman.

madden to make angry or mad.

madonna a picture or statue of the Virgin Mary.

magazine a paper containing stories, pictures etc., sold every week or month.

maggot the larva of a fly, sometimes found in bad meat, for example.

magic 1 strange and wonderful things which happen by a strange power. 2 clever or strange tricks done to amuse.

magician 1 (long ago) a person thought to be skilled in magic. 2 a conjuror, someone who does magic tricks to amuse people.

magistrate a person appointed to judge cases in the lowest courts of law.

magnesium a whitish metal which burns with a very bright light.

magnet a piece of iron or steel which attracts other pieces of iron or steel.

magnificent splendid.

magnify to make (something) appear larger.

magnitude largeness, size, importance (of something).

magpie a black and white bird with a long tail which likes to pick up brightly-coloured objects.

mahogany a kind of very hard reddish-brown wood used to make furniture.

maid 1 a woman servant. 2 an old-fashioned word for a girl.

maiden 1 an unmarried woman. 2 a cricket over in which no runs are scored.

mail 1 letters and parcels sent by post. 2 a kind of armour worn by soldiers long ago.

maim to hurt badly and cripple.

main most important, chief.

maintain 1 to keep (in good condition). 2 to support (a family, for example). 3 to say that you believe (that).

maize a kind of grain used for food, sweet corn.

majestic very impressive, like a king or queen.

Majesty a title given to a king or queen.

major *noun* an officer in the army. *adjective* the chief, the most important.

majorette, *also* **drum majorette** a girl who marches in front of a band, twirling a baton.

majority the larger part of a group of people or things.

make 1 to build; to create. 2 to force (somebody) to do something.

makeshift used for the time being, until you have something better.

malady an illness, sickness.

malaria a serious feverish illness passed on by mosquito bites.

male a person or animal that can become a father; a man or boy.

malefactor a person who commits a crime.

malevolent wishing to do harm to others.

malice the wish to do harm to others.

malign *verb* to speak about (someone) in a bad way. *adjective* evil.

malignant 1 harmful, evil. 2 (of a disease) likely to cause death.

malleable 1 (of metal) able to be hammered or pressed into a new shape. 2 (of a person) able to be persuaded to another's point of view.

mallet a large, usually wooden hammer.

malt soaked and dried barley, used in making beer, for example.

maltreat to treat badly, injure.

mammal an animal which feeds its young with its own milk.

mammoth *noun* a kind of large extinct elephant. *adjective* very big, huge.

man a grown-up male person.

manage 1 to be able to do (something). 2 to take charge of (something).

mandatory compulsory.

mane the long hair on the neck of an animal, especially a horse or lion.

manger an animal's feeding box in a stable, barn etc.

mangle *verb* to cut up roughly. *noun* a machine for squeezing water out of wet clothes and smoothing them.

mango a kind of tropical fruit with sweet yellow flesh.

maniac a mad person, especially a violent one.

manicure a special treatment of the hands and fingernails.

manifest obvious to the eye or mind, clear.

manifesto a public statement of belief and intentions by a group, especially by a political party.

manifold having many parts, uses and forms.

manipulate to handle or use with skill or cunning.

mankind the human race.

manner 1 the way in which you behave. 2 the way in which a thing is done.

mannerism something different or unusual which a person says or does a lot.

manners behaviour, especially good behaviour towards other people.

manoeuvre [manoover] 1 a clever or cunning trick to get something done. 2 **manoeuvres** military or naval exercises.

mansion a very large house.

mantelpiece a shelf above the fireplace.

manual *adjective* done with the hands. *noun* a book of instructions.

manufacture to make things in a factory by using machinery.

manure a substance, especially animal dung, used to make soil more fertile.

manuscript something written by hand; something written by hand or typed before it is printed.

many a large number of, plenty.

map a drawing of a large surface, showing its main features, for example rivers, mountains, roads.

maple a kind of tree with winged seeds.

maple syrup a sweet liquid which comes from a kind of maple tree.

mar to spoil, damage.

marathon a race on foot over a long distance.

marble 1 a kind of hard stone which can be smoothly polished. 2 a small round glass or stone ball used in children's games.

march *verb* to walk in step with others.
noun 1 an act of marching. 2 a piece of music to which people, especially soldiers, march.

mare a female horse.

margarine a food made from vegetable oils which is often used instead of butter.

margin a border down the side of a page.

marginal having little importance, not central.

marigold a kind of plant with golden or bright yellow flowers.

marine of or living in the sea.

mariner a sailor, a seaman.

marionette a puppet moved by strings or wires.

marital concerning marriage.

maritime of the sea or ships; near the sea.

mark *noun* 1 a sign put on something. 2 a spot, a stain. 3 the number you reach in a test.
verb to put a mark on.

market a place, often in the open air, where goods are bought and sold.

marksman a person who shoots well.

marmalade a kind of jam made of oranges, lemons etc.

marmoset a kind of small bushy-tailed monkey of Central or South America.

maroon *noun* a very dark red colour.
verb to leave (someone) somewhere where they cannot get away (for example an island).

marquee a very large tent.

marriage 1 being married. 2 a wedding.

marrow 1 the soft substance found inside bones. 2 a kind of very large white-fleshed vegetable.

marry to become someone's husband or wife.

marsh wet land, a swamp, a bog.

marshmallow a kind of soft spongy sweet.

marsupial a kind of animal, for example the kangaroo, which carries its young in a pouch.

martial connected with warfare; warlike.

martin a kind of bird rather like a swallow.

martyr a person who dies for something he or she believes in.

marvellous wonderful.

marzipan a paste made from almonds, egg and sugar, put on cakes, for example.

mascot a charm, a thing or animal supposed to bring good luck.

masculine concerning or like men and boys.

mash to crush to a soft smooth state (for example potatoes).

mask a covering for the face.

mason a person who builds with stone.

mass 1 a large amount of something. 2 a crowd of people. 3 the communion service in a Roman Catholic church.

massacre the killing of a lot of people or animals in a cruel way.

massage to rub (a part of the body) to make it less painful or stiff.

masseur a man who gives massage (for payment).

masseuse a woman who gives massage (for payment).

massive very large, enormous.

mast the tall pole used to hold up the sails on a ship.

master 1 the chief man, the man in charge. 2 **Master** used as a title with a boy's name (instead of Mr).

masterpiece a very fine piece of work; someone's best achievement.

mastiff a kind of very large strong dog.

mat 1 a small rug. 2 a small piece of material for putting under dishes.

match *noun* 1 a small thin stick with a tip which catches fire when rubbed on a suitable surface. 2 a game between two teams.
verb to be the same as (something else).

mate 1 a companion. 2 a husband or wife; one of a pair of animals, birds etc. 3 an officer in the merchant navy.

material 1 anything from which things can be made. 2 cloth.

maternal of or like a mother; on your mother's side.

mathematics the study of numbers, shapes and measurements.

matinee [**mat**eenay] an afternoon theatrical or musical performance.

matrimony marriage.

matter *verb* to be important.
noun something you think about.

mattress a large thick layer of material for sleeping on.

mature fully developed or grown; grown-up, sensible.

maudlin tearful and insincere.

maul to handle roughly, beat, batter.

mauve a pale-purple colour.

mawkish foolishly sentimental.

maximum the greatest amount or number, the most.

maybe perhaps, possibly.

mayonnaise a sauce made from eggs, oil, vinegar etc., eaten with salads, for example.

mayor the chief official in charge of some towns.

maze a lot of paths or lines arranged so that it is difficult to find your way through them.

meadow an area of grassland.

meagre small in amount.

meal 1 the food you eat at a certain time of the day. 2 grain ground into a kind of flour.

mealy-mouthed afraid to speak your mind.

mean *adjective* not generous.
verb 1 to have a meaning. 2 **mean to** to have it in your mind to.

meander [me**and**er] to wander aimlessly; (of a river) to wind about.

meaning what you have in your mind when you say or write something, an explanation.

means 1 the money or possessions you live on. 2 a method, way of getting something done.

measles an infectious illness which gives you red spots.

measure *verb* to find out how long, broad, heavy etc. something is.
noun a unit for measuring.

measurement what something measures.

meat flesh from an animal used as food.

mechanic a person who makes or repairs machinery.

mechanical done with a machine; like a machine.

mechanism the parts which make something work.

medal a disc of metal etc. given as a reward for something you have done.

meddle to interfere with things which are not your business.

media ways in which information etc. is brought to people, for example newspapers, television.

mediate to act as a peacemaker between two enemies.

mediator a person who mediates.

medical to do with the treatment of illness.

medicine 1 the treatment of illness. 2 something you take to make you better when you are ill.

medieval to do with the Middle Ages (5th to 15th centuries).

mediocre neither good nor bad, of poor quality.

meditate to think hard and deeply about a subject.

medium not big or small, in between.

medley a mixture (of people, songs etc.).

meek gentle, humble.

meet 1 to come together. 2 to go to see and greet (someone).

megaphone an instrument like a large trumpet used to make your voice sound louder.

melancholy very sad.

mellifluous (of the voice or words) sweet, very pleasant.

mellow 1 (of light etc.) not harsh or blinding. 2 (of character) pleasant and relaxed.

melodrama a drama showing crude and violent action and feelings.

melody a tune.

melon a kind of large juicy fruit with a green or yellow skin.

melt to become liquid because of heat.

member a person who belongs to a group.

memento something you keep to remind you of someone or something.

memoir a written record of an event.

memory 1 the part of the brain with which you remember. 2 a thought about the past.

menacing frightening, alarming.

menagerie a collection of captured wild animals in captivity.

mend to put right, to repair.

mental to do with the mind.

mention to talk about.

menu 1 a list of things served at a meal or which can be ordered in a restaurant. 2 a list of things a computer program can do.

mercantile of or concerned with trade.

mercenary *adjective* doing something only for money.
noun a soldier hired to fight for another country.

merchandise goods for sale.

merchant a person who buys and sells.

merciful showing mercy.

mercury a heavy silvery liquid metal, used in thermometers etc.

mercy pity, not punishing someone.

merely only.

merge to join or come together, especially gradually.

meringue a light crumbly cake made of whites of egg and sugar.

merit *verb* to deserve, be worthy of (something).
noun something which merits praise.

mermaid an imaginary creature with a woman's body and a fish's tail.

merry happy, cheerful, joyful.

mesh material with small spaces between the threads of wiring in a net or sieve, for example.

mess things mixed together in an untidy, dirty way.

message news sent from one person or group to another.

metal materials such as iron, steel, gold, silver and brass.

metaphor using a word or words to describe something else, usually because it reminds you of it.

meteor a small object from space which travels very fast and usually burns out when it enters the earth's atmosphere.

meteorology the study of weather and climate.

meter a machine for measuring such things as gas or electricity.

method the way in which something is done.

meticulous very careful, especially about the details of something.

metre a measure of length in the metric system.

metric of the **metric system,** the system of measuring based on decimal units.

metropolis the capital city of a country.

mettle courage, bravery.

mew the noise made by a cat.

mezzanine a smaller floor in a building, between two larger floors.

microcomputer a small computer you can use at home or at school.

microphone an instrument which picks up sounds and either makes them louder or records them.

microscope an instrument used to make very small things look much bigger.

midday twelve o'clock in the day.

middle the part of something that is the same distance from all of its sides or its ends.

midge a kind of very small insect which bites.

midget a very small grown-up person; a very small thing.

midnight twelve o'clock at night.

midriff the front part of the body between the rib-cage and the abdomen.

midwife a person, usually a woman, who is trained to help women to give birth.

mighty very strong, powerful.

migraine [**mee**grain] a kind of very severe headache.

migrate to go to live in another country.

mild 1 gentle, not rough. 2 not too hot or cold.

mile a measure of length equal to 1760 yards (about 1.6 kilometres).

mileage the number of miles travelled.

militant (of) an aggressive or quarrelsome person.

military concerning soldiers or the army.

milk a white liquid given by human mothers and some female animals to feed their babies.

mill 1 a place where grain is ground into flour or meal. 2 a factory, especially one where cloth is made.

millenium 1 a period of a thousand years 2 a period of happiness and prosperity in the future.

millilitre a measurement of capacity equal to one thousandth of a litre.

millimetre a measurement of length equal to one thousandth of a metre.

milliner a person who makes and/or sells women's hats.

million a number, 1 000 000.

millionaire a very rich person who has at least a million pounds (or dollars).

millstone 1 one of the two large stones formerly used for grinding corn etc. 2 something which causes you trouble and holds you back badly.

mime to use actions instead of words to show the meaning of something.

mimic to speak or act like someone else.

minaret a tall slender tower above a mosque.

mince *verb* to cut up into very small pieces.
noun meat cut up in this way.

mincemeat a sweet mixture of dried fruit etc. used in pies.

111

mind *noun* a person's way of thinking; the power to think.
verb 1 to look after. 2 to object to (something).

mine *pronoun* belonging to me.
noun a place where minerals, for example coal, are dug from the earth.

mineral things such as rock which are dug out of the earth.

mingle to mix.

miniature very small, but made like something bigger.

minim a note in music.

minimal of the smallest size or amount.

minimum the least possible amount.

minister 1 a person in charge of a church, a clergyman. 2 an important member of a government.

mink a kind of small furry animal that lives near water; its fur.

minnow a kind of freshwater fish.

minor *adjective* smaller or less important.
noun the younger one.

minority the smaller part of a group of people or things.

minstrel (long ago) a person who went from place to place entertaining people with songs and poetry.

mint 1 a plant used to flavour food. 2 a sweet flavoured with mint. 3 a place where coins are made.

minuet (long ago) a kind of slow graceful dance.

minus less than, without; the sign −.

minuscule very very small.

minute *noun* [**mi**nit] a length of time of sixty seconds.
adjective [my**newt**] very small.

miracle a strange and wonderful happening which is thought to be the work of God.

miraculous happening by a miracle, amazing, very surprising.

mirage something you think you see which is not really there at all, especially in the desert.

mirror a piece of glass, metal or plastic in which you can see yourself.

mirth gentle laughter.

miscellaneous of several different kinds.

mischief stupid actions which cause trouble.

mischievous always doing mischief.

misconstrue to put the wrong meaning to (something), to misunderstand.

misdemeanor a small offence.

miser a person who has plenty of money, but tries not to spend any.

miserable 1 full of sadness. 2 worthless, wretched.

misery great unhappiness, sorrow.

mishap a small accident.

miss *verb* not to see or find; not to succeed.
noun **Miss** a title given to an unmarried woman or girl.

missile a weapon which is thrown or fired; a weapon which travels to its target under its own power.

mission an important task that someone is sent to do.

missionary a person who goes to other places to teach people about religion.

mist drops of water in the air which stop you from seeing properly, like fog.

mistake something you have done or thought which is wrong, an error.

mistletoe a kind of evergreen plant with white berries, often used as a Christmas decoration.

mistress the chief woman, the woman in charge.

misunderstanding a confusion about the meaning of something; a slight disagreement.

mitigate to reduce the severity of (a punishment for example).

mitre 1 the pointed hat worn by a bishop. 2 a sloping joint between two pieces of wood etc.

mitten a glove with only two parts, one for the fingers and one for the thumb.

mix to put things together (for example by stirring or shaking).

mixture things mixed together.

moan a low sound made when you are in pain or unhappy.

moat a ditch round a castle to keep it safe from attack.

mob a noisy disorderly crowd.

mobile *adjective* that can move (easily and readily). *noun* a hanging decoration made of movable parts.

moccasin a kind of shoe of soft deerskin (as) worn by North American Indians.

mock to make fun or a fool of (someone), especially by doing the same as they do.

mode a way or manner in which something is done.

model 1 a copy of something. 2 a pattern to be followed. 3 a person who displays clothes by wearing them.

moderate *adjective* [**mod**erit] neither high nor low, avoiding extremes, medium. *verb* [**mod**erayt] to lessen the strong effect of (something).

modern up to date, belonging to the present time.

modest 1 not too proud, humble, shy. 2 decent in dress and manner.

modify to alter, to tone down.

module 1 a unit or part of something larger. 2 a part of a spaceship.

mohair (yarn of cloth made from) the long silky hair of the Angora goat.

moist a little wet, damp.

molar one of the strong teeth at the back of the jaw.

mole 1 a kind of small furry animal which burrows underground. 2 a small dark spot on the skin.

molest to harm, hurt, annoy (a person).

mollusc one of various kinds of shellfish with soft bodies, and often hard shells, for example snails, mussels.

moment a very short space of time.

momentous having great importance.

momentum amount or force of movement.

monarch a ruler of the country who is a king or queen.

monastery a place where monks live.

monastic of or like monks, nuns or monastries.

money the coins and pieces of paper you use for buying and selling.

mongoose a kind of small weasel-like animal which can kill snakes.

mongrel a dog which is a mixture of two or more breeds.

monk a man who has given his life to his religion and who lives in a monastery.

monkey an animal with a long tail and with hands and feet like a human being. It lives in trees in hot countries.

monologue a long speech by a single actor on the stage, for example.

monopoly sole right to supply or control a commodity or service.

monotonous unchanging, dull, boring.

monsoon a fierce rain-carrying wind in some Far Eastern countries; the season of heavy rains that it brings.

monster 1 a large imaginary frightening animal. 2 a cruel and wicked person. 3 a thing which is very large of its kind.

month 1 one of the twelve parts of the year (for example August). 2 a period of four weeks.

monument something built to remind you of an important person or event.

mood the way you feel.

moon the planet that goes round the earth and is sometimes seen shining in the sky.

moor *noun* a large area of rough ground, covered with grass and heather.
verb to fasten (a boat) with a rope.

mooring the place where a ship or boat is moored.

moose a kind of very large North American deer.

mop soft material at the end of a long pole, used for cleaning floors, for example.

mope to be very sad.

moral *adjective* to do with right or wrong; of right behaviour.
noun a lesson about right and wrong, for example one you learn from a story.

morale good spirits.

morass a dangerously boggy place.

morning the part of the day before noon.

morose very sad, gloomy, bad-tempered.

morris dance a traditional English country dance by persons in fancy dress wearing ribbons and bells.

morsel a small piece (of food).

mortal 1 that can die. 2 causing death.

mortar 1 a mixture of lime, sand and water used to stick building materials together. 2 a short cannon for firing shells in a high curve. 3 a bowl for crushing things with a pestle.

mortify to cause to feel ashamed or humiliated.

mortuary a building in which dead bodies are kept before cremation or burial.

mosaic a form of art or decoration using very small pieces of coloured stone etc.

mosque an Islamic place of worship.

mosquito a kind of small flying insect that bites and can pass on disease.

moss a furry green plant which grows on wet stones and trees, for example.

moth an insect like a butterfly which usually flies at night.

mother a female parent.

motion movement.

motive a reason for doing something.

moto-cross the sport of racing on motor cycles over rough country.

motor an engine to make things move or turn.

motorbike a motor cycle.

motor cycle a large bicycle with an engine.

motor scooter a vehicle rather like a motor cycle but with smaller wheels.

motorway a road with four or more lanes specially made to take fast traffic.

mottled having different-coloured spots or blotches.

motto a short saying which has a special meaning for a person or a group.

mould *verb* to make (something) into a new shape.
noun 1 a container for shaping things. 2 a furry growth found especially on food which is going bad.

mouldy having mould on it, not fresh.

moult (of a bird) to lose feathers; (of an animal) to lose hair or fur.

mound a large heap; a small hill.

mount to get on to (a horse or a bicycle, for example).

mountain a very high hill.

mountaineer a person who climbs mountains for sport.

mountaineering climbing mountains for sport.

mourn to be very sad because of the death of someone or for the loss of something.

mouse a kind of very small animal with a long tail.

mousse a light frothy food from whipped up eggs, cream etc.

moustache hair growing on the upper lip.

mouth 1 the part of the head with which you speak, eat and drink. 2 where a river goes into the sea.

mouth organ a small musical instrument played by blowing into it.

movable able to be moved.

move to go or take from one place to another.

mow to cut grass.

Mr [**mis**ter] title given to a man.

Mrs [**miss**iz] title given to a married woman.

mud wet earth.

muddle a mixed-up state, when things are in a mess.

muesli a food made of cereals, fruit, nuts, honey etc. mixed with milk.

muffin a round flat cake eaten toasted, usually with butter.

muffle to wrap or cover up for warmth or to deaden sound.

mug a big cup with straight sides.

mule an animal whose parents were a horse and a donkey.

multiply to increase something a number of times.

multitude a large crowd, a large number.

mumble to speak in a way that is difficult to hear and understand.

mummy 1 a dead body that has been preserved. 2 **Mummy** a name for your mother.

mumps a painful illness causing swelling on the neck.

munch to eat noisily.

municipal concerning or owned by a city or town.

mural a painting done on a wall.

murder to kill (someone) on purpose.

murky dark, gloomy.

murmur to speak very quietly.

muscle one of the parts of the body that help you to move.

museum a building where old and interesting things may be seen.

mushroom a kind of plant shaped like a small umbrella, used as food.

music pleasant sounds made by voices singing or by instruments.

musical to do with music.

musician a person who makes music.

muslin a kind of very thin, fine cotton cloth.

mussel a kind of shellfish used as food.

mustang a kind of small wild horse found in America.

mustard a hot-tasting yellow powder or paste made from the seeds of the mustard plant, used to flavour food.

muster to gather together for a purpose (especially troops).

mutant an animal or plant that has been changed greatly from the others of its kind.

mutation great change, especially in the characteristics an animal or plant inherits from its parents.

mute silent, dumb.

mutilate to cut off a part of the body; to damage badly.

mutiny a rebellion by soldiers or sailors against their leaders.

mutter to speak or complain in a low voice.

mutton meat from sheep.

mutual felt, done etc. in the same way by two people for each other.

muzzle 1 an animal's mouth and nose. 2 a covering put over an animal's mouth. 3 the open end of a gun barrel.

mysterious very strange.

mystery something strange which cannot be explained.

mystify to cause to be confused or bewildered.

myth a story from long ago about people who are not real.

mythical not real, imaginary.

N

nadir the lowest point.

nag to keep finding fault with (someone).

nail 1 a small sharp-pointed piece of metal used to join pieces of wood together, for example. 2 the hard shiny covering at the end of a finger or toe.

naive [nah-**eev**] innocent, not experienced in the ways of the world.

naked not wearing any clothes, not covered, bare.

name what you call someone or something, the word you use when talking about a person or thing.

namesake someone with the same name as someone else.

nap a short sleep.

napkin a small piece of cloth or paper used when eating to keep your clothes clean.

nappy a piece of cloth or paper wrapped round a baby's bottom.

narcissus one of a number of kinds of usually white or yellow spring flowers, especially one with white petals and a red and yellow centre.

narcotic (a drug) that relieves pain or makes you sleep.

narrator a person who tells a story, especially when describing the parts of a play or film which you don't see.

narrow not far across, not wide.

nasal of the nose.

nasty not pleasant; not good to taste; not kind.

nation the people of one country.

national belonging to a nation.

nationalism the support of your own country, especially in order to make it independent.

native a person born in a certain place; a plant or animal that lives naturally in a certain place.

natural 1 made by nature, not man-made. 2 usual, expected, normal. 3 simple, lifelike.

natural history the study of the natural world, especially plants and animals.

naturalist a person who studies natural history.

nature 1 everything in the world not man-made, for example animals, plants, rocks. 2 the way people or other living things behave.

naughty badly behaved.

nausea a feeling of sickness.

nauseate to sicken, disgust.

nautical to do with the sea or sailors.

naval to do with a navy.

navigate to plan and direct which way a ship, aeroplane, car etc. should go.

navy 1 a country's warships and sailors. 2 a dark-blue colour.

near close to; not far away.

nearly almost, not quite.

neat tidy and clean.

nebulous 1 not definite in shape or meaning, vague. 2 cloudy.

necessary said about something you must have or that must be done.

necessitate to make necessary.

necessitous very poor or needy.

neck the part of the body joining the head and shoulders.

necklace a string of beads or jewels worn around the neck.

nectar a sweet liquid made by flowers which bees use to make honey.

nectarine a kind of smooth-skinned peach.

need 1 to want badly. 2 **need to** to have to.

needle 1 a thin sharp piece of metal with a hole at one end, used for sewing. 2 a thin pointed instrument for knitting etc. 3 a very thin tube for injecting medicine into the body.

nefarious wicked, evil.

negative *adjective* 1 saying no; not positive. 2 (of a number) less than zero.
noun a piece of film from which you can make a photograph.

neglect not to do something that should be done; not to look after.

negligence lack of proper care.

negligible of little or no size or value.

negotiate to bring something about through discussion with another person or other people.

neigh the sound a horse makes.

neighbour a person who lives next door or quite near.

neither not the one or the other.

nephew a son of your brother or sister.

nepotism favouritism shown to relatives by someone with power and influence.

nerve one of the small parts of the body which carry messages to and from the brain.

nerveless feeble, weak.

nervous afraid; easily frightened or worried.

nest a place used as a home by birds and some animals.

nest egg money saved for a special purpose in the future.

nestle to lie or sit closely or warmly (together).

nestling a bird too young to leave the nest.

net material made of string or wire with open spaces, used to catch solid objects but let through air or liquid.

netball a team game in which a ball is thrown into a high net.

nettle a wild plant which can sting when touched.

neural concerning the nerves or the nervous system.

neurosis a sickness of the mind in which the person has unreasonable fears etc.

neurotic (a person who is) abnormally anxious or emotionally upset, (a person) suffering from neurosis.

neuter not masculine or feminine.

neutral 1 not supporting one side or the other, in a war, for example. 2 of colours, not distinct or definite.

never not ever, not at any time.

nevertheless all the same, in spite of that.

new just made or bought; not used or known before.

news telling or writing about something that has happened.

newspaper folded sheets of paper giving news etc., printed every day or every week.

newt an animal rather like a small lizard which lives partly in water.

next 1 nearest, with nothing between. 2 following.

nib the point of a pen.

nibble to eat in tiny bites.

nice pleasant.

niche a hollowed-out space in a wall to hold a statue, for example.

nick 1 to make a small cut in (something). 2 (*informal*) to steal.

nickel a kind of greyish-white metal.

nickname a name you get that is not your real name.

nicotine a yellowish-brown poisonous substance found in tobacco.

niece a daughter of your brother or sister.

niggardly mean, stingy.

niggling slightly annoying.

night the time of darkness.

nightingale a kind of small red-brown bird which sings sweetly at night as well as during the day.

nightmare a bad or frightening dream.

nil nothing.

nimble quick and light on your feet.

nine a number, 9.

nineteen a number, 19.

ninety a number, 90.

nip to bite, pinch.

noble 1 of very good character. 2 of high rank in society.

nobleman a man of high rank.

nobody no one.

nocturnal of or in the night.

nod to bend your head forward quickly, often as a sign that you mean 'yes'.

nodule a small rounded lump.

noise a sound, often loud and unpleasant.

nomad a person who moves around with a group in search of new pastures for animals; any wanderer.

nominal 1 in name only. 2 (of price etc.) very small in comparison with the real worth of something.

nonchalant [**non**shalant] unexcited, calm, unworried.

nondescript having no noteworthy features, very ordinary.

none not any, not one.

nonentity a person of no importance.

nonsense words that have no sense or meaning, foolishness.

noodles ribbon-like strips of pasta.

nook a corner or narrow place, for example in a room where you can be private.

noon twelve o'clock midday.

noose a loop in a rope which can be made tighter by pulling.

nor and not.

norm the average, the standard for ordinary people.

normal usual, the same as others.

north the direction that is on the left as you face the rising sun.

nose the part of your face with which you breathe and smell things.

nostalgia longing for things past; longing for home.

nostril one of the two openings in your nose.

notable famous, worthy of note.

notation 1 the signs or symbols used in music or mathematics. 2 the act of noting (something) down.

notch a small v-shaped cut.

note 1 a short letter. 2 a single sound in music. 3 a piece of paper money.

notice *verb* to see something. *noun* a piece of paper, often pinned to a wall, which tells you something.

noticeable easily noticed, obvious.

notify to inform (someone) about something.

notion an idea or opinion, especially a vague one.

notorious well known for a bad reason.

nougat [**noo**gah] a kind of chewy sweet made from nuts, egg-white, honey etc.

noun a word which tells you what a person or thing is called.

nourish to keep strong and healthy with food.

nourishment food and drink that nourishes.

novel *noun* a book that tells a long story about people and their lives. *adjective* new, strange.

novelette a short novel that does not deal with very serious matters or feelings usually.

novelist a person who writes novels.

novelty something new or unusual.

novice 1 a beginner, someone who is new to a job or profession.
2 a person who is learning to become a monk or a nun.

now at this moment, at this time.

nozzle the open end of a tube or spout.

nuance a very fine shade of difference (in colour, meaning or tone for example).

nub the main point (of a story or incident, for example).

nuclear energy great power produced by splitting atoms.

nucleus the central part of an atom; the centre part of something.

nude not wearing any clothes.

nudge a slight push.

nugget a rough lump found in the earth, containing metal, especially gold.

nuisance something which annoys you or holds you up.

nullify to destroy, to make useless, to cancel.

numb not having any feeling.

number 1 a word or figure, such as one, two, three, 1,2,3, which tells you how many. 2 more than one person or thing.

numerate able to count, having an understanding of mathematics.

numerous many.

nun a woman who has given her life to religion and lives in a convent.

nurse a person trained to look after sick people or young children.

nursery 1 a room or building for very young children. 2 a place where young plants are grown.

nurture *noun* what helps the development of a child.
verb to feed, look after, train.

nut 1 the seed of some trees. 2 a piece of metal which screws on to a bolt.

nutcracker an instrument for cracking the shell of a nut.

nutmeg a kind of spice used in cooking

nutritious (of food) giving good nourishment.

nuzzle to press or rub with the nose.

nylon a kind of strong cloth made from artificial threads.

nymph an imaginary sea, wood or river goddess.

O

oak a kind of large tree with hard wood.

oar a long piece of wood, flat at one end, used to push a boat through the water.

oasis a place in the desert where water can be found and some plants grow.

oath 1 a solemn promise. 2 a swear word.

oats a plant which produces grain used for food, for example porridge.

obedience when you obey.

obeisance an act of accepting someone else as better than yourself, a bow or curtsy.

obelisk a stone pillar, square at the bottom with long sides rising to a point.

obese very fat.

obey to do as you are told.

obfuscate to make (something) unclear or confused.

obituary a short account of someone's life published in a newspaper on their death.

object *noun* [**ob**ject] something that you can see or touch.
verb [ob**ject**] to say that you do not like or agree (to something).

objective *noun* what you try to achieve.
adjective fair-minded, seeing both sides of a question.

obligation something you must do, a duty.

obligatory needing to be done.

oblige 1 to do someone a favour. 2 to force (someone) to do something.

obliging helpful to others, kind.

oblique at a slant; not direct.

obliterate to wipe out, destroy completely.

oblivious forgetful, acting as if you did not know something.

oblong a shape which is longer than it is broad, like this page.

obnoxious nasty, offensive.

oboe a kind of high-pitched woodwind instrument.

obscene disgusting, offensive.

obscure dim, not clear.

obsequious obeying someone in a slave-like way.

observance obeying a rule or law; keeping to a religious practice.

observant good at noticing things.

observatory a building from which scientists can look at the stars, observe weather etc.

observe to see, to look at, to notice.

obsessed thinking too much about something or someone.

obsolescent becoming out of date.

obsolete out of date, no longer in use.

obstacle something which is in the way.

obstinate not willing to change your mind or give way to others.

obstreperous noisy, rough, badly-behaved.

obstruct to block the way, to hold back.

obtain to get.

obtrude to become noticeable in an unwelcome way, to get in the way.

obtrusive getting in the way, unwelcome, obstructing.

obtuse 1 (of an angle) between 90° and 180°. 2 stupid.

obverse the face side or front of a coin etc. (the opposite of reverse).

obvious easy to see or understand.

occasion a time when something happens.

occasionally sometimes, not very often.

121

occult (concerning) magic or supernatural acts or practices.

occupation 1 occupying or being occupied. 2 your job, what you work at.

occupy 1 to live in. 2 to take up (space or time). 3 to hold (an enemy's land) in your power.

occur 1 to take place, to happen. 2 to come into your mind.

occurrence something which happens.

ocean a very large sea.

oceanography the study of the world's oceans.

ochre a kind of yellowish-red earth used for colouring paint etc.; its colour.

o'clock the hour shown by the clock.

octagon a flat eight-sided shape.

octave 1 a musical scale with eight notes. 2 a sound played at the same time as one eight notes higher.

octet 1 a group of eight singers or musicians. 2 a musical work for eight performers.

octopus a kind of large sea creature with eight arms.

ocular concerning the eyes.

oculist a doctor who looks after your eyes.

odd 1 not even: for example, 1, 3, 5 are **odd** numbers. 2 strange, unusual.

oddity 1 being odd. 2 an odd person or thing.

odds the chances that something will or will not happen, for example in betting.

ode a kind of poem, usually a long one written to a person or thing.

odious hateful, bad.

odium hatred, great dislike.

odour a smell.

offal the internal parts of an animal's body, such as the heart, liver etc.

offence 1 an illegal act. 2 something which hurts another's feelings.

offend to hurt someone's feelings.

offensive nasty, offending someone.

offer 1 to say that you are ready to do something. 2 to hold (something) out for someone to take.

offering a gift; money collected in church.

offhand 1 (of manner etc.) careless, not paying attention to others. 2 without thought or preparation in advance.

office 1 a place where people do business. 2 a position of importance in an organisation.

officer 1 a person who is in charge of other people (for example in the army). 2 a person with an important position in an organisation.

official *adjective* to do with public authority and duties.
noun a person who performs public duties.

officious interfering, giving someone help they don't need.

offshoot a twig or branch growing from the main stem of a plant; anything growing from something bigger.

offspring a child or children.

often many times.

ogle to look at (someone) in an unpleasant way, to stare at (someone) with great interest.

ogre (in stories) a giant who eats people.

oil 1 a greasy liquid which does not mix with water. 2 petroleum.

oilskin a kind of cloth made waterproof with oil.

oil slick a layer of oil floating on the surface of water.

ointment a healing cream put on cuts and bruises.

old

old 1 of great age, not new or young. 2 having lived for a certain number of years.

olive a small fruit which gives an oil (**olive oil**) used in cooking; the tree on which it grows; the dull green colour of unripe olives.

olive branch a sign that you are offering peace.

ombudsman an official appointed by the government to investigate citizens' complaints against the government or its services.

omelette eggs beaten together and fried.

omen a sign of something that will happen.

ominous threatening something bad.

omission 1 the act of omitting. 2 something omitted.

omit to leave out; to leave undone.

omnipotent all-powerful.

omnivorous 1 able to eat any kind of food, both plant and animal. 2 having an interest in, reading about all kinds of things.

once 1 one time. 2 in the past.

one 1 a number, 1. 2 a single person or thing.

onerous hard to do, burdensome, causing trouble.

onion a vegetable with a strong smell, made up of a lot of skins.

only 1 by itself, singly. 2 not more than.

onomatopoeia words which sound the same as the noise or action they describe.

onset the beginning of something, of an attack, for example.

onslaught a fierce attack.

onward on and on, forward.

onyx a kind of precious stone with bands of different colours.

ooze to flow slowly.

optician

opal a kind of precious stone with a milky appearance in different colours.

opaque not transparent.

open not shut, not covered over.

opera a play set to music.

operate 1 to work (a machine). 2 to cut the body open to make it healthy again.

operatic of or like opera.

operation the act of operating; being operated on.

operative *adjective* in operation, causing a particular effect. *noun* a worker especially one with a special skill.

operetta a light-hearted opera in which some of the words are spoken.

opinion what you think about something.

opium a drug made from poppies which makes you sleep and lessens pain.

opponent someone who disagrees with you or fights against you.

opportunist a person who is good at taking advantage of things or people.

opportunity the chance or the time to do something.

oppose to be or set yourself against (someone or something).

opposite *adjective* 1 on the other side of a place or an argument. 2 as different as possible. *noun* the side facing you.

oppress 1 to rule or govern cruelly. 2 to make sad and miserable.

oppressive oppressing, cruel.

opprobrium disgrace, shame.

opt 1 to decide on, choose. 2 **opt out** to decide not to (do something).

optical to do with the eyesight or what you see.

optician a person who fits you with glasses or contact lenses to improve your eyesight.

optimism looking on the bright side of things, expecting good things to happen.

optimist a person who shows optimism.

optimistic showing optimism.

option something that can be chosen, a choice.

opulent rich, wealthy; luxurious.

opus 1 a piece of musical composition with a number. 2 an important piece of work by a writer or artist.

oracle a place where prophecies are given, supposedly from a god.

oral 1 spoken, not written. 2 of or using the mouth.

orange 1 a juicy reddish-yellow fruit grown in some hot countries. 2 the colour of this fruit.

orang-utan [orang-**oot**an] a kind of large long-haired ape found in South-East Asia.

oration a public speech.

orator a person skilled in giving long public speeches.

oratory 1 the ability to speak well in public. 2 a small room for private prayer.

orbit the path of one body round another in space.

orchard a place where fruit trees are grown.

orchestra a large group of musicians playing together.

orchid a kind of beautifully shaped and coloured flower.

ordain 1 to make (someone) a priest or minister. 2 (of God, fate etc.) to order, destine.

ordeal a time when you suffer a lot of pain, fear or worry.

order *noun* neatly arranged things or ideas.
verb to say what must be done.

ordinary usual, what you expect.

ordination the ceremony by which someone becomes a priest or minister.

ore rock in which metal is found.

organ 1 a large musical instrument with many pipes, played like a piano. 2 a part of the inside of the body.

organisation 1 a system; a plan of work. 2 a society; a business.

organise to arrange, plan, put in good order.

organism a living animal or plant.

oriental *adjective* of the Orient, the eastern part of the world, especially Asia.
noun a person from the Orient.

orienteering a sport in which contestants race on foot over a large area of rough country using a map and compass.

origin the beginning of something; where a person or thing comes from.

original the earliest, the first one.

ornament something used for decoration, especially in a room.

ornate highly decorated, fancy.

ornithology the scientific study of birds.

orphan a child whose father and mother have both died.

orthodox in keeping with the accepted standards of a religion or behaviour, for example.

oryx a kind of large antelope with long straight horns.

oscillate 1 to move rapidly from side to side. 2 to keep changing your opinions.

osmosis the passage of liquids in solution through a thin sheet of material.

osprey a kind of large, fish-eating bird of prey.

ossify to make or become hard as bone, to make or become hard and unbending.

ostensible appearing on the surface, apparent (but not real).

ostentatious fond of showing off wealth, possessions etc., showy.

ostracise (of a group) to refuse to have anything to do with (a person).

ostrich a kind of very large African bird which cannot fly.

other not the same, different.

otherwise in a different way.

otter a kind of fish-eating animal which lives near water.

ounce a measure of weight, equal to one sixteenth of a pound (about 28 grams).

oust to remove (someone) from office, property etc.

out 1 not inside. 2 not lit.

outbreak a sudden beginning, of a disease among a lot of people, for example.

outcast a person who has been thrown out by his friends or by society.

outcome the result, what happened.

outfit a complete set of clothes or equipment.

outing a trip, a journey made for pleasure.

outlandish very strange or unusual.

outlaw (long ago) a person who continually broke the law and was put outside its protection.

outlet 1 a way out; a way of letting something out. 2 a way of selling things.

outline the outside edge or shape of something or someone.

outlive to live longer than (someone or something).

outlook 1 what you see, the view. 2 the way you think about things. 3 what is likely to happen in the future.

output the quantity of goods made, in a factory, for example.

outrageous shocking, very bad.

outright 1 without doubt or restrictions. 2 total, complete.

outset the beginning.

outside *noun* the part of something that is on the surface. *adverb* not inside.

outskirts the parts of a town which are not in the centre.

outstanding 1 much better than anyone or anything else. 2 still to be dealt with.

outwards moving away from the centre of something.

outwit to beat (someone) by skill or cunning.

oval egg-shaped.

ovation hearty applause at the end of a speech or public performance, for example.

oven a heated box used for cooking and baking.

over *adverb* 1 above. 2 done; finished. 3 more than. 4 across. *noun* (in cricket) a certain number of balls bowled by the same person.

overall(s) a special piece of clothing for working in, worn over ordinary clothes.

overboard over the side of a ship.

overcast cloudy.

overcoat a long coat worn over your clothes to keep you warm and dry.

overcome 1 to defeat. 2 to cause (someone) to lose control of their feelings or actions.

overhaul to examine and repair (an engine, for example).

overhead above you, in the sky.

overkill using much more force etc. than is necessary.

overlap to cover and extend beyond (something).

overleaf on the other side of the page.

overlook 1 to take no notice of. 2 to look down on.

125

overpower to defeat by force, conquer.

oversight a careless mistake, especially one made by not noticing something.

overtake to catch up with and then pass.

overwhelm 1 to defeat completely. 2 to make helpless, by grief, for example.

overwrought very upset, nervous.

owe to be in debt; to have to pay (someone).

owl a kind of large bird which hunts at night.

own *adjective, pronoun* belonging to yourself.
verb to have, to possess.

ox a kind of bull which is kept especially to pull heavy loads and ploughs.

oxygen a gas without taste, smell or colour which is an important part of air and water and necessary to keep you alive.

oyster a kind of shellfish used for food.

ozone a kind of oxygen.

P

pace 1 a step, stride. 2 the speed at which you walk, run or move etc.

pacifism the belief that wars can and should be abolished.

pacifist (of) a person who believes in pacifism.

pacify to make calm, to soothe.

pack *verb* put into a box, parcel or suitcase.
noun 1 a group of things such as playing-cards. 2 a group of animals that hunt together.

package a bundle or collection of things tied or wrapped together.

packet a small box or container made of paper or cardboard.

pad 1 several sheets of paper stuck together at the top edge. 2 a piece of soft material such as cotton wool. 3 the thick skin on the feet of some animals.

padding material used to stuff or fill out the inside of something.

paddle *noun* a piece of wood with a broad flat end for driving a canoe or small boat.
verb to walk in shallow water.

paddock a small field for keeping horses in.

padlock a small lock on a ring which is not fixed to the thing it is locking.

paella a Spanish dish of rice, chicken, seafood etc.

pagan 1 (long ago) a person who did not belong to one of the world's great religions. 2 a person thought to have no religion or religious sense.

page a leaf of a book or newspaper.

pageant a colourful parade or display of scenes from history.

pagoda a kind of temple found in Eastern countries.

pail a bucket.

pain a feeling of being hurt or suffering.

paint a coloured liquid put on with a brush etc. for example to colour something.

painting a picture which is painted.

pair two things of the same kind or which always go together, such as socks or gloves.

palace a large building where a king or queen or a bishop or archbishop lives.

palatable good to eat, tasting good.

palate 1 the roof of the mouth. 2 the sense of taste.

palatial like a palace, very grand.

pale with little colour.

palette a small board on which an artist mixes paints.

palindrome a word or group of words that reads the same backwards or forwards.

paling a row of posts making up a fence.

palisade a fence made of pointed, usually wooden, stakes.

pallid pale, sickly-looking.

pallor paleness due to poor health.

palm 1 a kind of tall tree with heavy leaves which grows in hot countries. 2 the flat front of the hand.

palmistry telling someone's fortune using the lines of the palm of the hand.

palomino a kind of golden or cream-coloured horse with a pale-coloured mane and tail.

palpable able to be touched or felt, obvious.

palpitation rapid beating of the heart.

paltry of little value, worthless.

pamper to be too kind to, to spoil with kindness.

pamphlet a small thin book, usually on some important subject.

pan a round metal pot with a long handle, used for cooking.

panacea a cure for everything.

panache [pa**nash**] a self-confident and showy way of doing something.

pancake a thin cake of flour, eggs, milk and sugar which is fried in a pan.

panda a kind of black and white animal like a small bear found in China.

pandemonium uproar, great din.

pane a piece of glass for a window.

panel a piece of wood or other material fitted into a frame or into a door.

panic sudden alarm or fear which makes a person or people behave in a stupid or thoughtless way.

pannier a basket or bag carried on either side of a horse or bicycle.

panorama a wide view or picture of an area.

pansy a kind of small brightly-coloured garden flower.

pant to breathe quickly as though you are short of breath.

pantechnicon a very large van for moving furniture, stage scenery etc

panther a kind of large black wild animal of the cat family.

pantomime a nursery story performed on the stage with music and songs.

pantry a room for storing food, usually in or near a kitchen.

pants 1 underpants. 2 trousers.

pap soft mushy food, given to babies and invalids usually.

paper 1 material for writing on, making books, wrapping things and so on. 2 a newspaper.

papier maché [paper **mash**ay] a mixture of paper, liquid and glue, used to make boxes, ornaments etc.

paprika a hot-tasting red powder made from a kind of pepper.

papyrus a kind of reed from which the Ancient Egyptians made paper; paper made from it.

par the normal amount or condition.

parable a story, usually from the Bible, which has a special meaning.

parabola a kind of curve such as that made by something as it is thrown in the air and falls to the ground again.

parachute cloth shaped like an umbrella, used when jumping from an aircraft.

parade *noun* a marching display by people in uniform.
verb to march up and down.

paradise a place of complete happiness where you go when you die, heaven.

paradox something which seems silly or unlikely but is actually sensible.

paraffin thin oil used in lamps and stoves.

paragon a model of excellence, a perfect person or thing.

paragraph a group of sentences.

parakeet a kind of small long-tailed parrot.

parallel (of lines) always the same distance apart.

paralysed unable to move some or all of the body, for example because of serious injury.

paralysis being paralysed.

paramedical (of people or services) supporting and additional to medical work, for example ambulancemen.

paramount supreme, most important, in supreme authority.

parapet a low wall on the top of a castle, roof, balcony etc.

paraphrase a form of words which shows the meaning of a larger piece of writing in a different way.

parasite 1 an animal or plant that lives on or in another. 2 a person who lives off others.

parasol a kind of light umbrella used to shade you from the sun.

paratroops parachute troops.

parcel something wrapped up for posting or carrying.

parched very dry or thirsty.

parchment writing material made out of dried skin.

pardon forgiveness for something you have done wrong.

pare to cut the edge, skin etc. off.

parent a father or mother.

pariah a social outcast, an outsider.

parish a district looked after by a clergyman.

parity equality, the state of being equal.

park *noun* 1 a piece of land usually with grass and flowers where you can go to play and enjoy yourself. 2 a games field.
verb to leave (a car) somewhere for a time.

parliament 1 a group of people who make the laws of a country. 2 the place where they meet.

parlour a sitting room.

parody 1 a feeble imitation. 2 a piece in which an author's style is mockingly imitated.

parole a form of early release from prison in return for the prisoner's promise to stay out of trouble.

parquet a kind of wooden flooring made of small interlocking pieces.

parrot a kind of bird which can learn to talk and which has bright feathers.

parry to turn aside, ward off (a blow etc.).

parsimonious mean, over-careful with money.

parsley a kind of herb used in cooking.

parsnip a kind of pale root vegetable.

parson a minister, a clergyman.

part *noun* 1 a piece or portion of a whole thing. 2 a share in some activity.
verb to split up, to separate.

partial 1 not complete. 2 **partial to** having a liking for.

participate to take part (in something).

particle a very small piece (of something).

particular 1 special, different from others. 2 hard to please.

partition 1 a thin dividing wall. 2 the dividing up into parts (of a country, for example).

partner 1 one of two people playing a game or dancing together, for example. 2 a person sharing in a business.

partridge a kind of small game bird.

party a group of people gathered together, usually to enjoy themselves.

pass *verb* 1 to leave behind, to go past. 2 to get through (a test).
noun 1 a gap in the mountains. 2 a piece of paper that allows you to get into places.

passable just good enough.

passage 1 a narrow way through. 2 a piece taken from a book or story.

passenger a person who travels by train, bus, ship or car.

passion very strong feelings of love, anger etc.

passionate feeling or showing passion.

passport an official document which allows you to travel abroad.

password a secret word which tells you are a friend and not an enemy.

past *noun* the time that has gone before.
adverb up to and away from.

pasta dried flour paste in many shapes such as macaroni, spaghetti etc.

paste a wet and sticky mixture.

pastel 1 a kind of chalk-like crayon used for drawing; a drawing done with this. 2 a soft pale colour.

pasteurise to make (milk) free of bacteria by a special kind of heating.

pastime a hobby, interesting work done in your spare time.

pastoral 1 to do with shepherds and flocks etc. 2 to do with a religious group and its leader.

pastry the crispy baked casing of pies and tarts etc.

pasture a piece of grassy land for grazing animals.

pat to touch gently with the hand.

patch a small piece of material used to repair a hole, for example in clothes.

patchy with some parts better than others.

patent *adjective* 1 obvious, clear to see. 2 protected by a patent.
noun (a document giving) the exclusive right to sell something you have invented.

paternal of or like a father; on your father's side.

path a narrow track for walking.

pathetic causing pity or sadness or contempt.

patience 1 being patient. 2 a kind of card game played by one person.

patient *adjective* taking something calmly, able to wait for things to be right.
noun someone who is ill and seeing a doctor or dentist.

patina gloss produced by age on the surface of something.

patio a paved area near a house where you can sit outside.

patois [**pat**wa] the dialect of a local group of people.

patriarch 1 the father and ruler of a family or tribe. 2 the head of some Eastern Christian churches.

patriot a person who loves his or her country very much and is willing to give it support.

patriotic loving your country very much.

patrol 1 a small group of policemen or soldiers, for example, on the lookout for something. 2 a small group of Scouts or Guides.

patron 1 a person who supports an organisation or person, by giving money for example. 2 a regular customer of a shop etc. 3 **patron saint** a saint regarded as the protector of a particular place etc.

patter the sound made by: 1 raindrops. 2 running feet.

pattern 1 a design, a careful placing together of shapes and colours. 2 a plan to follow when making something.

pauper a very poor person.

pause a short stop or wait.

pavement the part at each side of the street you walk on.

paw the foot of an animal such as a dog or cat.

pawnbroker a shopkeeper who lends money in return for things which are left with him.

pay *verb* to hand over money for something.
noun money you are given for working.

pea a small vegetable which grows in a pod, used as food.

peace 1 quietness, stillness, calm. 2 not being at war.

peach a kind of soft juicy fruit with a yellowy red skin and a large hard seed inside.

peacock a large male bird which makes its tail go into a huge brightly-coloured fan-shape. The female is called a **peahen**.

peak 1 the top of a hill or a mountain. 2 the front part of a cap which sticks out.

peal 1 the sound of very big bells. 2 the sound of thunder.

peanut a small round hard seed like a nut, used as food.

pear a juicy fruit with a greenish-yellow skin and a pointed shape.

pearl a precious gem found in the shells of some shellfish, especially oysters.

peasant a worker on the land, a person with a small farm.

peat remains of old plants found in boggy soil, used as fuel and fertiliser.

pebble a small smooth rounded stone.

peck to pick up food with the beak, to poke at.

peckish rather hungry.

pectoral of, on or for the chest.

peculiar strange, unusual.

pecuniary of or about money.

pedal a bar or lever which you move with the feet to drive a machine or play an organ, for example.

pedantic being overfussy about details.

pedestrian a person who walks.

pedigree a list of a person's or animal's ancestors, in animals a sign that they have been purely bred.

pedlar a person who goes from place to place selling small articles.

peek to take a quick or sly look at something or someone.

peel *noun* the outside skin of fruit or vegetables.
verb to take off the skin from (fruit or vegetables).

peep to look at quickly and secretly, to glance.

peer *verb* to look at closely.
noun a person of high rank.

peevish slightly bad-tempered.

peg 1 a small hook for hanging clothes. 2 a small clip for fixing clothes to a washing-line.

pelican a kind of large bird which stores food in a pouch under its beak.

pellet 1 a tiny ball, for example of metal to fire from a gun. 2 a small pill.

pell-mell in a mad rush, in disorder.

pelt *noun* an animal's skin, especially one with the fur or hair still on.
verb 1 to throw (things) at (someone or something). 2 (of rain) to fall heavily. 3 to rush along.

pelvis the curved group of bones where the top of the legs join the spine.

pen 1 a tool which is used when writing with ink. 2 a place fenced in to keep animals together.

penal concerned with legal punishment.

penalty a punishment for breaking a rule or the law.

penance a punishment you give yourself to show sorrow for something you have done wrong.

pence *see* **penny**.

pencil a writing-tool made of wood with a grey or coloured centre.

pendant an ornament hung from a necklace etc.

pending awaiting (a decision, for example).

pendulous drooping, hanging down.

pendulum a swinging weight that controls the workings of a clock.

penetrate to enter; to find a way through or into, to pierce.

penguin a kind of large black and white sea bird which cannot fly, found near the South Pole.

penicillin a kind of medicine which kills many disease-causing germs.

peninsula a piece of land almost surrounded by water.

penitence being penitent.

penitent sorry for something you've done because it was wrong.

penknife a small knife with a folding blade.

pennant a long narrow triangular flag.

penny, *plural* **pennies** or **pence,** a small British coin worth a hundredth of a pound.

pension money paid regularly to someone who has retired, who is too ill to work etc.

pensive thoughtful, as if in a dream.

pentagon a shape with five straight sides.

pentathlon an athletic contest of five different events.

penultimate the last but one.

penurious very poor.

peony a kind of large red, pink or white garden flower.

people men, women and children.

pepper 1 a hot-tasting powder which is used for flavouring. 2 a kind of red-, green- or yellow-skinned vegetable.

peppermint a kind of strong-tasting plant, used especially to flavour sweets and toothpastes.

peptic ulcer an ulcer in the digestive system.

perambulate to walk over, through or about.

perceive to see, observe, understand.

perceptible able to be seen or understood, noticeable.

perception the act of perceiving; the ability to perceive; clear understanding.

perceptive able to understand quickly and clearly.

perch *noun* a bar on which a bird can rest.
verb to sit on the edge of something.

percussion musical instruments played by striking, for example drums.

perennial 1 living or lasting a long time. 2 (of plants) growing from year to year without being replanted.

perfect without fault, complete.

perforate to make small holes in.

perforations small holes in a sheet of paper etc., so that it can be torn apart easily.

perform to act, to do.

performance 1 something you do, especially in front of an audience. 2 when a play or a ballet etc. is put on the stage.

perfume scent, a pleasant smell.

perfunctory done in a hasty, offhand way.

perhaps maybe, possibly.

peril great danger.

perimeter the border or outside edge of a field, camp, shape etc.

period a length of time.

periphery the outer edge of a surface or area.

periscope an instrument with mirrors which allows you to see things at a higher level, for example from a submarine.

perish to die, waste away.

perjury telling a lie in a court of law.

perky full of life, in a good mood.

permafrost the subsoil which remains below freezing point in the polar regions.

permanent not coming to an end, for all time.

permeate to penetrate through every part of.

permission being allowed to do something.

permit to allow, to let (someone) do something.

permutation variation in the order of things.

perpendicular upright, at right angles (to a level line).

perpetrate to commit (a crime), to do (something bad or foolish).

perpetual continual, going on for ever.

perplexed puzzled, not knowing what to think or do.

persecute to keep hurting or giving (someone) trouble.

persevere to keep on doing something.

persist to do something again and again, to refuse to stop.

person a man, a woman or a child.

personal belonging to a particular person.

personnel the employees of an organisation, the staff.

perspective the way things look when viewed from a particular position.

perspire to sweat.

persuade to talk to a (person) until he or she does as you wish.

pertinacious stubborn, persistent.

perturbed upset, anxious, disturbed.

peruse to read thoroughly or closely.

pervasive spread throughout something, found everywhere.

perverse doing the wrong thing on purpose.

pessimism looking on the black side of things, expecting that things will be bad.

pessimist a person who thinks pessimistically.

pessimistic showing or feeling pessimism.

pest a person, an animal or an insect that annoys you or causes damage.

pester to keep annoying (somebody).

pestilence a fatal disease which affects many people.

pestle a short stick with a round end used for crushing substances in a mortar.

pet an animal which you keep for pleasure.

petal one of the usually brightly-coloured separate parts of a flower.

petition a letter or form, usually signed by a lot of people asking for something.

petrified very frightened.

petrol the liquid that drives the engine of a motor car.

petroleum a kind of oil found under the earth's surface, used to make many other substances, for example petrol.

petty small and unimportant.

petulant irritable, impatient without much reason.

pew a seat or bench in a church.

pewter a kind of dull grey metal, made from tin and lead.

phantom a ghost.

pharmacist a person skilled in pharmacy.

pharmacy 1 the preparation of medicines. 2 a shop where medicines are prepared and sold.

phase a stage which a person or thing goes through, for example in growing up or developing.

pheasant a kind of large colourful game bird with a long tail.

phenomenal extraordinary, outstanding.

philanthropy helping others, for example by giving money.

philatelist a person who collects postage stamps.

philosophy the study of the ways people think about life, morals etc.

phoenix a bird in fables which was supposed to rise from the ashes after it had burnt itself.

phone a telephone.

photocopy a copy of a page etc. made by photographing it.

photograph a picture taken using a camera.

phrase

phrase a few words which are part of a sentence.

physical belonging to the natural world or the body.

physician (old-fashioned) a doctor, especially one who treats illness with medicines and not with surgery.

physics the study of matter and energy and the relationship between them.

physique bodily build and fitness.

pianist a person who plays the piano.

piano a kind of large musical instrument played by pressing the keys.

piccolo a small high-pitched flute.

pick *verb* 1 to gather. 2 to choose. *noun* a pointed metal tool with a wooden handle for making holes in hard ground.

picket a person or group standing outside a factory etc. to stop workers going in during a strike.

pickles vegetables etc. kept in vinegar.

picnic a meal eaten in the open air.

pictorial of or expressed in pictures, illustrated.

picture a drawing, a painting or a photograph of something.

picturesque attractive to look at.

pie fruit or meat cooked in a pastry case.

piebald (a horse) with black and white markings.

piece a part of something larger.

pier a landing-stage for ships built out into the water.

pierce to make a hole in (something), to stab.

piety devotion to God, holiness, being pious.

pig a kind of fat short-legged animal kept for its meat.

pigeon a kind of greyish bird which makes a soft noise.

piglet a baby pig.

pink

pigment a colouring material used to make paint.

pigmy *see* **pygmy.**

pigsty a pen for pigs.

pike 1 a kind of large freshwater fish. 2 a long heavy spear.

pilchard a kind of small sea-fish.

pile a large heap.

pilfer to steal small things.

pilgrim a person who travels to visit a holy place.

pill a small ball of medicine for swallowing.

pillar an upright post, usually of stone, often used to hold up a part of a building.

pillow a cushion to rest your head on, especially on a bed.

pilot 1 a person who controls an aeroplane. 2 a person who goes on board a ship to guide it into harbour.

pilot light 1 a small flame kept alight to fire the main burner in a gas appliance. 2 a small light which shows that an electrical appliance is on.

pimple a small, usually red or yellow, swelling on the skin.

pin a thin sharp piece of pointed metal used for holding things together.

pinafore 1 an apron. 2 *also* **pinafore dress** a dress without sleeves or collar.

pincers 1 a tool with jaws which grip when closed. 2 the claws of a crab or lobster, for example.

pinch *verb* to nip tightly with the fingers. *noun* a very small amount, of salt, for example.

pine *verb* to long for something or somebody very much. *noun* a kind of tall evergreen tree on which cones grow.

pineapple a kind of juicy fruit grown in hot countries.

pink a very light red colour.

pinnacle a small pointed tower; a pointed mountain top; a high point.

pint a measure of liquid, equal to just over half a litre.

pioneer one of the first people to go to live in a new land; someone who does something for the first time.

pious very religious.

pip a small seed, for example in an apple or an orange.

pipe 1 a tube often made of metal or rubber. 2 a bowl with a stem for smoking tobacco. 3 a tubelike musical instrument played by blowing.

pique [peek] a bad mood because your pride is hurt.

piracy capturing and robbing a ship or robbery at sea.

piranha a small, flesh-eating South American freshwater fish.

pirate a sea robber.

pirouette (of a dancer) to spin on one foot or toe.

pistil the part of a flower which produces the seed.

pistol a short handgun, a revolver.

piston a disc which moves up and down inside a tube in an engine etc.

pit 1 a hole in or under the ground. 2 a coalmine.

pitch *noun* a stretch of ground used for playing games.
verb 1 to put up (a tent). 2 to throw.

pitcher 1 a large jug with a narrow neck and two handles usually. 2 (in baseball) a bowler.

pitta a kind of flat round bread with a pocket inside for holding food, originally from the middle East.

pity 1 feeling sorry for somebody. 2 something you are sorry about.

pivot a point on which something turns.

pixie a small fairy.

pizza [**pee**tsa] a flat Italian pie topped with cheese, tomatoes etc.

pizzeria a place where pizzas are made and sold.

pizzicato (in music for the violin family) by plucking the strings with the finger.

placard a large notice or poster hung up or carried publicly.

place 1 a position on the earth's surface. 2 a space for something.

placid calm, untroubled.

plague a terrible disease which spreads very quickly.

plaice a kind of flat sea-fish, used as food.

plain *adjective* 1 ordinary, simple. 2 easily seen or heard.
noun a flat piece of land.

plait [plat] to twist together, one over another, three or more strands of hair, rope etc.

plan *noun* a drawing of something.
verb to arrange.

plane 1 an aeroplane. 2 a tool for smoothing wood. 3 *also* **plane tree** a kind of broad-leaved tree.

planet one of the large bodies, like the earth, that go round the sun.

plank a long flat piece of wood.

plankton the tiny animals and plants which live near the surface of the sea, lakes, rivers etc.

plant *noun* something which grows from roots in the ground.
verb to put (seeds) into soil so that they will grow.

plaque 1 an ornamental plate, often commemorating someone or something. 2 a film on the teeth where bacteria breed easily.

plaster 1 a paste used to cover walls which goes hard when dried. 2 a covering you put on a cut to protect it. 3 *also* **plaster of Paris** a kind of paste which hardens to form moulds, casings for broken limbs etc.

plastic a light and strong man-made material used to make many different objects.

plate a flat dish from which you eat food.

plateau [**plat**o] an area of high flat land.

platform 1 a raised place, usually in a hall. 2 the place in a station where you get on and off trains.

platinum a kind of very valuable silvery-coloured metal.

platoon a small group of soldiers.

platter a large flat plate for serving food.

plausible sounding reasonable without necessarily being so.

play *noun* a story which is acted. *verb* 1 to enjoy yourself, especially in a game. 2 to make sounds on a musical instrument.

plea a serious request, an act of pleading.

plead 1 to ask for something in a begging way. 2 to give as an excuse. 3 to answer a charge in court. 4 **plead guilty/not guilty** to state in court that you are guilty/not guilty.

pleasant delightful, pleasing.

please 1 to make (somebody) happy. 2 a polite word used when asking for something.

pleasure happiness, joy.

pleat a fold which is pressed into clothes.

plectrum a small piece of plastic, wood etc., for plucking the strings of a musical instrument such as a guitar.

pledge 1 to promise. 2 to give something as a promise.

plenty more than enough.

pliable easily bent or influenced.

pliers a tool with handles and a head for gripping and cutting things.

plight a situation of danger or difficulty.

plod to walk or do something slowly and heavily.

plop the sound made by an object falling into a liquid.

plot 1 the story of a play. 2 a secret plan. 3 a piece of ground.

plough a machine with blades for breaking up the soil.

pluck 1 to take the feathers from (a dead bird). 2 to gather (flowers, fruit from a tree etc.). 3 to pull and then let go (the strings of a guitar, for example).

plucky brave.

plug 1 a stopper for a bath or a bowl. 2 a fitting put into a socket to get electricity.

plum a kind of soft red or purple fruit with a large hard seed in it.

plumage a bird's feathers.

plumber a person who fits and repairs water and gas pipes.

plume 1 a large feather, especially one used for decoration. 2 a shape of smoke for example that looks like a feather.

plummet to fall far and quickly.

plump pleasantly fat.

plunder (especially of soldiers) to rob (a place) violently.

plunge to dive or thrust in.

plural numbering more than one.

plus added to; the sign +.

plush *noun* a kind of fabric with a soft and warm feel. *adjective* splendidly comfortable, luxurious.

plywood a tough kind of wood made by gluing several thin sheets of wood together.

pneumonia [new**moan**ia] a serious lung disease.

poach 1 to cook gently in water (for example an egg). 2 to hunt animals or catch fish without permission.

pocket a bag sewn into your clothes to hold money and things.

pod a long case on a plant with seeds in it.

podium a small raised platform used by speakers to address a meeting.

poem a piece of poetry.

poet a person who writes poems.

poetry words written in lines of a certain length and often rhyming at the ends.

poignant [**poy**nant] very sad and upsetting.

point *noun* 1 the sharp end. 2 a dot. 3 a place or time.
verb to show with a finger.

pointer 1 a stick etc. used to point things out. 2 a kind of hunting dog which points its nose towards the hunted bird or animal.

poise being self-confident about yourself, especially about how you look.

poison a substance that can kill or harm you if it gets into your body.

poisonous containing poison.

poke to push with a stick or a rod.

poky small, cramped for space.

polar connected with the **North Pole** or the **South Pole**, the two points on the earth's surface furthest from the equator.

polar bear a large white bear which lives near the North Pole.

pole a long rounded stick, a rod.

police people whose job it is to make sure that the law is obeyed.

policy 1 a settled plan of action. 2 an insurance document.

polish to make smooth and bright by rubbing.

polite well-behaved, well-mannered.

political connected with the government of a country.

politician a person who is involved in politics, for example a member of parliament.

politics political matters.

poll 1 voting at an election. 2 *also* **opinion poll** a way of finding out what people are thinking by asking a number of them.

pollen fine yellow dust found in flowers.

pollution things which make dirty and destroy the environment, water, plants, etc.

polo a team game played on horseback with a ball and a stick.

polo-neck a high collar which goes right round the neck.

polygamy the practice of being married to more than one woman at the same time.

polythene a kind of lightweight plastic.

pomp splendour, great show or ceremony.

pompom a small ball of wool, silk etc. worn, especially on a hat, for decoration.

pompous self-important.

pond a small, usually man-made, lake.

ponder to think deeply about something.

ponderous 1 heavy, difficult to move or carry. 2 dull and uninteresting.

pony a small horse.

ponytail hair tied in a bunch at the top of the head.

poodle a kind of curly-haired dog kept as a pet.

pool 1 a small area of still water. 2 a pond prepared for swimming.

poor 1 not having much money, not rich. 2 not very good.

pop 1 a soft sudden noise. 2 a kind of modern music, especially popular with young people.

popcorn a kind of maize that puffs up when heated (and is good to eat).

poplar a kind of tree with a tall straight trunk.

poppy a kind of plant with large, usually red, flowers.

populace the ordinary people of a country or area.

popular well-liked by people.

population the number of people who live in a particular place.

populous containing many inhabitants.

porcelain a kind of fine china; articles made of this.

porch a shelter over an outside door of a building.

porcupine a kind of animal like a large hedgehog.

pore *noun* a tiny opening in the skin through which sweat for example passes.
verb **pore over** to study very closely.

pork meat from a pig.

porpoise a kind of sea animal rather like a dolphin.

porridge a breakfast food made of oatmeal boiled in water.

port 1 a place where ships land their cargo. 2 the left-hand side of a ship as you face forward. 3 a kind of strong, often red, wine from Portugal.

portable able to be carried about.

portent a sign that something (bad) is going to happen.

porter 1 a person who carries other people's luggage at a railway station or a hotel, for example. 2 a person who looks after the entrance to a building.

porthole an opening in a ship's side to let in air and light.

portion a part or a share of something.

portrait a picture of a person.

portray 1 to make a portrait of. 2 to describe in words.

pose 1 to sit or stand in a particular way, for example for a photograph. 2 to sit or stand in a way that attracts attention.

position 1 the place where something or somebody is. 2 a job.

positive 1 certain, quite sure. 2 saying 'yes'.

possess to have; to own.

possible able to be done; likely to take place.

post 1 an upright pole fixed in the ground. 2 the system for sending and getting letters. 3 a job, a position.

postage the cost of sending something by post.

poster a large piece of paper with a message printed, drawn or painted on it which is put up in public places.

postpone to put off till later.

postscript something added at the end of a letter, for example.

posture the way you carry yourself, stand, sit etc.

posy a small bunch of flowers.

pot 1 a round container, for example a **jampot** or a **teapot**. 2 a deep container with a handle for cooking.

potato a kind of oval or round-shaped vegetable which is dug out of the ground.

potent powerful.

potential *adjective* possible, able to happen or develop.
noun ability to happen or develop, for example.

pothole 1 a deep hole in the ground or rock, a deep cave. 2 a hole in the surface of a road.

potholing exploring holes and caves underground as a sport.

potion a drink containing medicine, poison or something magic.

potter *noun* a person who makes pottery.
verb to work or do things in a slow unhurried way.

pottery 1 pots and dishes etc. made of baked clay. 2 a place where these are made.

pouch a small bag.

poultry farmyard birds, for example chickens, ducks.

pounce to jump upon, to seize suddenly.

pound *noun* 1 an amount of British money equal to a hundred pence. 2 a measure of weight equal to 16 ounces (about 450 grams). *verb* to beat very hard.

pour 1 to make (liquid) flow out of a container. 2 to rain heavily.

poverty being poor.

powder dust made by crushing a hard substance.

power strength, force.

practical 1 able to do or make a number of useful things. 2 able to be used, likely to be useful. 3 **practical joke** a trick played on someone.

practice 1 the act of practising. 2 the actual doing of something, rather than thinking about it.

practise to do a thing again and again in order to get better at it.

pragmatic (of a person) sensible, practical, acting by experience.

prairie a large stretch of grassland in North America.

praise to say good things about (someone or something).

pram a small carriage for a baby or doll.

prance (especially of a horse) to jump about with quick light steps.

prank a joke, trick.

prattle to talk on and on in a foolish way.

prawn a kind of small shellfish used as food.

pray to speak to God.

prayer what you say when praying.

preach to give a religious or moral talk.

precarious unsafe, dangerous, uncertain.

precaution care taken before something to avoid danger etc.

precede to go in front of (someone or something).

precedence coming before in rank or position; the right to come before.

precedent something which happened before, taken as an example for future action.

precept a command, a law, a rule.

precious very valuable, greatly loved.

precipice a very steep cliff.

precise exact; definite.

precocious (of a child) behaving like someone older.

precursor a person or thing which went before.

predator an animal that kills for food.

predecessor a person who held a post or place before you.

predict to say that something will happen, to foretell.

predominant that predominates.

predominate to be the most outstanding, the most obvious or the most important.

preen 1 (of a bird) to tidy the feathers with the beak. 2 (of a person) to smarten yourself up.

preface a short introduction to a book.

prefer to like (one person or thing) more than the others.

preferable preferred, more acceptable.

preference what you prefer.

pregnant (of a woman or female animal) producing young, about to give birth.

prehistoric belonging to the time before history was written.

prejudice bias, an opinion formed without knowing all the facts about something.

preliminary taking place before something else, leading up to an event.

premature born before the right time; happening too soon.

premier *adjective* first, chief, leading. *noun* a prime minister.

première the first performance of a play etc.

premises a house or other building and its grounds.

premium 1 an amount paid regularly to an insurance company. 2 **at a premium** highly valued and therefore difficult to get.

preparations things you do to get ready for something or someone.

prepare to make or get ready.

preposterous ridiculous, absurd.

prerequisite (something) needed before something can happen or be done.

prescribe 1 to state, usually in writing, what medicine should be given. 2 to say what should be done.

prescription 1 what a doctor prescribes. 2 the act of prescribing.

presence being present.

present [present] *noun* a gift. *adjective* 1 in a place or with people. 2 **at present** now. *verb* [present] to hand over to someone else.

presently in a short time, soon.

preserve to keep (something) from harm or from going bad.

preside (**over**) to be in charge of a (meeting or a group).

president the head of a country or of an organisation.

press *verb* 1 to push hard. 2 to make smooth with an iron. *noun* a machine for printing.

pressing urgent, needing to be done immediately.

pressure pressing or being pressed; weight or force against something or someone.

prestige being well-known and well-thought of because you are successful.

prestigious having prestige.

presumably probably, as can be presumed.

presume to suppose, take for granted.

pretence the act of pretending.

pretend 1 to act as though you were somebody or something else. 2 to act as though something is true, which isn't.

pretty attractive, delightful to see.

prevail 1 to win through, to get control (over). 2 to be the commonest, most usual.

prevalent common, usual.

prevent to stop (something) from taking place; to stop (someone) from doing something.

preview a showing of a play, exhibition etc. before it is open to the public.

previous coming before.

prey a bird or animal that is hunted.

price what you must pay to buy something, the cost.

priceless very valuable.

prick to make a small hole with something pointed.

prickly 1 having sharp points or thorns, for example like a holly leaf. 2 bad-tempered, easily annoyed.

pride being proud.

priest someone who performs religious ceremonies.

prim neat; easily shocked; almost too well-behaved.

primary 1 first; earliest. 2 **primary colours** those from which others can be made by mixing (for example, red, blue and yellow for mixing paints).

primate 1 a member of the group of mammals which includes man, apes and monkeys. 2 an archbishop.

prime minister the head of a government.

primrose a kind of small yellow spring flower.

prince a man or boy in a royal family.

princess a woman or girl in a royal family.

principal *adjective* most important, chief, head.
noun the head of some colleges or schools.

principle a rule which you must keep or live by.

print 1 to press letters on to paper by a machine. 2 to write without joining up the letters.

printer 1 a person who prints books, newspapers etc. 2 a machine which prints, especially output from a computer.

printout the printed paper from a computer printer.

priority what should be done or seen to first.

prison a place where people who have broken the law may be kept.

privacy being away from other people or where they cannot see or hear you.

private *adjective* 1 belonging to one person or group only. 2 kept hidden or secret.
noun a soldier of the lowest rank in the army.

privet a kind of evergreen bush often used to make hedges.

privilege something special you are allowed to have or do.

prize a reward for winning something.

probably likely.

probe to search deeply, to examine closely.

problem a difficult thing to settle, or to work out.

procedure the proper way of doing something.

proceed to move forward.

proceeds the money made from a show, sale etc.

process a course of action, the series of actions involved in doing or making something.

procession an orderly, often ceremonial, march or forward movement.

proclaim to announce in public.

procrastinate to put off something till a later time, waste time.

procure to obtain, get.

prod to poke (with a stick, for example).

prodigious very big, amazing.

prodigy 1 a very exceptional person, especially a child. 2 an exceptionally wonderful thing.

produce *verb* [pro**duce**] 1 to bring out; to show. 2 to make.
noun [**pro**duce] something produced by growing.

product something produced.

profanity swearing, bad language.

profession an occupation which needs very special training and knowledge, for example being a lawyer or doctor.

proficient good at something, skilful.

profile 1 the outline of someone's face seen from the side. 2 a short description of a person, their character and life.

profit money that you make when you sell something for more than you paid for it, gain.

profound 1 very deep. 2 very wise, showing great understanding.

profuse plentiful.

progeny the offspring of a person, animal etc.

program a number of instructions for a computer which you use to tell it what to do.

programme 1 a list of performers and information about what will happen, for example at a concert or competition. 2 something broadcast on television or radio.

progress *noun* [**pro**gress] moving forward, getting better.
verb [pro**gress**] to go forward, to advance.

prohibit to forbid, usually by order.

project *noun* [**pro**ject] 1 a plan for something special. 2 a long piece of work, for example finding information about a subject.
verb [pro**ject**] 1 to stick out. 2 to show (films etc.) on a screen.

projectile something which is fired, from a gun, for example.

projector a machine for projecting pictures.

prolific producing many offspring; producing large quantities.

prologue an introduction to a play, book etc.

prolong to make (something) last longer.

promenade a paved public walkway near the sea usually.

prominent clearly seen, standing out clearly; well-known.

promise to say firmly that you will do something.

promote 1 to give (someone) a higher position or a more important job. 2 to help to sell or encourage.

prompt in good time, at the right time.

prong one of the sharp spikes of a fork.

pronoun a word used in place of a noun (for example, he, she, it).

pronounce 1 to say (a word or sound) in a certain way. 2 To declare, especially officially. 3 **pronounced** very noticeable.

pronunciation the way you pronounce words.

proof what shows or proves something to be true.

propel to push forward.

propeller curved blades on a ship or aeroplane which drive it forward.

proper correct, right.

property 1 something which belongs to someone. 2 land or buildings which belong to someone.

prophecy [**prof**essie] something prophesied.

prophesy [**prof**e-sye] to foretell what will happen in the future.

prophet a man who is thought to know what is going to happen in the future.

propose to suggest; to offer.

proprietor an owner, especially of a shop or business.

propulsion driving forward; the force which does this.

prose ordinary written or spoken language, not verse.

prosecute to accuse (someone) of a crime in a court of law.

prospect *noun* [**pros**pect] 1 a hope, expectation. 2 a view, a landscape.
verb [pros**pect**] to search for gold or other minerals.

prospectus a printed document describing the good points of a house, school, business etc.

prosper to do well, to succeed.

prosperity being prosperous.

prosperous successful, rich.

protect to prevent (someone or something) being harmed or damaged.

protein an important element in all living things and in food, for example.

protest to say strongly that you are against something.

protractor an instrument for measuring angles.

protrude to stick out.

proud thinking very well of yourself or of someone or something connected with you.

prove to show that something is true.

proverb a short well-known saying.

provide to give what is needed, to supply.

provident careful with money etc.

providential fortunate, happening by good luck, just at the right time.

province 1 a division of a country. 2 **the provinces** the parts of a country away from the capital city.

provincial of a province, like the provinces; dull, unexciting.

provision 1 providing something. 2 **provisions** supplies of food and drink.

provoke to make angry.

prow the bow of a ship.

prowess skill, especially where physical effort is needed.

prowl to creep about, for example like a cat in search of prey.

proximity closeness, nearness.

prudent careful, cautious.

prune *noun* a dried plum. *verb* to cut off unwanted branches from (a tree etc.).

psalm a Bible poem or song.

psychiatrist a doctor who specialises in the treatment of mental illness.

psychiatry the study and treatment of mental illness.

psychologist a person who studies psychology.

psychology the scientific study of the mind.

puberty the stage in life of growing up from childhood to adulthood, when you become able to produce children.

public 1 for everybody to use. 2 in open view.

publication 1 the act of publishing. 2 a published book, magazine etc.

publish to put into print for sale.

puck a thick rubber disk used in ice hockey.

pudding a soft cooked food, often a sweet one eaten at the end of meal.

puddle a small pool of usually dirty water.

puff a short burst of breath or smoke.

puffin a kind of sea-bird with a large brightly-coloured beak.

pugnacious fond of fighting, quick to start a fight.

pull to drag (something) towards you.

pullover a usually woollen garment for the upper body.

pulp 1 squashed fruit or vegetables. 2 a soft mass of something, especially of wood for making into paper.

pulpit a raised platform in a church from which a sermon is preached.

pulse the beating of the heart.

pulverise to crush or grind into powder.

puma a kind of large fierce animal of the cat family found in North and South America.

pummel to beat with the fists again and again.

pump *verb* to force air or liquid into or along something. *noun* a machine which does this.

pumpkin a kind of very large round fruit with a thick yellow skin.

punch 1 to hit with the fist. 2 to make a hole in something.

punctual arriving at the exact time.

punctuation full stops, commas and other marks used in writing.

puncture a small hole made by something pointed.

pungent having a very strong smell or taste.

punish to make (someone) suffer for something bad they have done or are thought to have done.

puny small and weak.

pup a young dog; the young of certain other animals, for example a young seal.

pupa a chrysalis.

pupil a person who is being taught, especially in a school.

puppet a kind of doll which can be made to move by pulling strings or by placing it on the hand like a glove.

puppy a young dog.

purchase *verb* to buy. *noun* something that has been bought.

pure with nothing added; clean, free from dirt etc.

puree [**pure**-ay] food, such as apples or tomatoes, in a soft, boiled state.

purge 1 to make clean, clear out. 2 to get rid of unwanted people.

purify to make pure.

purple a colour made by mixing red and blue.

purpose 1 what you mean to do. 2 **on purpose** meaning to do something, not by accident.

purr the noise made by a cat when it is pleased.

purse a small bag for holding money.

pursue to follow, to run after.

push to press against (something) to try to move it.

put to move (something) into a place.

putrid very rotten, (smelling) very unpleasant.

putt to hit a golf ball gently on the smooth grass near the hole.

putter 1 a golf-club used when putting. 2 a person who putts.

putty a soft mixture which hardens to hold glass in a frame.

puzzle 1 something which is difficult to understand. 2 a game which has to be worked out.

pygmy, pigmy (in Africa) one of a race of very small people.

pyjamas trousers and jacket worn in bed.

pylon a metal tower used to hold up electric cables.

pyramid a solid shape with flat sides, usually square at the bottom, and pointed at the top.

python a kind of large snake which squeezes its victims to death.

Q

quack the noise made by ducks.

quadrant 1 a quarter of (the circumference of) a circle. 2 an instrument used formerly in navigation.

quadrilateral a four-sided figure.

quadruped a four-footed animal.

quadruple *adjective* 1 four times as much or as many. 2 made up of four parts.
verb to make four times as much.

quadruplet one of four children born to the same mother at the same time.

quagmire a bog, wet and muddy ground.

quail *noun* a kind of bird like a small partridge.
verb to be afraid.

quaint unusual, strange, odd.

quake to shake, tremble, quiver.

qualification something you have gained by knowledge or skill, which allows you to fill a position, for example.

qualify to get or give qualifications.

quality how good or bad something is.

qualm a slight uneasiness or worry about something.

quandary a difficult or puzzling situation.

quantity an amount.

quarantine a period of time during which a person or animal is kept away from others to make sure they do not spread disease.

quarrel to disagree angrily with someone.

quarry 1 a place where stone is taken out of the ground. 2 an animal that is being hunted.

quart a liquid measure equal to two pints (about 1.14 litres).

quarter one of the four equal parts of something.

quarterly *adjective* (happening, coming out) every three months.
noun a publication that comes out four times a year.

quartermaster an army officer in charge of supplies.

quartet 1 a set of four musicians. 2 a musical work composed for four performers.

quartz a kind of hard mineral.

quaver *noun* 1 a note in music equal to half a crotchet. 2 a shaking in the voice.
verb (especially of the voice) to shake, tremble.

quay [key] a landing place for ships.

queasy 1 feeling sick. 2 having an easily upset stomach.

queen 1 a woman who is the ruler of a country. 2 the wife of a king.

queer strange, odd, peculiar.

quell to overcome, especially by force.

quench 1 to end (someone's thirst). 2 to put out (a fire).

querulous complaining and bad-tempered.

query a question, especially about something you think might be wrong.

quest a search, especially over a long period of time or distance.

question something that needs an answer.

questionable of doubtful quality, not clearly correct or honest.

questionnaire [question**air**] a list of questions to be answered on a form.

queue [Q] a line of waiting people or vehicles.

quibble to question or argue about very small details.

quiche [keesh] an open tart with a usually savoury filling made with eggs.

quick fast, at great speed, done in a short time.

quicksand loose wet sand into which things can be sucked.

quiet with no sound or very little, not loud.

quill 1 a long feather. 2 (long ago) a pen made from such a feather.

quilt a cover for a bed filled with feathers or other soft material.

quinine [kwineen] a drug used to treat fevers, especially malaria.

quintessential of or about the most essential part or aspect of something.

quintet 1 a set of five musicians. 2 a musical work composed for five performers.

quintuplet one of five children born to the same mother at the same time.

quip a clever remark, witty joke.

quirk an odd or unusual habit or happening.

quisling a person who co-operates with an enemy who is occupying his or her country.

quit to leave; to stop.

quite 1 completely, fully. 2 a little, but not very.

quits on even terms, for example after the score has been evened.

quiver *verb* to shake, tremble. *noun* a holder for arrows.

quiz a game in which a lot of questions have to be answered.

quizzical mocking, questioning.

quoits [koits] a game in which rings, called **quoits**, are thrown on to a peg.

quorum the fixed number of members needed to make a meeting of a group of assembly proper.

quota a share, an agreed limited amount.

quotation 1 the act of quoting. 2 something quoted.

quotation marks marks like this " " or this ' ' to mark the beginning and end of someone else's words.

quote to repeat exactly what someone has said or written.

R

rabbi a Jewish religious leader and teacher.

rabbit a small furry animal with long ears and long back legs which lives in holes in the ground.

rabble a noisy mob.

rabid 1 suffering from rabies. 2 mad, violent.

rabies a very serious disease caused by a bite from an infected animal, especially a dog.

race 1 a test of speed. 2 people of the same kind or colour.

racial concerning a person's race.

racism, racialism believing that some races of people are better than others.

rack a frame or bar for holding things.

racket 1 a kind of bat used in tennis, for example. 2 a lot of very loud noise.

radar a way of helping to guide ships and aeroplanes by using radio waves.

radiant 1 bright, shining. 2 very happy looking.

radiate 1 to send out rays of light, heat etc. 2 to spread out from a centre like the spokes of a wheel.

radiation 1 radiating. 2 radioactive rays.

radiator 1 a device that sends out heat. 2 the front part of the engine of a motor car, which cools the engine.

radio 1 a machine for sending out messages or programmes by electrical waves. 2 the sending or receiving of messages etc. in this way.

radioactive giving off rays of nuclear energy, often harmful to living things.

radish a kind of small red or white sharp-tasting vegetable used in salads.

radius, *plural* **radii** [**raid**-i-eye] a straight line from the centre to the outside edge of a circle.

raffia straw-like fibre made from palm leaves, woven into mats and baskets.

raffle a game of chance used to make money. Tickets with numbers are sold and some numbers win prizes.

raft a platform of logs made to float on water.

rafter a beam which holds up a roof.

rag a piece of old or torn cloth.

rage great anger, a violent temper.

raid a sudden unexpected attack.

rail a fixed wooden, plastic or metal bar, for example for hanging things on.

railings a fence made of metal bars.

railway 1 the rails on which trains run. 2 anything to do with trains.

rain drops of water falling from the clouds.

rainbow curved stripes of different colours sometimes seen in the sky in rainy weather.

raise 1 to lift, to move up. 2 to bring up (a family or animals). 3 to collect (money).

raisin a dried grape.

rake a garden tool with spikes for scraping the earth, gathering dead leaves, etc.

rakish 1 jaunty. 2 (behaving) like a rake.

rallentando (a piece of music) performed with reducing speed.

rally a large gathering of people, for example a car rally.

ram *noun* a male sheep.
verb to crash into.

ramble *noun* a long country walk.
verb to talk foolishly, to wander off the point.

rambler 1 a person who goes on rambles. 2 a rambling rosebush.

rambling 1 (of speech or writing) not making sense, mixed-up. 2 (of a plant) climbing, growing in different directions.

ramp a slope between two different levels.

rampage to rush about wildly and violently; **on the rampage** rampaging.

rampant wild, violent, out of control.

rampart a bank or broad wall built round a castle etc. for defence.

ramrod 1 a stick for cleaning a gun or for pushing gunpowder into an old-fashioned gun. 2 something that is very stiff.

ramshackle (of a house, car etc.) badly put together, tumbledown.

ranch a large cattle or sheep farm in North America.

rancid (of fat or oil) stale and bad-smelling.

rancour hate, bitterness, spite.

random: at random by chance.

range 1 the limit that something can reach. 2 a variety of different things, such as goods in a shop. 3 a row of mountains or hills.

rank 1 a line or row, for example of soldiers. 2 a person's official position, for example a captain in the army.

rankle to continue to cause annoyance.

ransack to search thoroughly and wildly, to plunder.

ransom a sum of money to buy a prisoner's freedom.

rant to speak or preach in a wild sort of way.

rap a sharp blow or knock.

rapacious greedy, grasping.

rapid very fast, very quick.

rapier a kind of light narrow-bladed sword.

rapture very great joy.

rare scarce, not often seen.

rarity 1 something considered very rare or unusual. 2 being rare.

rascal 1 a very wicked person. 2 a badly-behaved child.

rash *adjective* not thinking enough, doing things too quickly.
noun a large number of spots on the skin.

rasher a thin slice of bacon.

rasp 1 a coarse file. 2 the harsh grating sound made by this tool, for example.

raspberry a kind of red juicy berry.

rat an animal like a large mouse.

ratchet a set of teeth on the edge of a bar or wheel set to make sure there is movement only in one direction.

rate 1 the speed of something. 2 the price which has been fixed.

rather 1 more willingly, sooner. 2 quite, a little.

ratify to accept and confirm officially.

ration to give out (food, for example) in fixed amounts.

rational sensible, reasonable, wise.

rationalise 1 to find a reason or excuse for doing something you wanted to do anyway. 2 to make (a system etc.) more reasonable, better organised.

rattle 1 the noise of things being shaken together. 2 a baby's toy that rattles.

raucous harsh-sounding, loud.

ravage to destroy, damage, plunder.

rave to speak wildly, to rage and roar.

raven a large black bird of the crow family.

ravenous very hungry.

ravine a very deep steep-sided narrow valley.

raw 1 not cooked. 2 cold and wet.

ray a beam or shaft of light.

raze to destroy completely, to level to the ground.

razor a very sharp tool for shaving the skin.

reach 1 to stretch and touch. 2 to arrive at, to get to.

react 1 to do something because something else was done or said. 2 to change chemically.

reaction reacting.

reactionary a person who usually opposes changes in society.

reactor a place where controlled nuclear activity takes place, for example.

read to understand the meaning of written or printed words.

readily quickly, promptly, willingly.

ready 1 prepared and willing to do something. 2 prepared for use.

real true, not false.

realign to put (something) into a new or former state of order.

realise to come to understand (something), especially suddenly.

realist a person who accepts facts as they are.

realistic lifelike; seeing things as they really are.

reality what really exists.

really truly.

realm 1 a kingdom. 2 an area of knowledge etc.

reap to cut and gather in (a crop).

rear *noun* the back part. *verb* 1 (of a horse) to stand up on the hind legs. 2 to look after (children or small animals) until they are fully grown.

reason the explanation, the cause.

reasonable sensible; not asking too much.

reassure to make (someone) feel better, less worried about something.

rebate an amount of a payment which is repaid.

rebel *verb* [ribel] to turn against a leader and stop obeying orders. *noun* [rebel] a person who rebels.

rebound to spring back (from something).

rebuke (to give) a scolding (to).

recall 1 to call back. 2 to remember.

recapitulate to repeat the main points or headings of something.

recede to go further back from something, to withdraw into the distance.

receipt a paper stating that something has been received.

receive to take, to get something that is given or sent.

recent just happened.

receptacle a place or object for holding things.

receptionist a person whose job it is to receive guests at a hotel, patients at a doctor's surgery etc.

receptive willing to understand and accept new ideas.

recipe a list of instructions telling you how to cook something.

recipient the person who receives something.

reciprocal in return for something else.

reciprocate to give in return for something given.

recital a performance, especially of music, by one person or by a small group.

recite to say aloud and from memory.

reckless foolishly brave, heedless of danger, having no caution.

reckon 1 to count, to add up. 2 to think.

reclaim to get or ask for something back.

recline to lie or lean back.

recluse a person who lives completely alone.

recognise 1 to know (a person or thing) when you see them. 2 to admit (something).

recoil to spring back; to move back suddenly.

recollect to remember.

recommend to say or advise that a person would be good for a job or a thing good for a purpose.

recompense to reward or pay for something already done.

reconcile to make friendly again after a disagreement.

reconnaissance [re**con**esance] an examination of an area by the army etc., especially before taking action.

reconnoitre to look around, to spy out (land, for example).

record *noun* [**re**cord] 1 a disc for playing music or words on a **record-player.** 2 the best that has been done so far, for example in a sport. 3 something written down to tell you what has happened.
verb [ri**cord**] 1 to copy (voices or music) on a disc or tape. 2 to write down.

recorder a kind of wooden musical instrument played by blowing.

recount to tell (a story, for example).

re-count to count again.

recoup [ree**coop**] to recover what has been lost.

recourse a possible souce of help.

recover 1 to get better after an illness. 2 to get (something) back.

re-cover to put a new cover on.

recreation rest or play after you have been working.

recrimination accusations between quarrelling parties.

recruit *noun* a newcomer to the army, navy or air force, or other organisation. *verb* to find (new members) for the army etc. or other organisation.

rectangle a flat shape like the shape of this page.

rectify to put right.

recumbent lying down.

recuperate to recover health, get better after an illness.

recur to happen again.

red the colour of blood.

redeem 1 to buy back (what was your own). 2 to remove blame from. 3 to free from sin or evil.

redouble to intensify, to increase greatly (effort, for example).

redress *verb* to put right (a wrong). *noun* something which makes up for a wrong done to you.

reduce to make (something) less or smaller.

reed a kind of long thin plant that grows near water.

reef a line of rocks just below the level of the sea.

reek to give off a smell or smoke.

reel *noun* 1 a cylinder used for winding something on to, for example a **fishing reel**, a **reel of cotton**. 2 a lively Scottish dance.
verb to stagger about.

referee the person who makes sure that a game is played fairly.

reference book a book in which you can look things up, such as a dictionary or an atlas.

refer to 1 to talk about. 2 to be concerned with.

refine to purify.

refined having good manners and taste.

refinery a place where something, for example oil, is refined and made ready for use.

reflect 1 to show or shine back, like a mirror. 2 to think.

reflex a movement or action done automatically, without thinking beforehand.

reform to improve, make better.

refrain *verb* to hold back (from doing something).
noun the chorus of a song, sung at the end of each verse.

refreshment something to eat or drink.

refrigerator a special kind of container for keeping food cold.

refuge a safe place where you can go if you are in danger.

refugee a person who has had to leave his or her country because of persecution.

refund *verb* [ri**fund**] to pay back (money) especially for something which was not satisfactory.
noun [**ree**fund] money refunded.

refuse *verb* [ri**fuse**] not to accept; to say 'No'.
noun [**ref**use] rubbish.

refute to prove the error of (an opinion, judgement etc.).

regal like a king or queen.

regalia the badges of office etc. of royalty, for example.

regard to think of in a certain way.

regatta [re**gat**a] a sports meeting for boats or yachts.

regent a person who rules in place of a king or queen.

reggae [**reg**ay] a kind of West Indian music with a strong beat.

regiment a large group of soldiers, a part of an army.

region a part of the world or of a country.

register a list of names etc. kept for a special purpose.

regret to be very sorry about.

regrettable that should be regretted.

regular happening often, at the same time of the day etc.; usual.

regulate 1 to control, especially by rules. 2 to adjust (a machine etc.), make it work in a particular way.

rehearse to practise something such as a play or a concert.

reign *verb* to rule as a king or queen.
noun the length of time a king or queen reigns.

reimburse to pay (someone) back money they have already spent.

reindeer a kind of deer with long horns which lives in cold northern countries.

reinforce to give extra strength to.

reins straps used to control and guide a horse etc.

reject *verb* [ri**ject**] to put (something, someone) aside as not suitable; not to accept.
noun [**ree**ject] a thing or person rejected.

rejoice to feel great joy.

relate 1 to tell a story, to say what happened. 2 to connect something with something else.

related 1 connected. 2 belonging to the same family.

relation 1 someone in the same family. 2 **relations** connections. 3 **relations** how people get on with one another.

relative *noun* someone in the same family.
adjective 1 connected (with). 2 compared (to something else).

relax to make or become less active or tight; to stop working too hard or worrying.

relay a race in which each person in a team runs or swims a different part of the course.

release to allow to go free.

relegate (in sport) to transfer to a lower division or league.

relent to become less angry or severe with someone.

relentless 1 never giving up, unyielding. 2 pitiless.

relevant having to do with what you are doing or saying.

reliable able to be trusted.

relic a thing left from past times, often something holy.

relief 1 the feeling when pain, fear, worry stop. 2 help for people in trouble.

relieve 1 to bring relief to. 2 to take over a duty etc. from (someone).

religion a way of believing in God or in gods.

religious to do with religion; following a religion.

relinquish to give (something) up.

relish *noun* 1 enjoyment. 2 a strong-tasting sauce etc.
verb to enjoy (something) a lot.

reluctant not willing (to do something).

rely on to depend on, to count on, to trust.

remain to stay behind.

remainder what is left over.

remark something said about someone or something.

remarkable unusual, worth noting.

remedial providing a remedy, curing.

remedy a cure.

remember to bring back into the mind; not to forget.

remind to make (someone) remember.

reminisce to talk about things you remember.

reminiscence talking about the past.

reminiscent (of) reminding (you of something else).

remnant a small piece, of cloth for example, which is left over.

remorse sorrow for something you have done wrong.

remote far off, distant.

removal moving from one house to another.

remove 1 to take away. 2 to move from one place to another.

render 1 to give, to give back, to hand over. 2 to make, cause to be.

rendezvous [**ron**dayvoo] a meeting place; a meeting arranged in advance.

renegade a traitor.

renounce to give up, especially by saying so in public.

renovate to make something as good as new.

renown fame.

renowned famous.

rent the money you pay for the use of a house, a television set etc.

repair to mend, to put right.

repartee a smart witty reply.

repast a light meal.

repatriate to send (someone) back to his or her own country.

repay to pay back.

repeat to say or do something again.

repel 1 to drive back (an attack, for example). 2 to disgust.

repent to be sorry for something you have done wrong.

repercussion what results (later) from an event, incident or happening.

repertoire the stock of pieces that a company or a performer is able to perform.

repetition the act of repeating; something repeated.

replace to put back.

replenish to fill up again.

replete filled, completely full (of food).

replica an exact copy.

reply to answer.

report a description of something which has happened; a statement of what someone has done.

repose rest, sleep.

represent 1 to make a likeness of, to draw. 2 to act on behalf of (another person or a group). 3 to be a sign or symbol of (a group, for example).

reprieve the cancelling or delaying of a punishment.

reprimand an official scolding.

reproduce 1 to produce young. 2 to copy, make copies of.

reptile an animal with cold blood such as a snake or a lizard.

republic a country ruled by an elected government headed by a president.

repugnant disgusting, loathsome.

repulse to drive or push back (an enemy, for example).

repulsive disgusting, hateful.

reputation what a person or thing is known or thought to be like.

request to ask politely for (something).

require to need, to want.

rescue to save, to take out of danger.

research careful study of a thing or subject, especially in order to find out something new about it.

resemble to look or sound like.

resent to feel angry about (something).

reserve *verb* to keep (something) until it is needed.
noun 1 something spare or extra. 2 an area of land set aside for wildlife.

reservoir a large lake which has been specially made to supply an area with water.

reside to live (in a particular place).

residential 1 suitable for or occupied by private housing. 2 involving living in the place where you work or study, for example.

residual remaining, left over (after something has been taken away).

residue what is left over, the remainder.

resign to give up a job, for example.

resilient able to recover from illness or disappointment.

resist to fight back against (someone or something).

resolute determined, bold.

resonant (of sound) echoing, continuing to sound.

resource something which can be used.

respect to admire, to look up to.

respectable of good character.

respectful showing respect.

respiration breathing.

respond to reply.

response an answer, reply.

responsible 1 being the cause of. 2 being the person in charge of something, the person who is blamed if something goes wrong. 3 trustworthy.

rest *noun* 1 the others; what is left over. 2 a time of resting.
verb to be still, not to work or do anything tiring.

restaurant a place where you can buy food to eat there.

restitution returning something to the proper owner.

restore 1 to give or bring back. 2 to clean and repair.

restrain to hold back.

result 1 what happens because of something. 2 the final score in a sporting contest.

resuscitate to bring back to life or consciousness.

retail the selling of goods to the public.

retain 1 to keep (something for your own use, for example). 2 to keep in position.

retaliate to hit someone who has hit you.

retard to delay, to hold (something) up.

retentive able to hold things in memory, not forgetful.

retinue the group of people who attend upon an important person.

retire 1 to stop working, usually because you have reached a certain age. 2 to move back (from a particular place).

retort a quick, rather angry, but often witty reply.

retreat (especially of an army which is being attacked) to go back.

retrieve to get back (something which was lost).

retriever a kind of hunting dog which can bring in birds etc. which have been shot.

retrograde going in a backwards direction, especially to something less good.

return 1 to go or come back. 2 to give back.

reveal to show, to make known (especially something hidden).

revenge hurt you do to someone in return for something they did to you.

revenue income, the annual income of a government.

reverberate to echo again and again.

reverse *verb* 1 to go backwards. 2 to go in the opposite direction. *noun* 1 the opposite side or back, of a coin, for example. 2 *also* **reverse gear** the gear in a car which you use to drive backwards.

revert to return to a former state.

review 1 a description or criticism of a book, play etc., for example in a newspaper. 2 an inspection (of troops, for example).

revise to read over something and correct and improve it, or to prepare for an exam.

revive to bring back to life, health or use.

revoke to withdraw or cancel (a decree, promise etc.).

revolt 1 to rebel. 2 to disgust, horrify.

revolution a great change, especially a change in the government of a country made by force.

revolve to spin round.

revolver a kind of small handgun which can fire several bullets without being reloaded.

revulsion great loathing, disgust.

reward something you are given for something good or brave you have done.

rheumatism [**roo**matizm] an illness which causes stiffness and pain in your joints.

rhinoceros a kind of large African animal with one or two horns on its nose.

rhododendron a kind of evergreen bush with large bright flowers.

rhubarb a garden plant with juicy stalks that can be eaten.

rhyme 1 word endings which sound alike. 2 a piece of poetry with rhymes in it.

rhythm the steady beat or time of poetry or music.

rib one of the bones across the chest.

ribbon a narrow band of material, for example for tying things.

rice a kind of plant grown in hot countries; its grain is an important food.

rich 1 having a lot of money or other valuable things. 2 of food, having a lot of fat, sugar etc.

riches great wealth.

rickety shaky, ready to fall apart.

ricochet [**rik**oshay] (of a weapon etc.) bouncing off a wall, the ground etc.

rid to be free of.

riddle a word puzzle in which a question has a funny answer.

ride / robot

ride *verb* to move about on an animal or a bicycle or in a carriage.
noun a journey or trip on an animal or a bicycle or in a car, bus or other vehicle.

ridge the long narrow part along the top of something, for example a roof.

ridiculous so silly that it may be laughed at.

rifle a kind of gun with a long barrel.

rift 1 a crack, in earth or rocks for example. 2 (of people) a quarrel or falling-out.

right *adjective* 1 correct; not wrong. 2 good; true.
noun the opposite of the left.

righteous of good character, obeying moral laws.

rigid stiff; unyielding.

rigorous harsh, stern, strict.

rim the edge of something round, such as a bowl or a wheel.

rind the outer covering, for example of an orange or lemon or a cheese.

ring *noun* 1 a round piece of metal, for example one worn on the finger. 2 a circle.
verb 1 to make a sound like a bell. 2 to telephone.

ringleader a person who is the leader of a group doing wrong.

ringlet a long curly lock of hair.

rink a place made specially for ice skating or roller skating.

rinse to wash with clean water, usually after washing with soap.

riot fighting and disturbance by a lot of people.

riotous wild, violent; noisy, excited.

rip to tear roughly.

ripe fully grown, ready to eat.

riposte 1 a quick returned thrust in fencing. 2 a quick witty reply.

ripple a tiny wave.

rise *verb* 1 to stand up. 2 to increase or swell up. 3 to make a revolt or rebellion.
noun 1 an upward slope. 2 an increase, in wages, for example.

risk the danger of something going wrong.

risotto an Italian dish made with rice, stock, meat, vegetables etc.

rissole a fried ball or cake of meat or fish mixed with breadcrumbs etc.

rite a ceremony, especially a religious one.

ritual *noun* a set religious act or practice.
adjective to do with a rite or ritual.

rival a person who tries to equal or to do better than another person.

river a long wide stream of water, usually flowing into the sea.

rivet *noun* a kind of metal pin for fastening pieces of metal together.
verb 1 to fasten with rivets. 2 to attract very strongly. 3 to fix.

rivulet a very small river or stream.

roach a kind of freshwater fish.

road a wide track, usually covered with tar, on which cars, buses, lorries etc. can travel.

roadie a person who carries and sets up the equipment for a rock or pop group.

roam to wander about.

roar a loud deep sound, the noise made by a lion or by thunder.

roast to cook in fat in an oven or over a fire.

rob to take something that does not belong to you, to steal from.

robbery the act of robbing.

robe a long loose piece of clothing.

robin a kind of small red-breasted bird.

robot a machine that can do some of the work a person can do.

robust strong and healthy.

rock *noun* 1 stone; a large piece of it. 2 a sticky sweet shaped like a stick. 3 a kind of popular music.
verb to move from side to side.

rockery part of a garden with lots of rocks, where certain plants grow well.

rocket 1 a long tube driven into the air by gas or an explosion. 2 a kind of firework. 3 a spaceship.
verb to rise rapidly.

rod a thin bar of wood or metal.

rodent one of the family of animals to which rats and mice belong; they have strong front teeth for gnawing food.

rodeo a show where cowboys show their skills with horses, cattle etc.

roe 1 the eggs of a fish. 2 *also* **roe deer** a kind of small deer.

roebuck a male roe deer.

rogue a very wicked person that you cannot trust.

role a part played, especially one played by an actor.

roll *verb* to turn over and over.
noun 1 something wrapped round and round itself, for example a **roll** of wallpaper. 2 a long sound made by drums. 3 a small piece of bread, like a small loaf.

roller skate wheels attached to a boot or shoe to allow you to move along quickly.

romance 1 a love story; a love affair. 2 a story of unlikely adventures etc., especially one of far away or long ago.

romantic to do with romance.

roof 1 the top covering of a building. 2 the top part of the inside of the mouth.

rook 1 a black bird of the crow family with a grey beak. 2 a chess piece, also called a castle.

room 1 a part of a building, with its own floor, walls and ceiling. 2 space for something.

roost *noun* a place where a bird perches.
verb to perch or sleep on a roost.

root 1 the part of a plant which is in the soil and absorbs water to feed the plant. 2 the beginning or origin of something, for example a problem.

rope a thick cord.

rose a brightly-coloured, sweet-smelling flower, often found in gardens and hedges.

rosehip the fruit of some rose bushes.

rosemary a kind of evergreen bush with sweet-smelling leaves used as a herb in cooking.

rosette a large round badge made of ribbons, especially one used to show that you support something or someone.

rosy pink in colour.

rot to go bad (and die).

rota a list of jobs in the order they are to be done and of the people who are to do them.

rotate 1 to go round and round, to revolve. 2 to do things in turns, one after the other.

rote learning something by repeating it

rotor the blades of a helicopter.

rotten 1 gone bad. 2 nasty, unpleasant.

rotund round, fat.

rough 1 not smooth; coarse. 2 wild and stormy. 3 not in its final state (of a drawing, plan etc.).

roulette a gambling game using a numbered wheel with slots into which a spun ball drops.

round the same shape as a ball or ring.

roundabout 1 an island at a road junction that traffic moves around. 2 a revolving machine, for example at a fair, on which children can ride for amusement.

rounders a game played by two sides with a bat and a ball.

rouse to wake (someone) up, stir up, make more lively.

rousing thrilling, exciting.

rout [rowt] when the enemy are chased away from a battle.

route [root] the way to go somewhere.

routine *noun* doing things in a regular orderly way.
adjective ordinary, usual.

rove to wander.

row [rhymes with 'low'] 1 to move a boat with oars. 2 a line of people or things.

row [rhymes with 'now'] a noisy quarrel.

rowdy behaving noisily and roughly.

rowing boat a boat driven by oars.

rowlock a support for an oar on the side of a boat.

royal connected with kings and queens.

rub to move one thing against another many times.

rubber 1 a kind of tree grown in hot countries. 2 elastic material made from the sap of the rubber tree, used for making tyres, keeping out water etc. 3 a small piece of rubber or plastic used for rubbing out writing.

rubbish 1 waste things that are of no use. 2 nonsense.

rubble rough broken stones or bricks.

rubicund (of the face) ruddy, highly-coloured.

ruby a kind of deep-red precious stone.

rucksack a bag you can carry on your back.

rudder a piece of wood or metal fixed at the back to steer a boat or an aeroplane.

ruddy 1 (especially of the face) freshly or healthily red. 2 (informal) used to describe something annoying.

rude not polite, vulgar.

rudimentary of the rudiments.

rudiments the basic parts or principles of something.

rue to regret, be sorry about.

ruffian a wild rough violent person.

ruffle *verb* to disturb the smoothness of (a surface, feathers, temper, for example).
noun a folded band of cloth etc. round the neck of a garment, for example.

rug 1 a small carpet; a mat. 2 a kind of blanket, sometimes used to keep the knees warm when sitting down.

rugby a game like football, played with an oval ball.

rugged rough, uneven; strong and harsh.

ruin *noun* a building which has fallen down.
verb to wreck, to spoil.

rule *noun* a law that must be followed.
verb to have power over other people.

ruler 1 a person who rules. 2 a strip of wood or other material used for measuring or drawing straight lines.

rum a kind of strong alcoholic drink made from sugar-cane.

rumble a deep roll of sound like the sound of thunder.

ruminant an animal that chews the cud, like a cow or a deer.

rummage to search carelessly for something.

rumour something you hear which may or may not be true.

rump the rear end of an animal.

rumple to crease (cloth etc).

rumpus a noisy disturbance.

run to move very quickly on foot.

rung a step on a ladder.

rupture 1 a break or tear, often in a part of the body. 2 a break in friendship etc., a quarrel.

rural belonging to or concerning the country as opposed to the town.

ruse a clever trick played on someone.

rush *verb* to move very quickly; to hurry.
noun a kind of long thin plant that grows near water.

russet reddish-brown.

rust a reddish brown coating sometimes found on iron and steel.

rustic *noun* a country person.
adjective of or like the country or country people.

rustle a gentle rubbing sound.

rusty covered with rust.

ruthless without showing mercy, cruel.

rye a kind of grass. Its grain is made into bread in some countries.

S

sabbath the day for the worship of God in the Jewish and Christian religions.

sable a kind of small dark-furred animal of northern regions; its fur.

sabotage damage done on purpose, for example by an enemy.

sabre a heavy sword with a curved blade.

sachet a small bag containing dry perfumed material or shampoo etc.

sack *noun* a large bag, usually made of rough cloth.
verb to remove (somebody) from a job.

sacrament a very important religious ceremony.

sacred holy; to do with religion.

sacrifice the giving up of something that you like very much.

sad unhappy; miserable.

sadden to make sad.

saddle the seat of a bicycle; a seat for the rider of a horse.

safari a journey in Africa to see wild animals or to hunt them.

safari park a park where you can see wild animals roaming about.

safe *adjective* not in danger, free from possible harm.
noun a strong locked metal box used to keep valuable things in.

safeguard something which protects and keeps you from danger.

safety being safe; a safe place.

saffron a yellow dye used to colour and flavour food.

sag to hang or bend downwards, often in the middle, to droop.

saga 1 a story about Vikings long ago. 2 a long story.

sagacious wise, having good judgement.

sagacity being sagacious.

sage 1 a wise man. 2 a kind of herb used in cooking.

sago a kind of starchy white food made from the pith of certain palm trees, used in puddings, for example.

sail *noun* a large piece of strong cloth used on a sailing boat to make it move in the wind.
verb 1 to travel in a boat. 2 to travel in or control a sailing boat.

sailboard a flat board with a single sail, on which a person stands in the sport of windsurfing.

sailboarding windsurfing.

sailor 1 a person who works on a ship. 2 a person who sails a yacht.

saint a very good and holy person.

salad a dish of cold, usually raw, vegetables etc.

salary payment for work, usually given at the end of each month.

sale 1 the selling of things. 2 a time when things are sold at a lower price than usual.

salient jutting out, conspicuous, prominent.

saline salty, concerned with or containing salt.

saliva the liquid in your mouth.

sallow (of the face) of a pale yellowish colour, unhealthy-looking.

salmon a large fish with pink flesh.

salmonella a kind of germ which causes food poisoning.

salon a place where people's hair is cut and dressed, for example.

saloon 1 a dining room or sitting room on a ship. 2 a closed-in motor car. 3 a saloon bar.

saloon bar a bar which is slightly more comfortable and expensive than a public bar.

salt *noun* a mineral used to flavour or preserve food.
verb to put salt in or on.

salubrious (making you) healthy.

salutary good for you.

salute *verb* to greet, especially by raising the hand to the forehead.
noun an act of saluting.

salvage *verb* to save or recover things which have been lost or damaged.
noun an act of salvaging; something salvaged.

salvation saving someone from danger or wickedness.

salvo several guns being fired at the same time.

same not different: exactly like.

sample *noun* a small piece to show what something is like.
noun to test, try out.

samurai (long ago) a high-ranking Japanese warrior.

sanatorium a place where people who are ill for a long time are looked after.

sanctify to make holy.

sanction *noun* 1 approval, agreement. 2 **sanctions** actions such as stopping trade by one or more countries to try to persuade another to do something. 3 a penalty for disobeying a law.
verb to approve, agree.

sanctity holiness.

sanctuary 1 the holiest part of a church. 2 a place where you are safe from arrest or danger. 3 a place where birds or animals are kept safely.

sand powdered rock or shells often found at the seaside or in the desert.

sandal an open-topped shoe fastened with straps or cords.

sandalwood a sweet-smelling tree; a perfume made from it.

sandpaper paper coated with sand, used for smoothing wood for example.

sandstone a kind of rock formed from sand.

sandwich two slices of bread with a filling between them.

sandy like or made of sand.

sane not mad; sensible.

sanguine having high hopes, confident.

sanitary healthy, clean, good for health.

sanitation services, especially drainage and sewage, to keep the community healthy.

sanity being sane.

sap *noun* 1 the liquid in the stems of plants and trees. 2 a silly soft person.
verb to weaken, take away (someone's strength).

sapling a young tree.

sapphire a bright-blue precious stone.

sarcasm being sarcastic.

sarcastic being hurtful to someone by saying something but meaning the opposite.

sardine a small sea-fish used as a food.

sardonic using a forced and unpleasant laugh, sneering.

sari a long length of cloth wrapped into a dress, worn by some Indian women.

sash 1 a long wide ribbon worn round the waist or over the shoulder. 2 a window-frame.

Satan the Devil.

satchel a schoolbag.

sated completely satisfied, usually with (too much) food.

satellite a natural or man-made object moving in space round a planet.

satin a kind of smooth cloth with one shiny side, usually made of silk.

satire a form of speech or writing which uses ridicule and mockery.

satirical using satire.

satisfaction

satisfaction being satisfied.

satisfactory good enough, giving satisfaction.

satisfy to make content and happy.

saturate to soak completely; to cover or fill completely.

saturation being saturated.

saturnine (of a person) having gloomy looks.

satyr an imaginary creature, half-man, half-goat.

sauce a thick liquid food eaten with other food to add flavour.

saucepan a metal container with a handle used for cooking.

saucer a small round plate on which a cup stands.

sauna a place where you can have a steam bath.

saunter to stroll, wander about aimlessly.

sausage a mixture of minced meat, breadcrumbs, fat etc. in a thin skin.

savage fierce, wild, cruel.

save 1 to help (someone) to be safe. 2 to keep (something) till you need it. 3 to use less of (something).

savings money you save up.

saviour 1 a person who saves another from danger. 2 **the Saviour** Jesus Christ.

savour *noun* a taste, flavour, smell. *verb* 1 to enjoy the savour of. 2 to have a savour (of).

savoury appealing to the taste or smell, but not sweet.

saw a metal cutting-tool with sharp pointed teeth.

sawdust tiny pieces of wood from sawing.

sawmill a place where wood is cut up by saws.

saxophone a metal wind instrument often used for jazz or dance music.

scarce

say to speak, tell in words.

saying something which people often say.

scab a hard covering which forms over a wound or spot.

scabbard a sheath or cover for a sword or dagger.

scaffold 1 a framework on which builders etc. work. 2 a platform used when a person is hanged.

scald *verb* 1 to burn with hot liquid. 2 to clean by using boiling water. *noun* a burn on the skin from hot liquid.

scale 1 a set of numbers or marks for measuring. 2 a set of musical notes going up and down. 3 a small piece of flat shiny material on the skin of a fish or snake etc.

scales a machine for weighing things.

scalp the skin and hair on the top of the head.

scalpel a surgeon's small light knife held like a pen.

scaly having scales.

scamper to run quickly and lightly.

scan 1 to look at very closely. 2 to look at quickly. 3 to pass a beam over. 4 to examine the pattern of beats in a poem; (of a poem) to have a regular pattern of beats.

scandal something said or talked about which shocks other people.

scandalise to shock, horrify.

scandalous shocking, containing scandal.

scant slight, in short supply.

scanty not enough, too small.

scapegoat a person who is blamed for the fault of others.

scar *noun* a mark left on the skin by a wound.
verb to make a scar on.

scarce not often found because there are not many.

scarcely hardly at all.
scarcity shortage.
scare to frighten badly.
scarecrow an object, usually shaped like a man, used to frighten birds off crops.
scarf a square or length of cloth used as a covering for the neck and shoulders etc.
scarlet a very bright red colour.
scarlet fever an infectious disease causing red spots on the skin.
scathing (of speech) bitter, unpleasant.
scatter 1 to throw (something) about in different directions. 2 to move away quickly in different directions.
scavenge 1 to search for useful things among rubbish. 2 (of an animal) to feed on dead bodies.
scenario 1 a written description outlining a film, play etc. 2 a description of events which might happen in the future.
scene 1 a view. 2 a part of a play. 3 the place where something happened.
scenery 1 the landscape round about. 2 painted pieces of cloth, wood etc. used in a play, for example.
scenic 1 of or like a theatrical show. 2 having fine, natural scenery.
scent *noun* 1 a pleasant smell, a perfume. 2 the smell an animal leaves behind it.
verb 1 (especially of an animal) to smell, find by smelling. 2 to put perfume on, give a pleasant smell to.
sceptic a person who doubts a lot.
sceptical doubting a lot, not believing.
sceptre a short ornamental stick which represents the authority of a king or queen.
schedule *noun* 1 a list of details. 2 a plan, especially for timing something.
verb to arrange for a certain time.

scheme *noun* 1 a plan. 2 a plot, something planned to hurt or upset someone.
verb to plan something, especially to harm someone.
schizophrenia a serious mental illness in which the person's thoughts and feeling become disconnected.
scholar a person who has studied a subject a great deal and knows a lot about it.
scholarly like a scholar; making sure all details are correct.
scholarship 1 a sum of money you are given to help you to study. 2 the knowledge a scholar has.
school 1 a place where people, usually children, go to learn. 2 a large group of fish swimming together.
schooner 1 a kind of sailing ship with two or more masts. 2 a kind of tall drinking glass.
sciatica pain in a nerve in the lower back, hip or thigh.
science knowledge of and learning about nature and how things are made.
scientific following the rules of science.
scientist a person who studies science.
scimitar a kind of curved sword.
scintillate to shine brightly, sparkle.
scissors a cutting tool with two blades fastened together in the middle.
scoff at to make fun of; to mock.
scold to talk harshly to (someone) because they have done something wrong.
scone a small soft semi-sweet cake.
scoop *noun* 1 a hollow instrument for lifting amounts out of a larger mass of something, for example a round spoon for serving ice cream, a large shovel for digging up earth. 2 a piece of interesting news printed by a newspaper before others have heard it.
verb to lift with or as with a scoop.

scooter 1 a child's toy with an upright handle attached to a board on wheels pushed by one foot. 2 a motor scooter.

scope 1 the space or opportunity to do something. 2 the area or range something covers.

scorch to burn (something) slightly, often making it brown, to singe.

scorching very hot.

score *noun* 1 the number of points, runs, goals etc. made in a game or competition. 2 a long scratch, especially on a smooth surface. 3 a (group of) twenty; **scores** a large number.
verb 1 to make points, runs, goals etc. in a game or competition. 2 to count the number of such points etc.

scorn *verb* to look down on.
noun the act of scorning.

scornful showing scorn.

scorpion a creature like a large insect with a poisonous sting in a curving tail.

scot-free unharmed; unpunished.

scoundrel a rascal, rogue.

scour to clean by hard rubbing.

scout 1 a person who is sent out to find out information, for example about an enemy. 2 **Scout** a member of a youth organisation called the Boy Scouts Association.

scowl to give a very angry look, to frown.

scrabble *verb* to try awkwardly to grip or find something.
noun **Scrabble** trade name for a word game played with counters on a board.

scramble *verb* 1 to climb or crawl quickly, often over rough ground. 2 to mix up.
noun a rush to be first, a struggle.

scrap 1 a tiny piece. 2 rubbish thrown away. 3 a fight.

scrape *verb* to rub and clean with something hard.
noun a difficulty.

scraper a tool for scraping.

scrappy made up of odd bits and pieces.

scratch 1 to mark or tear slightly with something sharp or pointed. 2 to rub the skin because it is itchy. 3 to withdraw from a competition.

scrawl *verb* to write badly, to scribble.
noun writing that is untidy and can't be read easily.

scream to make a piercing cry, usually because of fear or pain.

scree the loose stones that slide down a steep hillside.

screech a harsh high sound.

screed a long boring piece of writing.

screen *noun* 1 a large white surface on which a film is shown; the front viewing part of a television set or computer. 2 a large covered-in frame used for example as shelter from the cold or to divide up a room.
verb 1 to cover or protect. 2 to show on a screen. 3 to separate off, for example parts of a room.

screw *noun* a nail with grooves round it so that it can be turned by a **screwdriver**.
verb 1 to fix with a screw. 2 to twist or turn (like the turning of a screw).

scribble to write so quickly and carelessly that the writing can hardly be read.

scribe (long ago) a person employed to write things down.

script something written down to be spoken, for example the words of a play.

scriptural concerning the Scripture.

Scripture(s) the Bible.

scroll a roll of parchment or paper.

scrounge to get by begging, without paying.

scrounger a person who is always scrounging.

scrub *verb* to clean with water and, usually, a brush.
noun (land covered with) bushes and low trees.

scruff the back of the neck.

scruffy untidy and dirty.

scrupulous very careful and exact.

scrutinise to look closely at, to inspect.

scuba a device which allows you to breathe under water.

scuba diving the sport of swimming under water using a scuba.

scud (especially of clouds or ships) to move along quickly and smoothly.

scuff 1 to walk with feet dragging. 2 to brush against or scrape; to damage in this way.

scuffle a struggle with a lot of pushing, a kind of fight.

scull *noun* a kind of short oar; a small boat with two of these.
verb to move a boat using sculls.

scullery a small room for doing the washing-up.

sculptor a person who makes artistic shapes out of stone, metal, wood etc.

sculpture 1 the work of a sculptor. 2 a piece of work by a sculptor.

scum 1 dirt and froth at the top of a liquid. 2 worthless people.

scupper to sink (a ship); to defeat.

scurrilous (of a person or language) abusive, foul.

scurry to run about with short quick steps.

scurvy a disease caused by lack of vitamin C from fresh fruit and vegetables.

scuttle *verb* 1 to sink (a ship) on purpose. 2 to hurry off.
noun 1 an opening on a ship's deck or side. 2 a container for coal.

scythe a tool with a long curved blade for cutting grass etc.

sea the salt water which surrounds the land on the earth's surface.

sea anemone a kind of small soft flowerlike sea creature.

sea horse a kind of very small fish with a head and neck rather like a horse.

seal *verb* to close or fasten tightly, for example an envelope.
noun 1 a design used as the special badge of an important organisation, often stamped into wax. 2 a kind of sea animal which lives partly on land.

sea-lion a kind of large seal found in the Pacific Ocean.

seam 1 a line of stitches where cloth is joined. 2 a layer of coal etc. under the ground.

seamanship skill in handling a ship or boat.

seance [**say**ons] a meeting where someone claims to receive messages from dead people.

search *verb* 1 **search for** to look for. 2 to look very hard in order to find something.
noun the act of searching.

seasick feeling sick because of the movement of a boat or ship.

season *noun* 1 one of the four main parts of the year: spring, summer, autumn, winter. 2 a special time of year, for example the **festive season**.
verb to add seasoning to (food).

seasoning something, such as salt or pepper, added to food to improve the flavour.

season ticket a ticket which can be used as often as you like during a certain time period.

seat *noun* something to sit on.
verb to cause to sit down; to arrange seats for.

seat-belt a belt you wear in a motor car to stop you being thrown out if there is an accident.

seaweed plants which grow in the sea.

secede to withdraw formally from an organisation or from a union of states.

secluded away from others, isolated, lonely.

second *adjective* after the first.
noun 1 a very short measure of time; a division of an angle. 2 a person who helps or supports another, for example in a boxing match.

secondary coming second, less important.

secondary school a school for children between the ages of 11 and 18.

second-hand not new, already owned by somebody else.

secrecy being secret.

secret (something) known only to a few people.

secretarial of the kind of work done by a secretary.

secretary a person whose job it is to write letters, make arrangements etc. for another person or for an organisation.

secrete 1 to hide away. 2 to form liquid in the body, for example saliva, sweat.

secretion something secreted in the body.

secretive fond of keeping things secret.

sect a group of people who hold different religious beliefs from others.

sectarian (of a person) belonging to a sect in a bigoted way.

section a part of something.

sectional 1 made up of sections.
2 applying to one section, in the interests of one group (in a community usually).

sector 1 a portion of an area or of a group. 2 the part of a circle between two radii.

secular not concerned with religion.

secure *adjective* firm: safe, free from danger.
verb 1 to make secure. 2 to get possession of.

security 1 being secure. 2 something valuable given by a borrower as a guarantee that he will pay back.

sedate calm, settled, dignified.

sedative something, for example a drug, which makes you calm.

sedentary involving a lot of sitting.

sedge a grass-like plant which grows in marshy ground.

sediment solids that settle at the bottom of liquid.

seduce to tempt, to attract someone into doing something wrong.

sedulous hard-working, painstaking, careful.

see *verb* 1 what you are able to do with your eyes. 2 to understand.
noun a district over which a bishop has authority.

seed a tiny grain from which a plant grows.

seedling a very young plant.

seedy 1 rather unwell.
2 shabby-looking.

seek to search for, to look for.

seem to appear to be.

seemly proper (to do), suitable.

seep to flow very slowly through or out of something.

seepage the act of seeping; liquid which has seeped.

seesaw a plank balanced on something on which children sit at opposite ends and go up and down.

seething 1 very angry, upset.
2 bubbling and moving like boiling liquid.

segment a part cut off or able to be cut off or separated from the other parts of something.

segregate to separate one part or group from others, especially a racial group.

seismology the study of earthquakes.

seize to take hold of roughly; to grab quickly; to capture.

seizure 1 the act of seizing; a capture. 2 a sudden attack of illness.

seldom not often, rarely.

select *verb* to choose, to pick out from amongst others. *adjective* (of a group etc.) small and carefully chosen.

selection 1 choice. 2 a group of specially chosen things.

self one's own person.

self-centred always putting yourself first.

self-conscious shy, uncomfortable with others.

self-evident obvious, needing no proof.

selfish thinking only about yourself.

self-raising (of flour) containing baking powder.

self-respect a feeling of your own worth.

self-service (of shops, restaurants etc.) where you can collect your own goods and pay at a cash desk.

self-sufficient able to provide yourself with what you need without help.

sell to give (something) to someone else in exchange for money.

semaphore a system of signalling using flags or your arms.

semi- prefix meaning half or partly.

semi-colon a punctuation mark ; used to separate parts of sentences or items in a list.

semi-detached (of a house) having a shared wall with one other house.

semi-final one of two matches, the winners of which play in the final.

semolina grains of wheat left after milling, used for puddings and pasta.

send to make (someone or something) go somewhere.

senile affected by old age.

senior 1 older than others. 2 having a higher position in an organisation or having been there longer.

sensation 1 feeling. 2 an exciting and unusual event.

sensational exciting, causing a sensation.

sense 1 the ability to think in a reasonable way. 2 the power to see, hear, smell, taste or touch. 3 a meaning.

senseless 1 without sense; stupid. 2 unconscious.

sensible having good sense, reasonable; showing good sense.

sensitive feeling or reacting to things very keenly or quickly.

sensory of the bodily senses.

sensual 1 depending on the senses. 2 indulging the senses or appetite too much.

sensuous of or feeling the pleasures of the senses.

sentence 1 a group of words that make sense together. 2 a punishment given by a judge at the end of a trial.

sentiment 1 a feeling. 2 a thought or idea.

sentimental having tender feelings or thoughts.

sentinel a guard, a soldier on guard.

sentry a soldier on guard at a door or gate.

separate divided, not joined to something else.

separation parting; a division.

septic poisoned, infected with germs.

sepulchral of or like a grave, gloomy, dismal.

sepulchre a tomb.

sequel 1 what follows after something, the result. 2 the continuation of a story or film in another story or film.

sequence the order in which things follow one another.

sequential forming a sequence, following in sequence.

serenade 1 music for playing in the open air at night, originally under a lady's window. 2 a piece of music, usually divided into parts.

serendipity the act of making helpful discoveries by accident.

serene calm, untroubled.

serenity being serene.

sergeant [**sar**jint] 1 a low-ranking officer in the army. 2 an officer in the police between constable and inspector.

sergeant-major a low-ranking officer in the army above a sergeant.

serial a story told or written in parts.

series a number of things in a certain order.

serious 1 of great importance. 2 causing great harm, for example an illness, a crime. 3 not cheerful or funny.

sermon a talk given as part of a service in a church.

serpent a snake.

serrated having a jagged edge like a saw.

servant a person who does work for another person, especially housework.

serve 1 to work for (someone). 2 to give out goods, for example in a shop. 3 to give food to. 4 to play the first shot in a game, of tennis for example.

service 1 something you do for others. 2 something people can use to help them. 3 a ceremony in church. 4 the checking and repair of a machine or car.

servile acting like a slave.

sesame a tropical plant, the seeds and oil of which are used for food.

session 1 people meeting for business. 2 a single span of time for some activity.

set *verb* 1 to put (something) in a place. 2 (of a jelly, concrete etc.) to (cause to) become solid or hard. *noun* 1 a group of people or things which are alike in some way. 2 a radio or television receiver. 3 the scenery on a stage. 4 a section of a tennis match.

setback a disappointment, something unsuccessful.

settee a long seat with a back and sides.

setter a kind of long-haired game dog.

settle 1 to sink to the bottom. 2 to become still or calm. 3 to go to live in a place (for a long time). 4 to fix, decide on. 5 to pay (a bill).

settlement 1 the act of settling. 2 a small community where people have come to live.

settler a person who settles in another country.

sever to cut off.

several some, a few, not many.

severe 1 very serious or bad, for example an illness or a frost. 2 very strict, harsh.

severity being severe.

sew [rhymes with 'so'] to join together with stitches using a needle and thread.

sewage waste matter carried away in a sewer.

sewer a drain for carrying waste matter from the human body away from buildings.

sex one of the two groups, male and female, that people and animals belong to.

sextant an instrument used in navigation.

sextet 1 a group of six musicians. 2 piece written for six performers.

sexton a person who looks after a church, digs graves etc.

shabby 1 almost worn out. 2 mean, nasty.

shack a roughly-made hut or shed.

shackle *noun* a chain to fasten the leg (of a prisoner, for example) to something else.
verb to fasten with or as with shackles.

shade 1 (a place where there is) shelter from the sun or other strong light. 2 the depth of a colour, its lightness or darkness.

shadow 1 a dark part where something is keeping out the light. 2 a dark shape seen where something comes between the light and another surface.

shady 1 in the shade; giving shade. 2 not very honest.

shaft 1 the long handle of a spade, an axe, a golf club etc. 2 the long part of an arrow, spear etc. 3 a long space going up or down, for example into a mine.

shaggy having long untidy hair.

shake to move quickly from side to side or up and down, often because of cold or fear.

shaky unsteady, likely to shake.

shale a kind of soft slate-like rock from which you can get oil.

shallow not deep.

sham *noun* something false.
verb to pretend to be.

shamble to walk clumsily and awkwardly.

shambles a mess.

shame a feeling of being unhappy because you have done wrong.

shameful disgraceful, very bad.

shameless too bold, having no shame.

shampoo a liquid soap for washing the hair.

shamrock a three-leaved plant like clover, the national plant of Ireland.

shandy a drink of lemonade and beer mixed.

shank 1 the lower part of the leg. 2 a long handle of an instrument.

shanty 1 a roughly-built hut. 2 a sailor's song.

shape *noun* the appearance or outline of something.
verb to make into a particular shape.

shapely having a good shape, well-formed.

shard a sharp piece of broken glass or pottery for example.

share *verb* 1 to divide into parts. 2 to use (something) along with someone else.
noun 1 one of the parts into which something is divided for sharing. 2 one of the parts into which a company's money is divided.

shareholder a person who owns shares in a company's money and therefore has a share in its profits.

shark a large dangerous fish with sharp teeth.

sharp *adjective* 1 pointed, able to cut, stab or stick into. 2 quick, sudden. 3 able to think, see or hear well and quickly.
noun a sign in music that the following note is a half-tone higher.

sharpen to make sharp.

shatter 1 to break into small pieces. 2 to upset very badly.

shave to remove hair from the skin with a razor.

shawl a covering worn on the head and shoulders or for wrapping a baby.

sheaf a bundle of things tied together, especially newly-cut corn.

shearing clipping the wool from sheep.

shears large scissors used for example for cutting hedges or wool from sheep.

sheath a close-fitting cover, especially for a sword or knife.

sheathe to put into a sheath or other protective covering.

shed *noun* a hut.
verb to let fall or pour out (for example tears, leaves).

sheen brightness on the surface of something.

sheep an animal kept for its wool and its meat.

sheepish bashful, shy, embarrassed.

sheer 1 complete, pure. 2 very steep, vertical. 3 (of cloth) very thin.

sheet 1 a large piece of thin cloth often used on a bed. 2 a thin flat piece of something, for example paper, glass, metal.

sheikh [shake] title of an Arab ruler or religious leader.

shelf a long flat board fixed to a wall or cupboard, for putting things on.

shell 1 the hard covering of an egg, nut, seed or snail, and of some sea creatures. 2 a large bullet.

shelter *noun* a place where you can be protected from bad weather or danger.
verb to give shelter to.

shelve 1 to put aside for a time, to postpone. 2 to put on a shelf.

shepherd a person who looks after sheep.

sherbet a sweet flavoured fizzy drink or powder.

sheriff 1 (in England and Wales) the chief representative of the king or queen in a country. 2 (in Scotland) a judge in a higher court. 3 (in America) an elected legal officer who keeps order etc. in an area.

sherry a kind of strong Spanish wine.

shield *verb* to protect from harm.
noun 1 a large piece of metal sometimes held by people to protect themselves when fighting. 2 a prize in the shape of a shield.

shift *verb* to move.
noun a group of people working in turns with other groups.

shiftless lazy, aimless.

shifty untrustworthy.

shilling (in Britain up to 1971) a coin worth a twentieth of a pound (5p).

shimmer to shine with a shaking light.

shin *noun* the front of the leg between the knee and the ankle.
verb to climb.

shine 1 to give out light. 2 to look bright, to sparkle.

shingle small stones covering the seashore.

shingles an infectious disease causing a painful skin rash.

ship a very large boat.

shipment a quantity of goods sent by ship.

shipshape in good order, tidy.

shipwreck the destruction of a ship, often in a storm.

shipyard a place where ships are built or repaired.

shire a county.

shirk to avoid doing something (you should do), to get out of doing something.

shirt a garment for the upper part of the body, of light cloth with sleeves and a collar, often worn by men.

shiver 1 to shake because of cold or fear. 2 to break into small pieces.

shoal a large group of fish of the same kind swimming together.

shock *noun* a sudden violent surprise or force.
verb to make (someone) feel shock.

shocking causing shock, dreadful, terrible, disgusting.

shod wearing shoes.

shoddy badly made or done, of poor material.

shoe 1 a covering for the foot. 2 an iron plate nailed to a horse's hoof.

shoot *verb* 1 to fire (a weapon). 2 to move very quickly.
noun a young growth on a plant.

shooting star a small meteor as seen in the sky.

shop *noun* a place where things are sold.
verb to go shopping.

shoplifter a person who steals from shops.

shopping 1 going to shops to buy things. 2 the things you buy in shops.

shore the land along the edge of the sea or of a lake.

shore up to support, strengthen.

short 1 small from end to end, not long, not tall. 2 not lasting a long time.

shortage not enough.

shortcoming a failure to reach a standard.

shorten to make shorter.

shorthand a way of writing down very quickly what someone is saying.

short-handed having fewer helpers than usual.

shortly soon.

shorts short trousers, with legs stopping above the knee.

short-sighted not able to see things which are far away.

shot 1 the shooting of a gun. 2 what is fired from a gun. 3 **a good shot** a person who is good at shooting. 4 a stroke etc. in a game. 5 a photograph.

shoulder *noun* the place where the arm joins the body.
verb 1 to take on your shoulder. 2 to push with your shoulder. 3 to accept (something) as a duty.

shout to speak or cry out in a loud voice.

shove to push hard.

shovel *noun* a broad-bladed tool for lifting loose things, for example coal.
verb to lift or move with a shovel.

show *verb* to allow to see.
noun where special things can be seen.

shower 1 a short fall of rain or snow. 2 a place to wash yourself where water sprays down on you from above.

showery raining in showers.

show-jumping a riding competition in which the horses are made to jump over fences etc.

showy flashy, attractive on the surface.

shrapnel bits of metal thrown out by an exploding shell.

shred *noun* a tiny narrow piece (torn off something).
verb to tear into thin strips.

shrew 1 a small mouselike animal. 2 a bad-tempered quarrelsome woman.

shrewd wise, cunning.

shriek *noun* a high-pitched scream of pain, surprise or laughter.
verb to make such a sound.

shrill (of a sound) high-pitched and piercing.

shrimp a very small kind of shellfish.

shrine a holy place.

shrink to make or become smaller.

shrivel to become wrinkled and withered.

shroud *noun* a garment to cover a dead body.
verb to cover as with a shroud.

shrub a small tree or bush.

shrubbery a clump or group of bushes.

shrug to move the shoulders up and down, often to show you are doubtful etc.

shudder to shake violently with fear or cold.

shuffle 1 to drag the feet along the ground when walking. 2 to rearrange the order of playing cards etc.

hun

shun to avoid.

shunt to move (a train, railway engine or wagon) on to another line.

shut *adjective* not open, covered over. *verb* to cause to be shut.

shutter 1 a wooden covering for a window. 2 a part of a camera which opens briefly to let light in.

shuttle 1 a part of a weaving machine which carries thread. 2 a transport service which makes regular journeys from one place to another. 3 a re-usable spacecraft.

shy afraid to speak; easily frightened.

Siamese cat a kind of cat, with cream and brown fur and blue eyes.

Siamese twins twins whose bodies are joined together at some point.

sibilant having a hissing sound like *s* or *sh*.

sibling a brother or sister.

sick 1 feeling that you will bring up food from the stomach. 2 ill, not well.

sicken to make or become sick.

sickening disgusting.

sickle a short-handled tool with a curved blade for cutting corn, for example.

sickly 1 unhealthy, pale, weak. 2 that make you sick.

sickness illness, being unwell.

side 1 one of the parts or surfaces of something which is not the top, bottom, back or front. 2 a team at games.

sideline work done for pay outside your usual work.

sidelong (of a look) to or from one side, not direct.

sideshow a small entertainment attached or close to a larger one.

sideways to or from the side.

sidle to move sideways, especially when you are trying not to be seen.

silicon chip

siege the surrounding of a place by soldiers or other people so that no help or food can reach it.

siesta a short sleep taken in the afternoon in hot countries.

sieve an instrument with small holes which only lets liquid and small objects through.

sift to separate coarse and fine parts, for example of flour, usually using a sieve.

sigh *verb* to make a low sound with a deep breath, especially because you are tired or sad.
noun such a sound.

sight 1 being able to see. 2 something seen.

sightseeing visiting interesting places.

sign *noun* a mark, movement or message which has a meaning.
verb to write your name on.

signal *noun* a sign, sound or light which tells you something.
verb to send a message by means of signals.

signature a person's name written by himself or herself, for example at the end of a letter.

signet a small seal, often part of a ring (**signet ring**).

significance importance, what something means.

significant important, worth noting.

signify to be a sign of, to mean.

silence being silent.

silent quiet, still, without noise; not saying anything.

silhouette a dark picture of a person or thing, seen in outline only.

silicon a substance, an element found combined with many other substances.

silicon chip a tiny slice of silicon processed to hold information in a computer etc.

silk a kind of smooth soft cloth made of thread which comes from a kind of caterpillar called a **silkworm**.

silken made of silk; like silk.

silky like silk.

sill a flat piece of stone or wood at the bottom of a window or door.

silly foolish, stupid.

silo 1 a pit or airtight container for pressing and keeping crops for animal feed. 2 an underground place for keeping a guided missile ready to fire.

silt sand or mud laid down by a river.

silver a valuable, rather soft, whitish metal, used for example to make jewellery, coins, spoons and forks.

silver-plated having a thin coating of silver.

silversmith a person who makes things out of silver.

similar like, almost the same as something else.

similarity being similar.

simile a comparison with something else, using 'like' or 'as': *as soft as butter.*

simmer to boil very gently.

simper to smile in a silly way.

simple 1 plain, without any decoration. 2 easy.

simpleton a silly person.

simplicity being simple.

simplification making simple.

simplify to make simple.

simply 1 easily. 2 barely, only just.

simulate to pretend; to imitate.

simulation the act of simulating; something simulated.

simultaneous at the same time.

sin doing something very bad, which is against the laws of your religion.

since 1 from that time until now. 2 because.

sincere meaning what you say, honest.

sincerity being sincere.

sinecure an office or job which is paid but has no duties attached to it or very few.

sinew a tough band of flesh that joins muscle to bone.

sinewy strong, wiry.

sinful wicked, bad.

sing to make music with the voice.

singe to burn slightly.

single 1 only one. 2 not married.

singlet a man's vest, or similar garment worn for sports.

singsong 1 a number of people singing together for pleasure. 2 an up-and-down tone of the voice.

singular 1 only one, on its own; (in grammar) showing only one. 2 unusual, remarkable.

sinister evil(-looking), threatening.

sink *verb* to go down slowly, especially in liquid.
noun a large fixed basin for washing dishes in a kitchen.

sinner a person who sins.

sinuous having many curves, moving like a snake.

sinus a hollow in a bone, especially one in the skull, connected to the nose.

sinusitis inflammation of the sinuses.

sip to drink in tiny amounts.

siphon *noun* a tube or pipe used to draw liquid out of a container.
verb to draw off liquid using a siphon.

sir 1 a title given to a man. 2 a polite title used in speaking to a man.

siren 1 a long loud warning sound which can be heard for a long distance. 2 (in stories of Ancient Greece) a kind of sea fairy whose singing drew people into danger of shipwreck.

sirloin a cut of beef from the back of the animal.

sister a girl or woman who has the same parents as another person.

sister-in-law the sister of a husband or wife or the wife of a brother.

sit to rest on your bottom with your back upright.

site a piece of ground set aside for building or where a building etc. was.

situate to put in a particular position.

situation 1 the place occupied by something. 2 the position in which a person finds himself or herself.

size how big something is.

sizeable of a fairly large size.

sizzle to make a spluttering sound like something frying.

skate *noun* a metal blade fitted to a boot to allow you to move quickly on ice.
verb 1 to move on ice using skates. 2 to move on roller skates.

skateboard a flat board on wheels on which you can stand and move about for fun.

skein a loosely-tied coil of thread or yarn.

skeleton the framework formed by all the bones in the body.

sketch *verb* to draw quickly and roughly.
noun 1 a rough drawing or outline. 2 a short one-scene play, usually funny.

sketchy unfinished, rough, incomplete.

skewer a long pin for holding meat during cooking.

ski *noun* a long thin piece of wood etc. fitted to a boot to allow you to move quickly over snow.
verb to move on snow using skis.

skid to slide out of control on a slippery surface.

skiff a small light boat.

skilful having skill.

skill cleverness, ability to do things well.

skilled having skill.

skim 1 to pass over a surface almost without touching. 2 to remove the surface from (a liquid), for example the cream from milk.

skimp to keep in short supply.

skimpy small in size, quantity, not quite enough.

skin *noun* the outer covering of a person or animal or of a fruit or vegetable.
verb to remove the skin from.

skinny very thin.

skip 1 to move with little jumping steps. 2 to jump over a turning rope.

skipper the captain of a ship or of a team.

skirmish a fight between small groups of soldiers.

skirt a woman's garment that hangs from the waist.

skittish (of a horse, young person) nervous, playful, lively.

skittle a wooden block knocked down by rolling or throwing a ball in the game of **skittles.**

skulk to move about in a cowardly or evil way.

skull the bones that cover your head.

skunk a kind of small black North American animal which has a white stripe and which gives off a bad smell.

sky the space above the earth where the sun, moon and stars are seen.

skylark a small bird which sings when it is flying high in the sky.

skylarking rough play.

skylight a window in a roof.

skyscraper a very high building.

slab a thick flat piece of something.

slack 1 loose. 2 careless, not working hard.

slacken 1 to make or become slack. 2 to slow down.

slag waste material left when producing metal from rock.

slake to satisfy (your thirst).

slalom a ski-race down a zigzag course marked with flags.

slam to bang or shut loudly.

slander to harm someone by saying something bad about them which is untrue.

slang words and phrases in common speech which are not used in formal writing, and sometimes used only by certain groups of people.

slant a slope.

slap a hard smack with the flat of the hand.

slash to cut with a long sweeping stroke.

slat a narrow thin length of wood etc.

slate 1 a kind of grey rock which splits easily into thin pieces. 2 a piece of this used as a tile on a roof or, formerly, for writing on.

slaughter 1 to kill (animals) for food. 2 to kill many people or animals.

slave a person who is owned by another person and is forced to work for them without pay.

slavery being a slave.

slavish 1 behaving like a slave. 2 behaving exactly like someone else.

slay to kill.

sleazy not admirable, squalid, shabby.

sledge a vehicle without wheels which will move smoothly on snow.

sleek smooth and glossy.

sleep to rest with the eyes closed and without being conscious.

sleeper 1 a person who sleeps. 2 a bar of wood etc. under a railway line. 3 a railway carriage with beds for overnight journeys; one of these beds.

sleepy feeling that you want to go to sleep.

sleet snow and rain falling together.

sleeve the part of a garment that covers an arm or part of an arm.

sleigh [slay] a large sledge drawn by animals.

sleight of hand quickness of hand movement to deceive an audience, a conjuring trick.

slender slim.

sleuth a detective.

slice a thin piece cut from something larger.

slick *adjective* 1 smooth and slippery. 2 done smoothly and easily.
noun an oil slick.

slide *verb* to move smoothly along a slippery surface; to slip.
noun 1 a hair fastener. 2 a small photograph for showing on a screen.

slight *adjective* 1 thin, small, not very strong. 2 small, of no importance.
verb to insult (someone), treat (someone) as unimportant.

slightly a little, a small amount.

slim *adjective* thin; small.
verb to (try to) become thinner.

slime wet slippery material.

slimy 1 covered with or like slime. 2 (of a person) unpleasant, insincere.

sling *noun* 1 a bandage to support a broken arm. 2 a piece of leather and string used for throwing stones.
verb to throw violently.

slink to move smoothly and quietly so as not to be noticed.

slip *verb* 1 to move quickly and quietly. 2 to lose your balance on a smooth surface. 3 to make a mistake.
noun 1 the act of slipping. 2 a small piece of paper. 3 an underskirt.

slippers light soft shoes worn in the house.

slippery so smooth that you are likely to slide on it.

slipshod untidy, careless.

slit a narrow cut or tear.

slither to slide, for example on ice; to move in a sliding way like a snake.

sliver [**sliv**ver] a long thin strip.

slobber to have liquid falling from the mouth.

slog to walk or work with effort.

slogan a short saying used in advertising, for example.

sloop a kind of one-masted sailing ship.

slop to spill liquid carelessly out of a container.

slope something that is higher at one end than at the other, a slant.

sloppy 1 careless, untidy. 2 wet and messy. 3 showing your feelings in a silly way.

slot a narrow opening.

sloth 1 laziness. 2 a slow-moving animal that lives in trees.

slouch a lazy way of walking, sitting or standing with your head and shoulders bent.

slovenly careless, lazy, untidy.

slow taking a long time, not quick.

slow-worm a kind of lizard with no legs, which moves like a snake.

sludge 1 thick, greasy mud. 2 sewage which has been processed.

slug a small animal like a snail, but without a shell.

sluggish slow-moving.

sluice a sliding door which controls a flow of water; the channel which it controls.

slum a very poor overcrowded uncared-for house or part of a town.

slumber sleep.

slump to fall suddenly.

slur 1 to speak unclearly. 2 to say bad things about.

slush half-melted watery snow.

sly not to be trusted, crafty, cunning.

smack *verb* to hit with a flat hand. *noun* 1 the act of smacking. 2 a kind of fishing boat.

small little, not big; not important.

smallpox a serious disease, formerly very common, causing spots which leave marks on the skin.

smart *adjective* 1 clever, quick to understand. 2 well-dressed. *verb* to have a stinging feeling.

smash to break into many pieces.

smattering a little knowledge, especially of a language.

smear to spread something dirty, sticky or greasy over something.

smell 1 to know about through your nose. 2 to have a smell.

smelter a furnace where metal is extracted from ore.

smile to show you are amused or happy by stretching the corners of your mouth.

smirk to smile in an unpleasant, often silly, way.

smith a person who shapes things out of metal; a blacksmith.

smithereens: into smithereens into many small bits.

smithy a place where a blacksmith works.

smitten struck down, badly affected (by something).

smock a loose overall or dress.

smoke *noun* the dark cloud which rises from something burning. *verb* to burn tobacco in a pipe or cigarette.

smooth flat, even, not rough.

smoothly evenly, easily.

smother 1 to stop someone breathing by covering the nose and mouth. 2 to cover thickly with something.

smoulder to burn slowly with a lot of smoke but no flame.

smudge a dirty mark.

smug too pleased with yourself.

smuggle to take things secretly into a country without paying tax on them.

smuggler a person who smuggles.

smut 1 a small piece of dirt or soot. 2 dirty language.

snack a small amount of food, especially if eaten between meals.

snaffle *noun, also* **snaffle bit** a kind of bit put in a horse's mouth.
verb to grab, take for oneself.

snag a difficulty, something which holds you back.

snail a small slimy animal with a shell on its back.

snake a smooth legless animal which glides on its body, often having a poisonous bite.

snap *verb* 1 to bite at something quickly. 2 to break with a sharp noise. 3 to make a sharp noise with the fingers.
noun 1 the act of snapping. 2 a snapshot.

snapshot a quickly-taken photograph.

snare a trap set for animals.

snarl 1 to growl showing the teeth. 2 to speak in an angry way.

snatch to grab quickly.

sneak *verb* to move secretly.
noun a person who tells something bad about someone else secretly.

sneer to speak in a way that shows you do not think much of someone.

sneeze a sudden noisy rush of air from the nose.

snick to make a small cut in.

snicker the noise made by a horse, a whinny.

snide sneering, saying unpleasant things about someone.

sniff to smell noisily with quick breaths.

sniffle to sniff slightly and repeatedly.

sniffles a cold in the head.

snigger to laugh in a quiet hidden way.

snip to make small quick cuts with scissors.

snipe a kind of marsh bird which is shot as game.

sniper a person who fires shots from a hidden position.

snippet 1 a small piece cut off something. 2 a short piece of news.

snivel to talk in a moaning, weeping way.

snob a person who thinks too much about money and position and looks down on others.

snobbery being a snob.

snobbish of or like a snob.

snooker a game played on a billiard table using several coloured balls which have to be played in sequence.

snooze a short sleep, a nap.

snore to breathe heavily and noisily while asleep.

snorkel a tube which brings you air from the surface when you are swimming under water.

snort to blow loudly down the nostrils.

snout an animal's long nose.

snow frozen raindrops which fall in white flakes.

snowdrift a bank of snow heaped up by the wind.

snowdrop a small white early-spring flower.

snowline the height on a mountain above which the snow does not melt.

snowplough a vehicle with a broad blade in front for clearing snow.

snowshoe a large net on a frame tied to a shoe to help you to walk over snow.

snub to insult (someone) by ignoring them.

snub-nosed having a short stumpy nose.

snuff powdered tobacco that is sniffed into the nose.

snuffle to talk with the nose blocked by a cold.

snug warm, cosy, comfortable.

snuggle to press close to a person or thing for warmth or comfort.

soak 1 to make very wet. 2 to leave for a time in a liquid.

soap a fatty substance used with water for washing.

soapsuds froth made in soapy water.

soar to fly or rise very high.

sob to weep noisily.

sober 1 not drunk. 2 serious, not bright or flashy.

sobriety not being drunk.

soccer an informal name for association football, a kind of football played with a round ball.

sociable fond of company, friendly.

social concerned with living together in a community.

socialise to make friends with others, to get to know people.

social security money paid by the government to help people who cannot earn enough for themselves.

society 1 the people in a community. 2 an organised body of people with similar interests.

sock a cloth covering for your foot and ankle, and sometimes the lower part of your leg.

socket a hole into which something fits, for example an electric plug.

sod a piece of turf.

soda-water water made fizzy by passing a gas through.

sodden soaked through.

sofa a seat for more than one person, a couch.

soft 1 not hard. 2 gentle, mild, not rough. 3 quiet, not loud.

software the programs which control a computer and are not part of a machine.

soggy soft and wet.

soil *noun* the earth in which plants grow.
verb to make dirty.

sojourn to stay in a place for a time.

solace comfort for someone in distress.

solar to do with the sun.

solarium a place covered in glass where you get the full benefit of the sun's rays on your body.

solar system the sun with the planets that move around it.

solder a substance which joins metals together when heated.

soldier a person whose job it is to fight, a member of an army.

sole *noun* 1 the bottom of a foot or of a shoe or boot. 2 a kind of flat sea-fish used as food.
adjective the one and only, single.

solely without another, only.

solemn 1 very serious. 2 in a religious manner.

sol-fa the musical scale when sung with a series of syllables (doh, ray, mee etc.).

solicit to ask earnestly or repeatedly.

solicitor a lawyer.

solicitous eager to help (someone).

solicitude being solicitous.

solid 1 hard, firm, not liquid or gas. 2 not hollow.

solidarity (people) sticking together, unity of aims and interests.

solidify to make or become solid, to harden.

solidity hardness, firmness.

soliloquy a special piece spoken by an actor to the audience which is not addressed to any other character in a play.

solitary alone, single.
solitude being alone.
solo *noun* a piece of music played or sung by one person alone.
adjective done by one person alone, for example a **solo** flight in an aeroplane.
soloist a person who sings or plays a solo.
soluble 1 able to be dissolved in water. 2 able to be solved.
solution 1 the act of dissolving; liquid with something dissolved in it. 2 the act of solving; the answer to a problem etc.
solve to find the answer to.
solvent *adjective* able to pay your debts. *noun* a liquid which dissolves or breaks down a substance.
sombre gloomy, dismal.
sombrero a kind of large-brimmed hat worn in Mexico.
somersault to turn over and over, head over heals.
somnambulist a sleepwalker.
somnolent sleepy, drowsy.
son a male child of a parent.
sonar *adjective* of or about sound waves.
noun a system for underwater detection of objects, especially submarines.
sonata a piece of music with three or four sections, usually for one instrument.
song a piece of music for the voice.
sonic to do with sound waves.
son-in-law the husband of a person's daughter.
sonnet a kind of poem with fourteen lines.
sonorous loud or deep-sounding.
soon in a short time.
sooner 1 earlier. 2 rather.
soot the black substance left behind after burning, for example in a chimney.

soothe 1 to bring relief of pain etc. to. 2 to comfort.
soothsayer a person who foretells the future.
sophisticated 1 having an easy manner in company, cultured, not simple. 2 (of machinery etc.) complicated.
soporific making you sleep.
soprano a woman or child with the highest singing voice.
sorbet [**sor**bay] a frozen dessert made of water with sugar, egg-white and flavouring.
sorcerer a person who uses sorcery.
sorcery magic arts, witchcraft.
sordid dirty, mean, nasty.
sore painful.
sorrow a feeling of sadness.
sorry feeling unhappy because you wish you had not done something or that something had not happened.
sort *noun* a kind, type.
verb to put into the right order, for example putting things of the same size together.
sortie a short, sudden attack.
SOS a signal or call for help.
soufflé a light spongy dish made with eggs and baked in the oven usually.
soul the part of a person that is not the body or the mind and is thought to live on after death, the spirit.
soulful full of feeling.
soulless having no feelings, dull.
sound *noun* something you hear, a noise.
adjective strong and healthy, in a good state.
sound effects noises made by machines etc. to sound like natural sounds for a film or broadcast.
soundings measurements made of the depth of water.
soundproof not allowing sounds to get in or out.

soundtrack the sounds and words which accompany the pictures on a film.

soup a food made by boiling vegetables, meat or fish in a lot of water.

sour 1 having a sharp bitter taste, like a lemon. 2 (of milk) not fresh.

source a place where something starts, for example a river.

south the direction that is on the right as you face the rising sun.

southern lying towards the south.

souvenir something you keep to remind you of something, for example a place you visit.

sou'wester a waterproof hat with a broad flap at the back.

sovereign 1 a king or queen. 2 (long ago) a gold coin worth one pound.

sow [rhymes with 'low'] to put (seeds) into the ground so that they will grow.

sow [rhymes with 'now'] a female pig.

soya bean a kind of bean used as food, sometimes instead of meat.

soy (sauce) a dark brown sauce made from soya beans, used in Chinese cooking.

space 1 the distance between things. 2 what is beyond the earth's atmosphere.

spacecraft a vehicle which can travel in space.

spacious having plenty of space, roomy.

spade 1 a flat-bladed tool for digging soil. 2 a small spade shape on one of the four kinds of playing cards.

spaghetti pasta formed in strings.

span 1 a measure of length or time. 2 the distance across an arch.

spangle a small thin piece of glittering material.

spaniel a kind of dog with a long silky coat and drooping ears.

spank to hit hard on the bottom.

spanner a tool which turns a metal nut to tighten or slacken it.

spar *noun* a strong pole.
verb to fight playfully with the fists.

spare *adjective* 1 not in use at present, extra. 2 thin, scanty.
verb to give up, to do without.

spark a tiny burning piece of material.

sparkle to shine with tiny movements of light.

sparkling glittering; (of wine etc.) bubbling.

sparrow a kind of small brown bird.

sparse thinly scattered.

spartan simple, basic, without luxuries.

spasm a sudden jerky movement of the body.

spasmodic occurring in fits and starts.

spastic (of) a person suffering from brain damage which makes them unable to move parts of the body easily.

spate a flood of water in a river.

spatula a broad-bladed tool for lifting and spreading soft substances or for holding the tongue down in a medical examination.

speak to use the voice to say something, to talk.

spear a sharp-pointed weapon with a long thin handle.

special 1 of a kind that is different. 2 made or done for one person or occasion.

specialise to keep mainly to one thing or subject in your business, study etc.

species a group of plants or animals that have a lot in common and can be interbred.

specific 1 clear, detailed. 2 definite, relating to a particular subject.

specify to mention in a definite way, to list (items).

specimen 1 an example of a particular kind. 2 a small amount of something which shows what the rest is like.

specious looking good on the surface but not underneath, false.

speck a tiny spot of something

speckled having many spots or markings of different colour on the skin, hair, feathers, etc.

spectacles glasses (to help you to see better).

spectacular amazing, exciting, extraordinary.

spectator a person who watches something, for example a football match.

spectre a ghost.

spectrum 1 the whole range of colours which vary slightly from one to another. 2 any similar range.

speculation 1 putting money into a business or property for example to make a profit. 2 thoughts about (something).

speech 1 the ability to speak. 2 a talk given to a group of people.

speechless unable to speak, usually because of shock or surprise.

speed the quickness or slowness with which something is done.

speedometer a dial on a motor car etc. which tells how fast you are going.

speedway a place where motor cycles are raced.

speedwell a small blue wild flower.

speedy quick, prompt, early.

spell *verb* to say or write letters one by one to make words.
noun 1 words used in magic or witchcraft. 2 a short period of time.

spellbound unable to speak or move because of amazement or surprise.

spend 1 to give (money) to pay for something. 2 to use (time) in doing something.

spendthrift a person who spends money wastefully or foolishly.

spent used up, exhausted.

sphere a round ball, a globe.

spherical round like a sphere.

sphinx (in fables) a monster with the body of a lion and a woman's head.

spice something used to give food a special, often hot, taste.

spick and span very tidy, clean and in good order.

spicy tasting of spice, having a hot taste.

spider a small eight-legged creature which weaves a web to catch insects for food.

spidery thin like the lines of a spider's web.

spike a pointed object, especially of metal.

spiked pointed.

spill to let (a liquid or powder) out of its container, especially by accident.

spin 1 to turn round and round very quickly. 2 to make cotton, wool etc. into thread.

spina bifida a split in the spine from birth causing serious problems such as paralysis.

spinach a kind of vegetable with dark-green leaves.

spinal concerning the backbone.

spindle a pin on which thread is twisted and wound as it is being spun.

spine 1 the backbone. 2 a thorn, prickle.

spineless having no courage, weak.

spinnaker a large triangular sail which goes in front of the main sail on a yacht.

spinster an unmarried woman.

spiral coiling like a screw.

spire the pointed upper part of a tower, often of a church.

spirit 1 the soul of a person. 2 a ghost. 3 life, energy. 4 a liquid containing a high level of alcohol.

spirited full of life and energy.

spiritual *adjective* to do with the soul rather than the body, religious. *noun* a kind of song usually sung by black people in North America.

spit *noun* the liquid that forms in the mouth. *verb* 1 to force something out of your mouth. 2 a rod on which meat is roasted.

spite bad feelings towards others, a wish to hurt.

spiteful full of spite.

spittle saliva spat from the mouth.

splash to throw or scatter liquid noisily.

spleen 1 an internal organ of the body. 2 ill-temper, spite, anger.

splendid 1 excellent, very good. 2 very grand.

splendour brilliance, magnificence.

splice to join together.

splint a flat piece of wood used to support a broken bone.

splinter a small sharp piece, usually of wood.

split *verb* to crack, to break (something) along its length. *noun* 1 a division, for example in a group of people. 2 a broken place, a crack.

splutter to make spitting noises; to speak quickly and unclearly.

spoil to ruin, damage.

spoilt (of a child) having been given everything you want so that you become badly behaved.

spoke a thin bar from the centre to the rim of a wheel.

spokesperson a person who speaks on behalf of others.

sponge 1 a soft substance which soaks up water, used for washing. 2 a soft light cake.

spongy soft, holding liquid like a sponge.

sponsor *noun* a person or organisation that helps another in some way, especially by giving money for something done for charity, for example a walk of a certain length. *verb* to act as a sponsor for.

spontaneous 1 behaving naturally and freely. 2 done by itself.

spoof a trick, deception, an imitation of something to amuse.

spook comic name for a ghost.

spool a reel on which thread, film etc. is wound.

spoon a utensil used for stirring tea, eating pudding etc.

spoor the track or scent of an animal.

sporadic happening here and there or at odd times.

sporran a kind of purse worn in front of a kilt.

sport 1 games played for exercise or pleasure, for example football, tennis. 2 fun, amusement.

spot *noun* 1 a tiny mark. 2 a place. *verb* to notice.

spotless very clean.

spotlight a beam of light that can be directed.

spouse a husband or wife.

spout *noun* a short tube through which a liquid is poured. *verb* to rush or gush out.

sprain *verb* to injure by twisting badly (for example the ankle or the wrist). *noun* an injury caused by spraining.

sprat a fish like a small herring used as food.

sprawl to spread out the limbs lazily.

spray *noun* 1 thin jets of water. 2 a bunch of flowers.
verb to spread or sprinkle in a fine spray.

spread 1 to take up more space. 2 to scatter about. 3 to cover a surface with something.

spree a lively period of activity such as a party.

sprig a twig or small shoot.

sprightly lively, active.

spring *noun* 1 to leap or jump. 2 a metal coil. 3 a place where water appears from below the ground. 4 the season between winter and summer.
verb 1 to jump suddenly. 2 to sprout.

springbok a kind of African antelope.

sprinkle to scatter (liquid or something powdery) in small drops or grains.

sprinkler a device for sprinkling water.

sprint *verb* to run quickly for a short distance.
noun a race over a short distance.

sprinter a person who runs sprint races.

sprocket 1 each of the teeth on a wheel that catches on a chain to turn it. 2 *also* **sprocket wheel** a wheel with sprockets.

sprout *verb* to begin to grow.
noun 1 a shoot, sprig. 2 a vegetable like a small cabbage.

spruce *noun* kind of fir tree.
adjective neat and tidy.

spry active, lively.

spur *noun* a sharp instrument used to make a horse go faster.
verb to drive (a person or animal) to further effort.

spurious false, not genuine.

spurn to reject with scorn.

spurt to gush or spout out.

spy *noun* a person who finds out and passes on information secretly.
verb 1 to catch sight of. 2 to explore or try to find out about secretly.

spyglass a small hand-held telescope.

squabble *verb* to quarrel noisily about small things.
noun a noisy quarrel.

squad a small group, for example of soldiers or workmen.

squadron a military group, especially of planes or ships.

squadron leader an officer in the Royal Air Force.

squalid horribly dirty, disgusting.

squall a sudden strong wind.

squalor the state of being squalid.

squander to waste (money or time).

square 1 a figure with four equal sides and four right angles. 2 an open space in a town, often of this shape, with buildings round it. 3 the result when a number is multiplied by itself.

square root a number which when multiplied by itself gives a particular number.

squash *verb* to crush, to squeeze tightly together or into a small space.
noun 1 the act of squashing. 2 a fruit drink which is mixed with water. 3 a game in which a small ball is hit with a racket against a wall.

squat *verb* 1 to sit on the heels. 2 to live in a building without permission.
adjective short, dumpy.

squatter a person who lives in a building without permission.

squaw a North American Indian woman, especially a wife.

squawk the loud harsh noise made by some birds, especially as a cry of alarm.

squeak a small sharp noise like that made by a mouse.

squeaky like the noise made by stiff or rusty hinges.

squeal *noun* a long shrill cry, often caused by pain or joy.
verb to make such a cry.

squeamish easily shocked or disgusted; feeling slightly sick.

squeeze *verb* 1 to press together, to squash. 2 to press to get something out (for example an orange, a toothpaste tube).
noun a firm grip.

squelch to make a noise as when walking through mud.

squib a kind of small firework.

squid a kind of edible sea creature with a long body and ten arms at one end.

squint *noun* a defect in which one eye looks in a different direction to the other.
verb to look with half-shut eyes.

squire an English country landowner.

squirm to twist about, to wriggle.

squirrel a small wild animal which has a bushy tail and which lives among trees.

squirt to force (liquid) out in a fast stream.

stab to make a wound with a sharp pointed weapon.

stabilise to make balanced or stable or steady.

stability steadiness; reliability.

stable *noun* a building where horses are kept.
verb to keep or put (a horse) in a stable.
adjective 1 standing firm. 2 reliable.

staccato (in music) (played) in an abrupt, sharp manner, with all the notes separate.

stack *noun* a large tidy pile.
verb to place (things) in a stack.

stadium a large open-air sports ground with rows of seats.

staff 1 a group of people who work together in an office, shop etc. 2 a long pole used by walkers.

stag a male deer.

stage *noun* 1 a platform in a theatre or hall where people act, dance etc. 2 a part of a journey etc.
verb to put a show on the stage.

stagecoach (long ago) a horse-drawn coach which made regular trips with passengers.

stagger 1 to sway as you walk, to walk unsteadily. 2 to amaze. 3 to arrange over a period of time, with breaks in between.

staggering astonishing.

staging a temporary platform or scaffolding to support (something or someone).

stagnant 1 (of water) not moving. 2 not active, not developing.

stag party a party for men only, especially one held by a bachelor the night before his wedding.

staid solemn and dull.

stain *noun* 1 a mark which spoils something. 2 a kind of dye, used especially for wood.
verb to mark with stains.

stainless 1 (of steel) not likely to rust. 2 (*literary*) without fault.

stair one of the steps in a flight of stairs.

staircase a set of steps and its side parts.

stairs a set of steps leading to another floor in a building.

stake *noun* 1 a strong pointed stick. 2 (long ago) a post to which people were tied when being burned to death as a punishment.
verb 1 to mark (your property) with stakes. 2 to place a bet.

stalactite an icicle-like deposit *hanging down* from the roof of a cave.

stalagmite an icicle-like deposit *growing up* from the bottom of a cave.

stale 1 old, not fresh; no longer fit to eat. 2 no longer interesting.

stalemate 1 a position in chess caused by one player having no move to make. 2 a position in an argument etc. from which neither side can move forward.

stalk *noun* the stem of a flower or plant.
verb 1 to walk with long proud steps. 2 to track (an animal) quietly.

stall *noun* 1 a counter for selling things, for example in a market. 2 a place where a cow, horse etc. is kept. 3 **the stalls** seats on the ground level of a cinema or theatre.
verb (of a vehicle or its engine) to stop suddenly.

stallion a male horse kept for breeding.

stalwart sturdy, courageous, steady.

stamen the part of a flower which contains the pollen.

stamina the ability to keep going although you are tired, ill etc.

stammer to have difficulty in saying words, to repeat words without meaning to, to stutter.

stamp *verb* 1 to put your feet down hard and noisily. 2 to press a mark or design on to (something).
noun 1 the little piece of paper stuck on a letter or parcel to show you have paid to have it sent through the post. 2 a heavy tread.

stampede a sudden rush of horses, for example, in fear; any sudden rush.

stand *verb* 1 to be in an upright position. 2 to rise up. 3 to put up with (something). 4 to be a candidate in an election.
noun 1 a support for an object. 2 a witness-box. 3 seats under cover at a sports ground. 4 firmness in holding an opinion.

standard 1 a level or measurement of ability to be reached. 2 a flag.

standardise to make (something) the same size or shape etc. as the standard.

standing reputation, position in society or group.

standing order 1 an order or rule that remains in force for some time. 2 an instruction to a bank to pay a certain amount regularly out of a bank account.

standpoint a person's point of view.

standstill a stop.

stanza a division of a poem or song.

staple 1 a U-shaped piece of wire used for holding things. 2 a small piece of thin wire which is bent to hold pieces of paper together.

star 1 a distant heavenly body seen as a small point of light in the sky on a clear night. 2 a very famous actor, sportsperson etc.

starboard the right-hand side of a ship when you are facing forward.

starch 1 a white substance found in some foods such as bread or potatoes. 2 some of this substance mixed with water and used to stiffen clothes.

starchy 1 of, like or containing a lot of starch. 2 (of a person) strict, unbending.

stare *verb* to look at something steadily for a long time.
noun a fixed look.

starfish a kind of sea animal with five limbs, giving it a star shape.

stark bare, clearly seen.

stark naked with no clothes on.

starling a small bird with very dark brown feathers.

start *verb* 1 to begin. 2 to make a sudden movement.
noun 1 a beginning. 2 a sudden movement (caused by fear or surprise).

startle to surprise or frighten suddenly.

startling surprising, astonishing.

starvation lack of food which causes death or suffering.

starve to die or suffer because of lack of food.

state *noun* 1 the condition of a thing or person. 2 a country or its government. 3 a part of certain countries, such as the **United States of America.**
verb to say in words, either by writing or by speaking.

stately grand, dignified, ceremonious.

statement something said or written down, especially for an important reason.

statesman a person who is skilled in government affairs.

static *adjective* at rest, not moving or changing.
noun the crackling noise sometimes heard on a radio or record player.

station 1 a place from which trains or buses set out or stop on a journey. 2 a place from which certain services are carried out, for example a **police station**, a **fire station**.

stationary not moving.

stationery writing materials such as notepaper, envelopes, pens etc.

statistics numbers collected together and arranged to give information.

statue an image or likeness in wood, stone etc.

statuesque like a statue, large and well-formed.

stature 1 the height of a person. 2 high reputation.

status social position, rank (compared with others).

statute a law passed by parliament.

staunch *adjective* loyal, steady.
verb to stop the flow of (blood, for example).

stave 1 one of the flat pieces of wood used to make a barrel. 2 the lines and spaces used in writing music.

stay 1 not to go away, to remain. 2 to live somewhere for a short time.

steadfast firm, determined.

steady firm, not moving, not changing.

steak a thick slice of meat or fish.

steal 1 to take something that is not yours, to rob. 2 to move quietly without being noticed.

stealth moving or acting secretly, without being noticed.

steam *noun* the mist or cloud that comes from boiling water etc.
verb 1 to give out steam. 2 to move by means of steam. 3 to cook in steam.

steamer a ship powered by steam engines.

steed (*literary*) a horse.

steel a hard and strong metal which is made from iron.

steep *adjective* sloping sharply.
verb to soak (something) in a liquid.

steeple a pointed tower on top of a church.

steeplechase 1 a long horse race with fences. 2 a running race with many jumps.

steeplejack a person who works on tall chimneys, towers, steeples etc.

steer *verb* to guide (a boat, a motor car etc.).
noun a young ox.

stellar to do with stars.

stem *noun* the stalk which holds the leaves or flowers of a plant.
verb to stop the flow of (a liquid).

stench a bad smell.

stencil a thin sheet with holes in it for making a design or copying letters.

step *noun* 1 putting your foot forward or back in order to move. 2 a flat place in a staircase or in front of a door, where you put your feet. 3 a stage in a process.
verb 1 to take a step. 2 to put the foot down (on something).

185

stepfather a man who marries your mother, for example after your father dies.

stepmother a woman who marries your father, for example after your mother dies.

stereo a machine for playing tapes and records which has two loudspeakers.

stereotype a thing or person said to be very like others of the same type.

sterile 1 unable to produce crops, fruit or young. 2 free of germs.

sterilise 1 to make (something) free of germs. 2 to cause (a person or animal) to be unable to produce young.

sterility being sterile.

sterling *noun* the type of money used in Britain, based on the pound. *adjective* of great worth.

stern *adjective* strict, harsh towards another person. *noun* the back part of a ship or boat.

stethoscope an instrument for listening to the heart and lungs.

stew *verb* to cook slowly in water. *noun* meat and vegetables cooked in this way.

steward 1 a man who serves food and helps passengers on a ship, aircraft or train. 2 a person who arranges things, for example at a large meeting.

stewardess a woman who serves food and helps passengers on a ship, plane or train.

stick *noun* a short thin piece of wood. *verb* 1 to fasten or be fastened by something such as glue. 2 to pierce.

sticker 1 a small piece of paper etc. which can be stuck on to another surface. 2 a person who works hard to complete a task.

stickleback a small freshwater fish with prickles on its back.

stickler a person who always insists on high standards in something.

sticky able to stick to something else.

stiff 1 difficult to bend. 2 not friendly or natural in manner.

stiffen to make or become stiff.

stiff-necked stubborn.

stifle 1 to suffocate. 2 to try or pretend to stop (a yawn, for example).

stifling very hot and airless.

stigma a stain on your reputation.

stile steps for climbing over a fence or wall.

stiletto a short dagger.

still *adjective* 1 not moving, quiet, peaceful. 2 the same now as before. *noun* an instrument for making alcohol.

stilt one of a pair of poles for walking on high above the ground.

stilted halting or stiff in speech.

stimulant something which excites or arouses you, or makes you more active.

stimulate to stir into action; to arouse interest etc.

stimulus something which stimulates.

sting *noun* a sharp pain caused by an insect or plant. *verb* 1 to pierce with a sting. 2 to (cause to) feel a sharp pain.

stingy mean.

stink *noun* a bad smell. *verb* to give off a bad smell.

stipend money paid at regular intervals as a kind of salary, especially to a clergyman.

stipulate to insist on, especially as a condition.

stipulation something stipulated, a condition.

stir *verb* 1 to move something round and round with a stick or spoon. 2 to begin to move about. 3 to arouse or excite. *noun* excited activity.

stirring thrilling, exciting.

stirrups rests hanging from a saddle for a rider's feet.

stitch *noun* 1 a loop made in sewing or knitting. 2 a sudden pain in the side.
verb to sew; to fasten by sewing.

stoat a kind of small animal like a weasel, with a brown coat and a black-tipped tail.

stock *noun* 1 a quantity of things or animals. 2 a liquid in which meat etc. is cooked, used for example to make soup.
verb 1 to keep for sale. 2 to provide with a stock of something.

stockade a fence built for defence round a camp for example.

stocking a close-fitting covering for the leg and foot, often made of nylon or wool.

stocks 1 in olden times, an instrument of punishment with holes for the legs. 2 shares in a company.

stock-still without moving.

stodgy (of food) thick, heavy, not easy to eat; (of people) dull.

stoic(al) having great self-control, able to put up with pain, disappointment, hardship etc.

stoke to add fuel to (a fire).

stoker a person whose job it is to put fuel on a furnace etc.

stole a long band of material worn round the shoulders.

stolid dull, not easily roused.

stomach part of the body which digests food.

stone *noun* 1 the hard material found on and below the surface of the earth; a piece of this. 2 a precious jewel. 3 a hard seed found in some kinds of fruit.
verb 1 to throw stones at. 2 to take the stones out of (fruit).

stony 1 full of stones. 2 cold, hard, unfeeling.

stooge a person who is made to seem foolish, especially on stage.

stool a seat without a back.

stoop *verb* 1 to bend the body forward. 2 to fall below your own standards of behaviour.
noun a forward bending of the body.

stop *verb* to end doing something.
noun 1 the act of stopping. 2 a place where buses etc. stop. 3 a punctuation mark like this . used at the end of sentences etc.

stopper something which stops the flow of liquid out of a container.

storage 1 a place for storing goods. 2 the storing of goods. 3 the price charged for this.

store *noun* 1 a place for keeping things. 2 a large shop.
verb to save (something) for later.

storey, story one floor of a building with its rooms.

stork a very large wading bird with long legs and a long straight beak.

storm *noun* 1 violent weather with wind and rain. 2 a sudden outburst of violent feeling.
verb 1 to attack (a castle etc.) suddenly. 2 to rage at someone.

story 1 an account of real or imaginary happenings. 2 *see* **storey**.

stout *adjective* 1 fat, plump. 2 strongly made. 3 firm in your determination, brave.
noun a kind of dark-brown beer.

stove a closed container for cooking or heating.

stow 1 to pack closely, in a ship for example. 2 **stow away** to hide in a ship etc. to avoid the fare.
stowaway a person who does this.

straddle to stand or sit over (something) with the legs apart.

strafe to hit repeatedly with bullets or bombs.

straggle 1 to wander away from the main group. 2 (of strands of hair etc.) to slip out of place or out of control.

straight 1 without a bend or turning. 2 honest.

straighten 1 to make straight. 2 to put in good order.

straightforward 1 direct, without any difficulties. 2 honest, truthful.

strain *verb* 1 to pull, usually too hard. 2 to try too hard. 3 to damage (a muscle etc.) by using it too hard. 4 to separate liquid from solids by passing it through a **strainer**.
noun 1 damage to a muscle etc. as in *verb* 3. 2 the state of mind or body caused by too much worry, work etc.

strainer an instrument with small holes for letting liquids through, a sieve.

strait a narrow channel of water between two pieces of land.

straitlaced narrow-minded, strict.

straits difficulties.

strand 1 a single thread of rope, wire, hair etc. 2 (in poetry) a stretch of sand by the seashore.

stranded left behind in a helpless position, for example after a shipwreck.

strange unusual, odd, remarkable.

strangely curiously, oddly.

stranger a person you do not know; a person who does not know the district.

strangle to kill by pressing or tightening something round the throat.

strap *noun* a long thin piece of leather etc. for example for fastening things together.
verb to fasten with a strap.

strapping big and strong.

stratagem a cunning plan to surprise or trick an enemy.

strategic in accordance with (a) strategy; important in achieving a purpose.

strategist a clever planner.

strategy skilful planning, especially of how to win a war etc.; a careful plan to get something done.

stratify to arrange in strata, layers, grades etc.

stratosphere an outer layer of the earth's atmosphere.

stratum *noun* (*plural* **strata**) a layer, especially of rock or soil.

straw 1 the stalks of wheat, barley etc. 2 a thin tube for drinking through.

strawberry a kind of soft juicy red fruit which grows on very small plants.

stray *verb* to wander away, to get lost. *noun* a lost animal or person. *adjective* 1 lost, away from its owner. 2 scattered, out of place.

streak *noun* 1 a band of colour. 2 a quick movement like a flash of light or someone running.
verb 1 to mark with streaks. 2 to move very quickly.

streaky with streaks.

stream *noun* 1 a small river. 2 a flow of liquid or air. 3 a number of people etc. moving steadily along.
verb to flow; to move in or like a stream.

streamer a long thin ribbon or flag.

streamline to give something the best possible shape for moving through air or water.

street a road with buildings along its side.

strength being strong, power, might.

strengthen to make or become stronger.

strenuous needing great effort, energetic.

stress *noun* 1 strain, pressure. 2 emphasis, for example on a word or part of a word.
verb 1 to emphasise. 2 to cause stress to or in.

stretch *verb* 1 to make longer or wider by pulling. 2 to exaggerate.
noun a length of something.

stretcher a frame to carry an injured or sick person lying down.

strew to scatter about.

stricken suffering a lot of trouble, illness etc.

strict 1 firm, severe, especially about rules. 2 exact.

stride *noun* a long pace or step. *verb* to walk with long steps.

strident loud, harsh.

strife fighting, quarrelling, trouble.

strike *verb* 1 to hit something hard. 2 (of a clock) to make a ringing sound. 3 to go on strike. 4 to come into your mind.
noun when workers stop work because of a dispute.

striking very impressive to look at.

string *noun* 1 thin cord or twine. 2 one of the thin pieces of wire etc. which makes the sound in a musical instrument. 3 a number of people or things one after the other.
verb to put on a string; to fasten with a string.

stringent very strict.

stringy like string; having tough stringlike parts.

strip *noun* a long narrow piece of something.
verb to uncover; to undress.

stripe 1 a thin band of colour. 2 a mark of rank worn on the sleeve.

stripling a youth, a young man.

strive to try hard, struggle.

stroke *noun* 1 a sudden blow. 2 a sudden illness which often makes you unable to move. 3 a single movement, for example of an oar when rowing. 4 the leading oarsman in a boat. 5 a pen or pencil mark.
verb to pass the hand gently over.

stroll to walk along slowly, often for pleasure.

strong 1 powerful; having great energy, able to do difficult things with the body. 2 having a lot of taste or smell. 3 very bright, dazzling.

stronghold a place which is difficult to attack.

structural concerned with structure.

structure 1 a building or framework. 2 the way something is made up or organised.

struggle 1 to fight, especially to get free of someone or something. 2 to try very hard to do something.

strut *verb* to walk in a proud or conceited way.
noun a support, for example in a framework.

stub *noun* the piece, for example of a cigarette, left over when the rest has been used up.
verb 1 to put out (a cigarette or cigar) by pressing it on something. 2 to knock (your toe, for example) against something.

stubble 1 stumps of corn stalks left after reaping. 2 short hairs on a man's chin.

stubborn not giving way easily, obstinate.

stubby short and thick.

stucco a kind of plaster, used for covering walls, for example.

stud 1 a collar-fastener. 2 a short thick-headed nail; a small round knob.

studded stuck all over with studs or with other small objects.

student a person who is studying, especially at a college or university.

studio 1 a room where an artist works. 2 a place where broadcasts or films are made.

studious fond of studying.

study *verb* 1 to spend time learning about something. 2 to examine closely.
noun 1 learning. 2 a room for studying in.

stuff *noun* things, materials.
verb 1 to fill something very full. 2 to put something into something else. 3 to fill with material (for example a cushion). 4 to fill (a chicken etc.) with stuffing.

stuffing 1 filling material. 2 a tasty mixture put inside meat, vegetables etc.

stuffy 1 having little fresh air. 2 boring or unpleasant to talk to.

stultify to make stupid, dull the mind.

stumble to fall or almost fall, especially by catching the foot on something.

stumbling block something which bars your way, a hindrance.

stump *noun* 1 what is left when the larger part (of a tree, for example) has been cut off. 2 an upright stick used to bowl at in cricket.
verb 1 in cricket, to put (a batsman) out by touching a stump with the ball. 2 to ask (someone) a question they cannot answer. 3 to walk about heavily.

stumpy short and thick.

stun 1 to amaze or shock (someone). 2 to strike (a person) until he or she is unconscious.

stunning very attractive, splendid.

stunt *verb* to stop the growth of. *noun* an act of daring done for an audience; something done to attract attention.

stupefy to make senseless, to stun.

stupendous very great, amazing.

stupid having no sense, foolish, silly.

stupidity being stupid.

stupor a state of not being in full possession of your senses.

sturdy strong, well-built, healthy.

sturgeon a large shark-like fish from which **caviare** is taken.

stutter to stammer.

sty 1 a place where pigs are kept. 2 a painful small swelling on the eye.

style 1 a way of doing, saying or making something. 2 a fashion, for example in dress.

stylish fashionable, showing good style.

stylus a needle-like object for reproducing sound from a gramaphone record.

suave smooth in manners, polite and charming.

subaqua of underwater sport.

subconscious not fully realised, thought by the unknown part of the mind.

subdivide to divide into even smaller parts.

subdivision a part of a part of something.

subdue to overcome, bring under control; to make quieter or less fierce.

subject *noun* [**sub**ject] 1 what is being talked about. 2 a person who belongs to a country.
verb [sub**ject**] to take power over.
adjective [**sub**ject] under the power of; depending on.

subjection being or causing to be under someone's power.

sublet to rent an already rented property (or part of it) to someone else.

sublime very high in glory or worth.

subliminal just below the level of a person's full awareness.

submarine *noun* a ship which can go along under water.
adjective living or found under or in the sea.

submerge to go or cause to go under water.

submission 1 the act of submitting. 2 something submitted.

submit 1 to give in, to surrender. 2 to suggest for consideration.

subordinate *noun* a person of lower rank than another.
adjective of lower rank; of less importance.
verb to put or take under control.

subscribe to agree to make payments for.

subscription money paid towards something, for example for membership of a society.

subsequent coming after or later.

subservient accepting the will or wishes of another, slavish.

subside to sink or fall lower; to become less.

subsidence a falling in or sinking.

subsidiary connected with, helpful to, aiding the main organisation, group, business etc.

subsidy money paid, especially by the government, to help an organisation.

subsist to live, especially on small amounts of food etc.

subsistence what you need to stay alive.

substance 1 something of which things are made, material. 2 wealth, possessions.

substantial 1 real, solid, strong. 2 of a considerable size.

substantiate to provide good evidence for (a fact, claim etc.)

substitute *verb* to use in place of another person or thing. *noun* a person or thing substituted.

substitution the act of substituting.

subterfuge a cunning trick.

subterranean underground.

subtle 1 cunning, doing things by clever ways. 2 (of a flavour etc.) delicate, faint but pleasant.

subtlety being subtle.

subtract to take one quantity away from another.

subtraction the act of subtracting, especially in counting.

suburb a district on the outskirts of a town.

suburban of or like a suburb or suburbs in general.

subversive trying to cause the destruction of the government, for example.

subvert to overthrow (a government or religion, for example).

subway 1 an underground tunnel for pedestrians under a road or railway. 2 (in North America) an underground railway.

succeed 1 to manage to do what you try to do; to do well. 2 to come after, to follow.

success 1 having a good result, doing well. 2 a person who or thing which achieves this.

successful having success.

successor a person who follows or takes the place of another.

succinct brief and to the point.

succour (*formal*) *verb* to help, to aid. *noun* help, aid.

succulent 1 juicy, good to eat. 2 (of a plant) thick and fleshy.

succumb 1 to give way under pressure. 2 to die.

suck 1 to take into the mouth by breathing inwards. 2 to move something, such as a sweet, about in your mouth without chewing it.

sucker 1 a part of an animal which can stick on to a surface. 2 a shoot of a plant from a root or from the base stem. 3 a person who is easily cheated.

suckle (of a mammal) to feed (its young) with milk from the breast.

suction the drawing away of a gas or a liquid, either to let in another substance or to make two surfaces stick together under the pressure of the air outside.

sudden quick, not expected.

suds a froth of soapy water.

sue to take (a person) to law, for example to get back property, money etc.

suede a kind of soft leather with a dull surface.

suet a kind of hard animal fat used in cooking.

suffer to feel great pain, sorrow etc.

suffering feeling pain, distress, sorrow.

suffice to be enough for something, to be adequate.

sufficient enough, as much as is needed.

suffix a syllable or letter added to the end of a word to change its meaning, for example badly.

suffocate to choke by making the breathing difficult or impossible; to find difficulty in breathing; to die from this.

suffocation the act of suffocating; being suffocated.

suffragette a woman who fought for women's rights to vote in Britain in the early 20th century.

sugar a sweet substance made from sugar canes or sugar beet.

sugar beet a kind of plant from whose roots beet sugar is made.

sugar cane a kind of tropical grass plant whose stems produce sugar.

suggest to say what might be done, to hint.

suggestion something suggested; a plan, a proposal.

suicide the act of killing yourself; a person who does this.

suit *noun* a set of clothes, for example a jacket with trousers or skirt.
verb to be good or right for, to fit.

suitable correct, just right for something.

suitcase a container with a handle and stiffened sides for carrying clothes and other belongings.

suite a set of rooms or pieces of furniture.

suitor (old-fashioned) a man who wants to marry a woman.

sulk to show you are in a bad mood by not saying anything, to take the huff.

sulky in a bad mood, in a huff.

sullen being silent because you are feeling gloomy or bad-tempered.

sully (*formal*) to soil, make dirty.

sulphur a yellow mineral used in medicine and in industry.

sulphuric acid a very strong acid containing sulphur.

sultan a Muslim ruler.

sultana 1 the wife of a sultan. 2 a kind of seedless raisin.

sultry 1 (of weather) hot and airless. 2 (of a person) passionate.

sum 1 something to be worked out with numbers. 2 to add numbers and find the total.

summarise to make a summary of.

summary an outline, the main points of something.

summer the warmest season of the year, between spring and autumn.

summit the top, especially of a mountain.

summon to order (a person) to come to you or to a court of law etc.

summons an order to appear in court.

sumptuous rich, magnificent, splendid.

sun the heavenly body seen as a large ball of fire in the sky which gives the earth light and heat.

sundial an instrument that tells the time by means of the shadow cast by the sun.

sundry various, of different kinds.

sunflower a very tall plant with large yellow flowers and seeds which are used as food.

sunrise the time when the sun first appears in the morning.

sunset the time when the sun goes down at night.

sunspot a dark-looking patch on the surface of the sun.

sunstroke an illness caused by being too much in sunshine.

superb excellent, splendid.

supercilious showing contempt for others, scornful.

superficial 1 (showing) on the surface. 2 shallow, not deep.

superfluous more than what is needed.

superintend to control or manage an organisation.

superintendent 1 a person who is in charge of something. 2 a rank in the British police force.

superior 1 higher or more important than others. 2 better than others in some way.

supermarket a large self-service shop.

supernatural not natural, beyond the laws of nature, miraculous.

supernumerary (a person or thing) over and above the normal number (needed).

superpower an extremely powerful nation.

supersede to take the place of.

supersonic faster than the speed of sound.

superstition belief in magic and the supernatural.

superstitious having superstitions.

supervise to oversee and check the work of others.

supervision the act of supervising.

supervisor a person whose job it is to supervise something.

supine cowardly, lazy.

supper a meal eaten in the evening.

supplant to take the place or position of another.

supple easily bent or shaped, not stiff.

supplement *verb* to add to (something).
noun something added, for example an extra section to a newspaper, magazine or book.

supplication (*formal*) asking for something, especially in prayer.

supply 1 to provide the things that are needed. 2 a quantity or store of things.

support *verb* 1 to help (someone) by giving what is needed. 2 to provide, especially money, for. 3 to hold up.
noun 1 a person or thing that supports. 2 the action of supporting.

suppose to think; to believe something to be true.

supposed 1 thought to be (often wrongly). 2 **be supposed to** ought to; thought likely to.

supposition something supposed.

suppress 1 to put down, to stop from happening (for example a rebellion). 2 to hide (information etc.) from others.

supremacy being in a supreme position, usually in a country.

supreme greatest, highest, most important.

surcharge an extra amount added to the price of something.

sure certain; not having any doubt.

surety a person who agrees to be responsible for another person doing something such as appearing in court, paying a debt.

surf foam on waves breaking on the shore.

surface 1 the outside of something. 2 the area at the top of something (for example water).

surfboard a board for riding on waves near the shore.

surfeit *noun* excess of eating or drinking.
verb to overfill with food or drink.

surge to move or swell up, like water moving forward.

surgeon a doctor who carries out operations.

surgery 1 a place where doctors and dentists work. 2 the treating of patients by means of operations.

surgical of or used for surgery.

surly gruff, grumpy, bad-tempered.

surmise to suppose, believe something to be true.

surmount 1 to overcome (a difficulty). 2 to be on the top of (something).

surname the family name, your last name.

surpass to outdo, go beyond, be better than.

surplice a loose white piece of clothing worn over a gown, for example by a priest.

surplus over and above what is needed.

surprise *noun* 1 something you did not expect. 2 the feeling that this causes, a shock.
verb 1 to be a surprise to. 2 to attack without warning.

surrender to give in, especially to an enemy.

surreptitious done in an underhand or sly way.

surrogate a deputy, substitute.

surround to be, come or put all round.

surroundings the country round about something; the people and things round about you.

surveillance a close watch kept on (someone) by the police, for example.

survey *noun* [**sur**vey] 1 an inspection, a look around. 2 the measuring and mapping of land or buildings.
verb [sur**vey**] to make a survey of.

surveyor a person whose job it is to make surveys.

survival (the act of) surviving; something which survives.

survive 1 to go on living, especially after some disaster or illness. 2 to live longer than.

survivor a person who survives, especially after a disaster.

susceptible easily open to (pain, illness, love kindness etc.), sensitive to emotion.

suspect *verb* [sus**pect**] to believe, to have reason to think, especially something bad (about a person). *noun* [**sus**pect] a person who is suspected.

suspend 1 to hang (something) up. 2 to take a job away from (someone) for a time, usually because of something they have done wrong.

suspense a state of anxious doubt or uncertainty.

suspension the act of suspending; being suspended.

suspicion suspecting; being suspected.

suspicious suspecting; causing suspicion.

sustain 1 to keep in existence, support. 2 to keep (a person or thing) going. 3 to suffer (an injury).

sustenance what you need to stay alive, nourishment.

swab 1 a small piece of cotton wool etc. used to clean a wound or to take away liquid from the body for testing. 2 a kind of mop for washing the deck of a ship for example.

swaddle to cover closely in bandages, clothes, blankets etc.

swagger to walk about in a conceited way.

swallow 1 to take in, especially food and drink, through the throat. 2 a kind of small bird with pointed wings and a long forked tail.

swamp *noun* soft wet ground, a marsh. *verb* to overwhelm, flood with large numbers or amounts.

swan a large white water-bird with a long neck.

swansong the last piece of work by an artist, performer etc.

swap, swop (*informal*) to exchange.

swarm *noun* a large number of insects etc. moving together; a large crowd of people or animals.
verb to gather in a swarm; be crowded (with).

swarthy dark-skinned.

swashbuckling of or like daring, wild, bold men in sword-fighting adventure stories.

swastika a symbol like a cross with bent arms used by the Nazis.

swathe to wrap in bandages or cloth.

sway *verb* to move from side to side.
noun power, authority (over).

swear 1 to use bad language. 2 to promise faithfully, to take an oath.

swear-word a use of bad or angry language.

sweat liquid coming through the skin, usually when you are too hot.

sweater a jersey, pullover.

swede a kind of turnip.

sweep *verb* 1 to clean (something) with a brush. 2 to make a curving movement.
noun a person who cleans chimneys.

sweet *adjective* 1 pleasant to taste, like sugar. 2 kind, charming, nice.
noun 1 a small piece of sweet food such as chocolate, toffee etc. 2 a sweet dish you eat at the end of a meal, a pudding.

sweeten to make sweet or sweeter.

sweetheart a lover.

swell to become bigger.

swelling a part which swells, especially on the body.

swelter to feel uncomfortable because you are too hot.

swerve to move sideways quickly.

swift *adjective* very fast, very speedy.
noun a kind of small bird with long narrow wings.

swig to take deep drinks of (something), to drink greedily.

swill *verb* 1 to wash with large amounts of water. 2 to drink a lot.
noun food for pigs.

swim to move along in water by moving parts of the body.

swindle *verb* to cheat, trick.
noun an act of swindling.

swine 1 (*old-fashioned*) a pig; pigs. 2 (*informal*) a very nasty person.

swing *verb* to move round or in a curve from a fixed point, to sway.
noun a moving seat on ropes; a ride on a swing.

swipe 1 to hit (a cricket-ball for example) hard and recklessly. 2 (*informal*) to steal.

swirl *verb* to spin round.
noun a circular movement, especially in a liquid.

swish the sound made by a cane cutting through the air or curtains being pulled along a rail.

swiss roll a kind of thin sponge cake rolled up with jam or cream.

switch *noun* 1 a device for turning electrical things on and off. 2 a sudden change of direction or plan.
verb 1 to turn an electric appliance on or off. 2 to change direction or plan.

swivel to turn round around a central point.

swoon to faint.

swoop to fall or come down suddenly.

swop see **swap**.

sword a sharp-sided metal weapon like a long two-sided knife.

sycamore a kind of tree with large leaves.

sycophant a flatterer, a hanger-on to people considered superior.

syllable a part of a word which can be pronounced by itself.

syllabus the list of the main subjects or topics in a programme or teaching course.

symbol something which is a sign or stands for something else.

symbolic of or like a symbol; acting as a symbol.

symmetrical having two parts which are exactly the same on either side of a dividing line.

sympathetic showing or feeling sympathy.

sympathise to show or feel sympathy.

sympathy understanding of the feelings of others; an expression of this.

symphony a long piece of music for an orchestra.

symphony orchestra a large orchestra.

symptom a sign, especially of an illness.

synagogue a Jewish place of worship.

synchronise 1 to make (something) happen at the same time as (something else). 2 to make (clocks) show the same time.

syndicate a group of people or companies who gather together to advance or protect their common interest.

synonym a word which has the same (or almost the same) meaning as another.

synopsis a summary or short outline of the main points of something.

synthetic artificial, not natural.

syringe an instrument for sucking in and squirting out a liquid.

syrup sugar boiled in water to make a thick sweet sticky liquid.

system 1 a way of putting things in order. 2 a group of people or things working together.

systematic using a system, orderly.

T

tab a small flap or strip of cloth or paper, for example.

tabasco (sauce) trade name for a very hot pepper sauce.

tabby 1 a female cat. 2 a cat with greyish or brownish stripes.

table 1 a flat piece of furniture which stands on legs. 2 a list of numbers, facts etc. in order.

tableau a group of people standing still and dressed in costume to represent a scene, from history for example.

tablet 1 a pill of medicine. 2 a cake of soap etc. 3 a flat piece of stone or metal with words on it.

table tennis a game played with bats and a small ball on a table with a net across it.

tabloid a popular newspaper printed on small sheets.

taboo something forbidden by society.

tabulate to arrange (figures, for example) in a table or list.

tacit agreed or understood without being spoken.

taciturn saying little.

tack *noun* a small nail with a large head.
verb 1 to fasten things together by using long stitches. 2 to change the direction of a sailing-boat.

tackle *verb* 1 to try to do (something). 2 (in football) to try to take the ball from another player.
noun the things which are necessary to do something, for example **fishing-tackle**.

tact the ability to do and say the right thing, without offending people.

tactful showing tact, careful and polite in manner.

tactical of tactics, using careful planning.

tactics careful plans you use to win a battle or game, for example.

tactile 1 connected with the sense of touch. 2 able to be touched or felt.

tadpole a small black water creature which has a long tail and which becomes a frog or toad.

tag 1 a label. 2 a children's chasing game.

tail 1 the part of a creature that sticks out at the back. 2 the end part of something. 3 **tails** the side of a coin that does not have a head on it.

tailor a person who makes clothes such as suits and coats.

tainted spoiled, gone bad, especially by touching something bad.

take 1 to get hold of. 2 to carry away. 3 to swallow (medicine, for example).

takings money taken in business.

talcum (powder) smooth, usually perfumed, powder put on the skin.

tale a story.

talent something a person is able to do well, an ability.

talisman an object that is supposed to bring you luck.

talk to speak, to say something.

tall bigger in height than usual.

tally to match with exactly.

talon a claw of a bird of prey.

tambourine a kind of small drum with jingling metal disks round the rim.

tame not wild; friendly; not exciting.

tamper with to interfere with, often so as to damage slightly.

tan *noun* a light-brown colour, especially the colour of your skin after you have been in the sun a lot.
verb 1 to make (animal skins) into leather. 2 to make or become brown, especially of the skin in the sun.

tandem a two-seater bicycle.

tang a sharp biting taste or smell.

tangent a straight line which touches the edges of a curve or circle without crossing it.

tangerine a kind of small sweet orange.

tangible able to be felt by touch, clearly there, definite.

tangle a jumble, a muddle, especially of twisted threads etc.

tango a kind of slow ballroom dance from South America.

tank 1 a container to hold large amounts of liquid or gas. 2 a large vehicle which is used in war and is able to move over very rough country.

tankard a large beer mug.

tanker a ship or lorry which carries liquids such as petrol or oil.

tantalise to tease by offering something but not giving it.

tantamount to equal to, the same as.

tantrum a fit of bad temper.

tap 1 a knob or handle which is turned to allow liquids to flow. 2 a tiny knock.

tape 1 a narrow piece of cloth, often used to hold things together. 2 a long narrow strip of plastic material used for recording.

taper *noun* a thin piece of wax candle.
verb to become thin at one end.

tape-recorder a machine for making a copy of music or words and playing them back.

tapestry pictures or patterns in silk or cotton worked on heavy cloth.

tapioca a white starchy food made from a tropical plant, used in puddings etc.

tapir a kind of wild animal like a large pig, found in some tropical countries.

tar a thick black liquid, used in making roads for example.

tarantula a kind of large poisonous spider.

tardy slow, late.

target something at which you aim.

tariff 1 list of charges for goods or services. 2 tax on goods coming into or leaving a country.

tarmac a kind of road-surfacing made of tar and small stones; an area covered with this, especially a runway for aircraft.

tarnish to spoil the appearance of (metal, for example, by making it dull).

tarpaulin (a large sheet of) canvas made waterproof (by tar).

tarry to delay, act slowly.

tart *noun* a piece of pastry with jam, fruit etc. in it.
adjective sharp, sour to the taste.

tartan woollen cloth with a pattern of stripes and squares, often used in Scotland for making kilts, for example.

tartar 1 a deposit of saliva, calcium etc. that forms on the teeth. 2 *also* **cream of tartar** a kind of white powder used in baking.

task a piece of work which has to be done, a job.

tassel a hanging bunch of threads often used as a decoration.

taste *noun* the flavour of food or drink.
verb to try a little of (some food or drink).

tasteful showing good taste.

tasty nice to eat, pleasant-tasting.

tattered in rags, in tatters.

tatters rags, shreds of cloth.

tattoo *verb* to make a picture etc. on (the skin) by pricking and putting in dye.
noun 1 a picture etc. on the skin made by tattooing. 2 a military display with music and marching, often at night. 3 the beating of drums.

taunt to annoy by mocking.

taut stretched very tight.

tautology saying the same thing twice over, using different words.

tavern old-fashioned word for a public house or inn.

tawdry showy but of little value, over-ornamented.

tawny (of) an orange-brown colour.

tax money which has to be paid to the government by the people.

taxi *noun* a car that can be hired by paying the driver.
verb (of an aeroplane) to move along the ground before take-off or after landing.

taxidermist a person skilled in preparing and mounting the skins of dead animals to make them lifelike.

tea 1 a hot drink made from the dried leaves of a bush grown in eastern countries. 2 an afternoon meal at which this is drunk.

teach to help to learn, to give lessons to.

teak a kind of very hard, light-brown wood from a tree grown in some hot countries.

teal a kind of wild duck.

team 1 a number of people who work or play together. 2 a number of animals working together.

tear [teer] a drop of water from the eyes.

tear [tare] to pull apart, to rip.

tease to make fun of.

technical belonging to a particular art or science.

technician a person skilled in the practical application of an art or science.

technique the exact method of doing something.

technology the science of practical or industrial methods.

tedious boring, wearisome.

tee (in golf) 1 a cleared space from which the players take their first shot at each hole. 2 a small piece of wood or plastic on which the ball is placed when taking the first shot at each hole.

teem 1 to be very full of. 2 (of rain) to fall very heavily.

teenager a person aged between thirteen and nineteen years old.

teethe (of a baby) to grow teeth.

teetotal never taking alcoholic drink.

telephone a way of carrying the sound of someone's voice by wire, using electricity.

telescope an instrument which makes far away things look bigger.

television a machine on which pictures are seen that are sent by radio waves.

tell to give news or information in words, to say.

teller 1 a person who gives out and receives money in a bank. 2 a person who counts votes.

temper 1 the state of the mind, the mood you are in. 2 when you are very angry or annoyed about something.

temperament a person's natural state of mind.

temperance moderation, control, especially of eating and drinking; never drinking alcohol.

temperate moderate, mild, not extreme.

temperature 1 the amount of warmth or cold. 2 a body temperature higher than it should be.

tempest a violent storm.

tempestuous 1 (of weather) wild, stormy. 2 (of a person) violent.

temple 1 a large church in some religions. 2 the part of the head between the forehead and the ear.

tempo 1 the speed at which music is performed. 2 the rate at which something happens or is done.

temporary lasting only for a short time.

tempt to persuade others to try to do what they really do not wish to do or ought not to do.

tenable able to be held against attack, for example a position, fortress or an argument.

tenacious 1 gripping tightly. 2 stubborn.

tenant a person who rents property.

tend 1 to look after. 2 to be likely (to).

tendency a slight leaning towards something.

tender *adjective* 1 gentle, kind, showing love. 2 not tough, soft. 3 feeling painful.
noun 1 an offer to do something for an agreed payment. 2 a small boat which helps a larger one. 3 a truck for coal and water behind a steam railway engine.

tendon a strong cord which joins muscle to bone.

tendril the part of some plants which curls round something else; a long thin curl of hair.

tennis a game played by two or four people who use rackets to hit a ball over a net.

tenor a man able to sing high notes.

tense *adjective* 1 nervous, worried. 2 stretched tightly.
noun the form a verb takes to show the time when something happens.

tension being tense.

tent a waterproof shelter held up by poles and ropes, used when you are camping.

tentacle a long thin feeler of an animal, for example of an octopus.

tentative done in a hesitant way.

tenuous thin, slender, very weak.

tepid slightly warm.

term 1 a part of the school or college year. 2 a period of time.

terminal 1 a building at an airport where passengers arrive and depart. 2 a place in a town where you can take a bus to an airport. 3 a part of a computer which receives and gives information.

terminate to come or bring to an end.

terminology the specialised names or terms used in a subject.

terminus the place where a railway or bus route ends.

tern a kind of small gull-like sea-bird.

terrace 1 a flat raised piece of ground. 2 a row of houses joined together.

terrapin a kind of small freshwater turtle.

terrestrial 1 of the earth (rather than from Outer Space). 2 living on the ground (rather than in water).

terrible very bad.

terrier a kind of small dog.

terrific 1 very large (and frightening). 2 very good, excellent.

terrify to frighten badly, to fill with fear.

terrine an earthenware dish containing pâté for example; the pâté etc. it contains.

territory a large area of land.

terror great fear, great fright.

tertiary of the third rank or stage, next after secondary.

test to try out, for example by looking at carefully, to examine.

testament 1 a will. 2 one of the two main divisions of the Bible (**Old Testament, New Testament**).

testify to state in a serious way, especially in court.

testimonial 1 a written description of a person's character or achievements. 2 an expression of thanks or respect for something someone has done.

testimony a statement that something is true.

tether to fasten (an animal) by means of a rope etc.

text 1 the actual words of a speech etc. 2 the main part of a book, not the notes, pictures etc.

textbook a special book for studying a subject.

textiles woven materials, cloth.

texture the way something is put together or feels to the touch.

thank to say that you are pleased about something that someone has given to you or done for you.

thatch roof covering made of straw or reeds.

thaw warmer weather which melts snow and ice.

theatre 1 a building where plays are acted, for example. 2 a room in a hospital where operations take place.

theft stealing, robbing.

theme 1 a subject of which a person thinks, writes or speaks. 2 a short tune on which others are based.

theology the study of God and religion.

theorem (especially in mathematics) a statement proved by reasoning.

theoretical concerned with theory rather than practice of a subject or skill.

theory something thought out but not yet proved in practice; the ideas of a subject.

thermal connected with heat, giving or causing heat.

thermometer an instrument that measures heat and cold.

Thermos trade name for a kind of container for keeping things hot or cold.

thermostat a device for keeping temperature, for example in a room, at the same level automatically.

thesaurus a list of words grouped according to their sense or meaning.

thick 1 wide, not thin, deep. 2 with a lot of things close together. 3 (of a liquid) not flowing easily.

thicket a group of closely-planted trees or bushes.

thief a person who steals.

thigh the part of the leg between the hip and the knee.

thimble a hard covering to protect the finger when you are sewing.

thin 1 narrow; not fat. 2 (of a liquid) flowing easily.

thing an object; a subject, idea; a happening.

think to use the mind; to believe.

third *adjective* coming after the second. *noun* one of three equal parts.

thirst the feeling of needing or wanting to drink.

thirsty feeling thirst.

thistle a wild plant with prickly leaves and purple flowers.

thong a narrow strip of leather, used for fastening, for example.

thorn a prickle or point on a plant stem.

thorough 1 taking great care that everything is done. 2 complete.

thoroughbred (especially of a horse) of pure breed.

thoroughfare a public road open at both ends.

thought thinking; an idea in the mind.

thrash to beat, especially with a stick or whip.

thrashing a beating.

thread a very thin line of material used in sewing, knitting or weaving.

threat saying or showing that you mean to harm or punish someone.

threaten to make threats to, to be a threat to.

thresh to separate (grain) from its plant by beating.

threshold a plank or stone slab under a doorway; an entrance; a beginning.

thrift care in using money and other things.

thrifty showing thrift, not wasting anything.

thrill a feeling of excitement.

thrilling very exciting.

thrive to grow well and healthily; to do well and succeed.

throat the front part of the neck, containing the tubes through which you swallow and breathe.

throb a strong steady beat.

throne a special chair, for example for a king or queen.

throng *noun* a crowd.
verb to gather in large numbers.

throttle *verb* to choke, strangle.
noun the part of an engine which controls the flow of fuel.

through 1 from one side to the other; from one end to the other. 2 because of.

throughout all through; in all parts of.

throw to make (something) move through the air from your hand.

thrush a kind of brown songbird with a spotted breast.

thrust *verb* to push hard.
noun the lifting power of an engine, for example of a rocket.

thud the noise of something falling or bumping heavily.

thug a violent unfeeling person, especially a criminal.

thumb the shortest and thickest finger of the hand.

thump 1 a heavy blow, usually struck with the fist. 2 a dull noise made by this.

thunder the crash of noise that follows lightning.

thwart to upset or stop (someone's plans).

thyme a kind of herb used in cooking.

tiara a semi-circular jewelled head-dress.

tic an uncontrolled movement of the muscles, especially round the face.

tick 1 a mark ✓ to show for example that something has been checked. 2 the small regular sound made by a clock or watch.

ticket a card or paper allowing you to go into a place or to travel by train, plane or bus.

tickle to touch (someone) lightly and so to make them laugh.

ticklish 1 easily made to laugh when tickled. 2 difficult, needing careful handling.

tidal concerned with the tides.

tide the rising and falling of the sea twice each day.

tidings information, news.

tidy neat and in good order, properly arranged.

tie *noun* a narrow piece of cloth worn round the neck.
verb 1 to fasten, for example by making a knot. 2 to be equal in a competition or test.

tiff a slight quarrel.

tiger a fierce Asian wild animal with black stripes on a yellow skin.

tight fixed or fitting closely together.

tightrope a tightly-stretched rope on which acrobats perform.

tights a close-fitting garment covering the feet, legs and lower part of the body.

tile a flat piece of baked clay, plastic etc. used to cover roofs, floors, walls etc.

till *preposition, conjunction* until.
noun a drawer for holding money in a shop.
verb to work (the land) to produce crops.

tiller the handle of a boat's rudder.

tilt to lean to one side.

timber wood for making things.

time 1 the passing of minutes, hours, days, months, years. 2 a moment in this or a part of it.

timetable 1 a list of activities arranged by time. 2 a list of times of departure or arrival of trains, buses etc.

timid easily frightened, likely to be afraid, shy.

timorous easily frightened.

timpani kettledrums.

tin 1 a shiny white metal. 2 a metal can.

tinder a dry substance which a spark will set on fire.

tinge to colour slightly.

tingle a prickly feeling often caused by cold, fear or excitement.

tinker a person who travels around and lives by mending pots and pans.

tinkle a sound like that of a small bell.

tinsel glittering material used for decoration.

tint a shade of colour.

tiny very, very small.

tip *noun* the pointed end of something. *verb* 1 to upset (something). 2 to give money for something done.

tipsy slightly drunk.

tiptoe to walk on your toes.

tirade a stream of angry words.

tire to become tired.

tired 1 feeling that your body is weak, usually because you have done a lot, needing to rest. 2 bored.

tiresome annoying, boring.

tissue 1 a piece of soft paper for wiping. 2 very thin paper used for wrapping.

titanic gigantic, colossal.

titbit 1 something small which is good to eat. 2 an interesting piece of news.

titivate to smarten up your appearance.

title 1 the name of a book, a play, a piece of music etc. 2 the first part of a name which shows the person's rank, for example **Lord** Nelson.

titter to laugh quietly.

toad an animal like a large frog with a rough skin.

toadstool a kind of fungus shaped like a mushroom, many are poisonous.

toast bread which has been made crisp and brown by heat.

tobacco a plant from which the leaves are taken and used for smoking.

toboggan a long narrow sledge for use on snow.

today this day.

toddle to walk with short uncertain steps, like a baby.

toddler a very young child who is just beginning to walk.

toe one of the five end parts of the foot.

toffee a sticky sweet made from sugar and butter.

toil to work hard.

toilet 1 a large bowl used for waste matter from the body. 2 a room with a toilet.

toiletries articles, for example soap, talcum powder, toothpaste, used in washing and dressing.

toilet water a kind of light perfume.

token 1 something which stands as a symbol for something else. 2 a sign.

tolerable 1 able to be endured. 2 fairly good.

tolerance being tolerant.

tolerant able to accept the views, beliefs and behaviour of others.

tolerate to allow (something) to happen or to be done, to put up with (a person or thing).

toll *noun* a payment made for the use of a bridge or road.
verb (of a heavy bell) to ring slowly.

tomahawk a Red Indian war axe.

tomato a soft round red fruit, often eaten in salads.

tomb a grave.

tomorrow the day after today.

tomtom a kind of long narrow drum played with the hands.

ton a large measure of weight, in Britain equal to 2240 pounds.

tone 1 the sound of the voice used in speaking or singing; the sound of a musical instrument. 2 a shade of colour.

tongs an instrument for grasping and picking up objects.

tongue the thick soft part inside the mouth used for tasting, eating and speaking.

tonic a medicine to make you stronger and livelier.

tonight this night.

tonne a large measure of weight, equal to 1000 kilograms.

tonsils two small lumps at the back of the mouth.

tonsillitis an illness causing painful tonsils.

tool an instrument used to help you to do some work.

toot the sound of a horn or trumpet.

tooth one of the bone-like parts growing out of the jaw, used for biting and chewing.

toothache a pain in a tooth.

top 1 the highest part, above all others. 2 a covering or lid for something, for example a bottle. 3 a toy which spins.

topic something you write or talk about.

topical concerned with what is going on at the present time.

topography the detailed description of an area including its natural and man-made features.

topple to make or become unsteady and fall over.

topsy-turvy upside down; in confusion.

torch 1 an electric light which can be carried about. 2 a burning stick carried to give light.

torment *noun* [**tor**ment] great pain and suffering.
verb [tor**ment**] to cause pain to someone, to tease, to annoy.

tornado a whirlwind, a violent and damaging storm.

torpedo a weapon which can be fired through water, usually against ships.

torpid dull, inactive, sluggish.

torpor the state of being torpid.

torrent 1 a swiftly-rushing stream. 2 a heavy downpour of rain.

torrid very hot, intense.

tortoise a slow-moving animal with a hard curved shell.

tortuous twisting, winding.

torture to cause great pain to someone on purpose.

toss to throw into the air.

total everything added together, the whole.

totter to move unsteadily, to stagger.

touch 1 to be as close as possible to something. 2 to feel gently with the hand or another part of the body.

touching very moving, pitiful.

touchy easily offended.

tough hard, strong; not easy to bite or cut.

tour a journey in which you visit a number of places.

tourist a person who travels for pleasure.

tournament 1 a series of sporting competitions to find an outright winner. 2 (long ago) a fighting competition between knights on horseback.

tourniquet a very tight bandage to stop the flow of blood from a wound.

tow to pull (something) along using a rope or chain, for example a car or a boat.

towards in the direction of.

towel a piece of cloth for drying the body etc.

tower a tall narrow building or part of a building.

town a large number of buildings grouped together, smaller than a city but bigger than a village.

toxic poisonous; caused by poison.

toy something you play with.

trace *noun* a very small amount left behind.
verb 1 to copy exactly by following the lines of a drawing etc. through transparent paper. 2 to find after searching and following clues.

track 1 a narrow path. 2 a place specially prepared for races. 3 the metal lines on which a train runs. 4 a mark left by a foot or a tyre, for example.

track suit loose trousers and top sometimes worn over sports clothes.

tract 1 a large area of land. 2 a short book or pamphlet.

tractable easily led or controlled.

tractor a strong machine used for towing heavy loads, used especially on a farm.

trade 1 buying and selling. 2 a job, especially one in which you use your hands.

tradition handing down of the customs, beliefs etc. of a country or group to those who come after.

traditional of the traditions of a people.

traffic movement of vehicles and people.

tragedy 1 something very sad that happens. 2 a serious play with a sad ending.

tragic of tragedy; very sad, disastrous.

trail 1 to follow a track or the scent of (an animal). 2 to drag or be dragged behind.

trailer 1 a vehicle pulled by a car or lorry. 2 a short piece of film to create interest in the full version.

train *noun* 1 railway coaches joined to an engine. 2 part of a dress which trails on the ground.
verb to prepare (yourself or someone else) for a job or a sport, for example.

trainer 1 a person who trains. 2 a kind of shoe often used for sports.

trait an aspect of a person's character, appearance or behaviour that marks them out as different.

traitor a person who tells secret things to the enemy and betrays his country.

trajectory the path up and then down followed by an object which is thrown into the air or fired from a gun, for example.

tramp *noun* a person with no home who wanders about begging.
verb to walk heavily.

trample to walk heavily on, often doing damage.

trampoline a large frame with springs covered with material on which you can bounce up and down.

trance a state like sleep, though you are awake.

tranquil peaceful.

tranquilliser a drug which makes you feel calmer.

transaction a piece of business which is done.

transcend 1 to rise above, surpass. 2 to be beyond understanding.

transcendent excellent, above all in beauty, goodness etc.

transcendental going beyond experience and knowledge.

transfer *verb* [trans**fer**] 1 to move to another place. 2 to hand over to another person.
noun [**trans**fer] 1 the act of transferring or being transferred. 2 a picture that can be transferred from one surface to another.

transfix 1 to pierce through. 2 to hold (a person) still by looking at them.

transform to change completely.

transformation being transformed; the act of transforming.

transformer a machine for changing one electric current into another.

transfusion a transfer of the blood of one person into the body of another.

transient quickly passing away, not lasting long.

transit carrying or moving from place to place.

transition a change from one state of being to another.

transitory lasting only a short time.

translate to change from one language into another.

translation the act of translating; something translated.

translucent letting some light pass through.

transmission the act of sending messages etc.; a radio or television broadcast.

transmit to send out (messages, radio signals etc.).

transmitter a device that sends out radio or television signals for broadcasting.

transmute to change (something) from one form into another.

transparent able to be seen through.

transpire to happen, take place.

transplant to remove from one place and fix in another.

transport *verb* [trans**port**] to move from place to place.
noun [**trans**port] the act of transporting; ways of doing this.

transverse situated, arranged or moving in a crosswise direction.

trap *noun* a device for catching animals, birds etc.
verb to catch in a clever way.

trapeze a short bar suspended on ropes from a roof on which acrobats perform.

trapper a person who traps wild animals.

trash worthless things, rubbish.

travel to move from one place to another.

travesty a very bad copy of the real thing.

trawler a fishing boat which catches fish by dragging a large net in the sea.

tray a flat piece of wood, plastic or metal for carrying small things.

treacherous disloyal, likely to betray.

treachery being treacherous.

treacle a dark sweet sticky liquid made from sugar.

tread *verb* to walk with a heavy step.
noun 1 a heavy step or its sound. 2 the part of a staircase on which you put your feet.

treason the crime of betraying your country.

treasure a thing or a number of things of great value.

treasurer a person who looks after the money which belongs to a group of people.

treasury the government department which controls the country's money.

treat *verb* 1 to behave or act towards. 2 to try to cure (a person of an illness).
noun something specially pleasant you are given.

treatment 1 a way of curing an illness. 2 a way of behaving towards someone.

treaty an agreement between countries.

treble *adjective* three times as much or as many.
noun the highest part in music; a person who sings this, especially a child.
verb to make or become three times as many or as large.

tree a large plant with a trunk, branches and leaves.

trek 1 a long journey of people from one land to another. 2 a long difficult journey.

trellis a screen made out of criss-crossing wood or metal slats, especially for plants to climb on.

tremble to shiver, to shake with excitement, fear or cold.

tremendous immense, huge, great; very good.

tremor a shaking, vibration.

tremulous quivering, nervous.

trench a ditch dug in the earth for a special purpose.

trend (a shift in) a general direction.

trepidation fear, anxiety.

trespass to go into private places without permission.

trestle a wooden board with two pairs of legs; two are used to support a table-top etc.

trial 1 a test. 2 an examination before a judge to decide whether or not a person is guilty.

triangle 1 a flat shape with three straight sides and three corners, like this △. 2 a metal musical instrument of this shape, played by striking it with a steel rod.

tribal of or belonging to a tribe.

tribe a group of people ruled by one chief.

tribulation great misery arising from trouble.

tribunal a kind of court of justice.

tributary a river or stream which flows into a larger one.

tribute 1 public praise or thanks given to someone. 2 a tax paid by one country to another.

trick *verb* to cheat.
noun something clever done either to cheat or to amuse people.

trickery cheating.

trickle a very small flow of a liquid.

tricky difficult to do.

tricolour a flag with three colours arranged in equal separate bands.

tricycle a cycle with three wheels.

triennial happening once every three years.

trifle 1 a small thing of no importance. 2 a kind of dessert made of cake, fruit, cream etc.

trifling of little importance or worth.

trigger a small lever which is pulled to fire a gun.

trill *verb* to sing or whistle like a bird.
noun 1 a trilled sound. 2 (in music) two notes repeated over and over again.

trilogy a group of three connected books or films for example.

trim *adjective* tidy, neat.
verb to cut and make tidy.

trinket a small cheap ornament or piece of jewellery.

trio a group of three people doing something together, for example singing or playing instruments.

trip *noun* a journey, especially one for pleasure.
verb to stumble and fall.

tripe 1 food made from a cow's stomach. 2 (*informal*) nonsense.

triplet one of three babies born at the same time to the same mother.

triplicate *verb* to make (something) in three identical parts.
adjective consisting of three identical parts.

tripod a three-legged stand, for example for a camera.

triptych a picture or carving with three sides which can fold into each other.

trite (of a saying etc.) used so often that it has lost its meaning.

triumph a great victory or success.

triumphant victorious, successful.

trivial of small value or importance.

trolley 1 a small light cart pushed by hand. 2 a small table on wheels for serving food.

trombone a long brass musical instrument with a sliding tube which you play by blowing.

troop a group of people, for example soldiers.

troops soldiers.

trophy something kept or awarded as a sign of victory, for example in a competition.

tropical in the tropics; of or like the tropics, very hot.

tropics the part of the world near the equator.

trot to run gently with short steps.

trouble *noun* a worry, a problem, a difficulty.
verb to cause worry or annoyance to.

trough a long narrow open feeding container for animals.

trounce to beat thoroughly.

troupe a group of actors or performers.

trousers a piece of clothing for the legs and the lower part of the body.

trousseau a bride's outfit of clothes.

trout a kind of fish that lives in fresh water, used as food.

trowel 1 garden tool like a small spade. 2 a small flat-bladed tool for spreading cement for example.

truant a person who stays away from school without permission.

truce an agreement to stop fighting for a time.

truck a vehicle for carrying heavy loads.

truculent aggressive, fond of fighting.

trudge to walk slowly and heavily as you do when you are tired.

true correct, accurate, honest.

truffle 1 an edible fungus which is highly valued in cooking. 2 a kind of soft sweet, often made with chocolate and rum.

trump 1 a playing card of a suit chosen to have a higher value than the others. 2 **turn up trumps** to behave unexpectedly in a very helpful way.

trumpet a brass musical instrument which you play by blowing.

truncheon a short thick stick used by a policeman.

trundle to roll or wheel along noisily and slowly.

trunk 1 the thick stem of a tree. 2 a large box for carrying things, especially on a journey. 3 an elephant's long nose. 4 the body (without the head, arms and legs).

trunks very short trousers worn by men and boys for swimming etc.

trust *verb* 1 to believe that someone is honest and can be relied on. 2 to believe to be true.
noun 1 the feeling that you can trust a person or thing. 2 reponsibility, being trusted to look after something.

trustworthy able to be trusted, reliable, honest.

truth what is true.

try 1 to make an effort to do something. 2 to test.

tub a large round container with an open top.

tuba a large low-pitched musical instrument which you play by blowing.

tubby fat and round.

tube 1 a thin pipe. 2 a soft metal or plastic container from which things such as toothpaste can be squeezed. 3 an underground railway, especially in London.

tubular in the form of a tube.

tuck to push or put (something) into or under something.

tuft a small bunch of grass, hair, feathers etc.

tug *verb* to pull hard and sharply. *noun* 1 the act of tugging. 2 a small powerful boat used to pull other boats.

tuition instruction given to an individual or a small group.

tulip a bell-shaped spring flower grown from a bulb.

tumble to fall heavily.

tumbler a flat-bottomed drinking glass.

tumour a swelling which can be the sign of a serious illness.

tumult an uproar, riot.

tumultuous noisy, rowdy, excited.

tuna a very large fish found in warm seas, used as food.

tundra the vast level Arctic region where the subsoil is permanently frozen.

tune a set of pleasant musical notes.

tunic a kind of close-fitting jacket worn by soldiers and policemen, for example.

tunnel a long covered passageway through hills or under rivers.

turban a head-covering made from a long strip of material wound in a special way round the head.

turbid (of water) muddy, not clear.

turbine an engine driven by jets of steam, gas or water.

turbot a kind of flat sea-fish, used as food.

turbulence 1 being turbulent. 2 uneven air currents (such as disturb the flight of an aircraft).

turbulent in disorder, disturbed; causing disorder.

tureen a large deep dish for holding soup.

turf short grass with its roots and the earth in which it grows.

turgid swollen, enlarged; (of writing etc.) pompous, dull.

turkey a large bird used as food.

turmoil uproar, riot, disturbance.

turn *verb* 1 to face a different way; to move round. 2 to change. *noun* 1 the act of turning. 2 a chance to do something after other people, for example in a game.

turnip a root vegetable with white or yellowish flesh.

turnover 1 all the money taken in by a company over a certain time. 2 a small pastry made of a round of dough folded over fruit etc.

turnstile a revolving barrier allowing one person to pass through at a time.

turpentine a kind of oil used for thinning paint or for cleaning it off something.

turquoise 1 a greenish-blue precious stone. 2 the colour of this.

turret a small tower on a building, aeroplane etc.

turtle an animal with a hard curved shell which lives mainly in the sea.

tusk a long pointed tooth found in some animals such as an elephant or a walrus.

tussle a struggle, a scuffle.

tutor a teacher, especially one who teaches one person or a small group.

twang a sound like that of a plucked string, for example of a guitar.

tweak to pinch with a sudden twist, for example someone's nose.

tweed a rough woollen cloth, used for suits and heavy coats, for example.

tweezers a small tool for getting hold of things.

twice two times.

twiddle to turn or twist (knobs, for example) round and round quickly.

twig a very small branch of a tree.

twilight dim light just after sunset.

twill a kind of hard-wearing cloth.

twin one of two babies born at the same time to the same mother.

twine *noun* thin strong string. *verb* to wind or twist (around something).

twinge a slight sharp pain.

twinkle to shine with small bright flashes.

twirl to twist round, to spin quickly.

twist 1 to wind things round each other. 2 to turn (a bottle cap for example).

twitch to move suddenly and quickly without meaning to.

twitter chirping sounds, like those made by birds.

type *noun* a special sort, a kind. *verb* to tap keys on a typewriter or keyboard in order to print words.

typewriter a machine with a keyboard used to print words on paper.

typhoid (fever) a serious infectious disease, often caused by bad food or water.

typhoon a great storm.

typical able to be used as an example of something, usual.

typist a person who is able to write with a typewriter.

tyrannical of or like a tyrant.

tyranny the rule of a tyrant; ruling like a tyrant.

tyrant a person who rules cruelly and unjustly.

tyre the rubber round the outside of a wheel, often filled with air.

U

ubiquitous being or seeming to be in a number of different places at the same time, being everywhere.

udder a baglike part of a cow etc. from which it gives milk.

ugly not nice to look at.

ulcer an open sore.

ulcerated covered with ulcers or open sores.

ulterior secret, hidden, especially for bad reasons.

ultimate final, last.

ultimatum a final demand or offer.

ultra(-) extremely, excessively; beyond, on the other side of.

ultraviolet (of light) beyond the purple end of the spectrum, involving radiation.

umbilical cord a tube which connects a baby or baby animal to its mother before birth.

umbrage: take umbrage (at) to take offence (at).

umbrella a covering you hold over your head to keep off the rain.

umpire the person who makes sure that a game is played fairly, a referee.

umpteen *(informal)* a lot of, a great many.

unabridged complete, not shortened.

unanimity being unanimous.

unanimous with the agreement of all.

unassailable that cannot be attacked or overcome.

unassuming shy, modest, not wanting to be noticed.

unavailing achieving nothing, useless.

unaware of not knowing about.

unawares without knowing, without meaning to.

unbend to behave less stiffly, in a more natural way.

unbending not changing your views, severe, strict.

unbridled not under control, wild.

uncanny mysterious, strange, supernatural.

unceremonious(ly) (done) without ceremony; (done) in an abrupt and unfeeling way.

uncertain not certain, doubtful; not secure or reliable.

uncertainty being uncertain.

uncivil ill-mannered, impolite.

uncle the brother of a father or mother; an aunt's husband.

uncommon unusual.

uncompromising firm, stubborn, not willing to give in.

unconditional without any conditions set in advance.

unconscious not conscious; not knowing what is happening.

unconventional (acting) in an unusual way, against the normal standards.

uncouth clumsy, awkward, rude.

uncover to take the lid or covering off (something); to reveal.

uncritical easily accepting what you are told or what is suggested to you, unquestioning.

unctuous trying to win (someone's) favour by excessive flattery.

undaunted fearless, brave, bold.

undecided hesitating, doubtful, uncertain.

undeniable certain, clear, obviously true.

under below, lower than.

undercarriage the landing gear, wheels etc. of an aircraft.

undercoat a layer of paint which is put under the final coat.

undercover acting secretly, spying on or investigating someone while appearing to be a normal part of the scene.

undercurrent 1 a current under the surface of the water. 2 something going on secretly, under the surface.

undercut to charge less than (a competitor) for goods or services.

undergo to suffer, experience.

underground *adjective, adverb* under the earth.
noun a railway which goes under the ground.

undergrowth the thick plants or grasses which grow under or around trees.

underhand secret, sly, deceitful.

underlie to be underneath, be the basis of.

underline to draw a line under; to emphasise, make to stand out.

undermanned with not enough people to get jobs done properly.

undermine to weaken bit by bit.

underneath below.

underpass a road or path which goes under another road or railway.

underpin to support firmly (from below).

underprivileged not enjoying the same benefits or rights as others in your society.

underrate to think less of than you should.

undersigned (the name of a person) whose signature is placed at the foot of a document.

understand to know what something means.

understanding *noun* 1 the ability to understand (well). 2 an agreement.
adjective able to understand (especially the problems of others).

understudy an actor ready to take on the part of another actor in an emergency.

undertake to agree or promise to do something.

undertaker a person whose job it is to arrange funerals.

undertow the current below the surface of the sea that moves in the opposite direction to the one on the top.

underwear clothes worn next to the skin under other clothes.

undeterred not held back (from doing something).

undifferentiated all part of a general group, not separated into different parts.

undisciplined unruly, wild in behaviour.

undo 1 to untie. 2 to destroy the results of.

undoubted certain, undeniable.

undue greater than is necessary, not welcome or needed.

undulating (of land) going up and down like waves.

unduly more than necessary, excessive.

unearth 1 to dig up. 2 to discover (after a long search).

unearthly strange, uncanny, not belonging to this world.

uneasy anxious, worried, disturbed in mind.

unemployed having no paid work.

unequalled better than any other.

unequivocal clear, unmistakable, plain.

unerring true, without mistakes.

unethical using dishonest practices, in business for example.

uneven 1 not level or smooth. 2 not of the same quality.

unexpected not expected, surprising.

unfair not fair, unjust.

unfamiliar not familiar, strange.

unfashionable not fashionable, out of date.

unfeeling unkind, unsympathetic.

unfold to open out (something folded).

unfortunate having bad luck.

ungainly clumsy, awkward in manner.

unguarded without taking proper care, especially about what you say.

unhappy not happy, miserable.

unhinged not sane, unbalanced.

unicorn an imaginary animal like a horse, with one horn.

uniform special clothing worn by people of the same group, such as policemen, soldiers and nurses.

unify to make into one.

unilateral (of a decision in a dispute, for example) decided by one side acting without taking account of the other.

unimpeachable above and beyond criticism, totally honest.

union a joining together.

unique being the only one of its kind.

unisex (of clothes, shops for example) designed to be used by either sex.

unison 1 the singing or playing of the same note(s). 2 complete agreement.

unit 1 one complete thing or set. 2 an amount used as a measurement. 3 a number under ten. 4 a separate part which helps to make up a whole.

unite to join together into one.

unity 1 formed of parts that make up a whole. 2 harmony, good relations between people.

universal of or belonging to all the people or places in the world.

universe all the suns and planets in space.

university a place where people may go to learn after leaving school.

unjust not fair.

unkempt untidy.

unleash 1 to let (a dog) free from a leash. 2 to release from control.

unless if not; except if.

unlikely not likely, not expected.

unlimited 1 very great in number or quantity. 2 not restricted.

unload to take something off (a lorry, for example).

unlock to open with a key.

unmask 1 to remove a mask from. 2 to expose the true character of (someone).

unmistakable plain, clear, obvious.

unmitigated not excused or lessened, total, absolute.

unmoved not affected by feelings, especially pity.

unnecessary not needed; more than is needed.

unnerve to make (someone) frightened.

unobtrusive not easily noticed, shy, modest.

unpack to take things out of a case or container.

unparalleled without an equal.

unperturbed calm, not excited.

unpopular not well liked by others or by the public.

unpretentious not trying to seem rich or important.

unquestionable certain, evident, obvious, not to be doubted.

unquestioning done without asking any questions.

unravel 1 to separate the strands of (wool, string etc.). 2 to solve (a mystery, a problem).

unreliable not reliable, not able to be trusted.

unremitting going on all the time, never relaxing.

unrest disturbance in a country or in a large group of people.

unruffled calm, not upset.

unruly out of control, badly behaved.

unsavoury wicked, unpleasant.

unscathed unhurt, not harmed.

unscrupulous without regard to the rules or to the needs of others, especially in business.

unseemly not proper, in bad taste.

unsettle to disturb, upset.

unsightly not nice to look at, ugly.

unsociable not friendly, not liking the company of others.

unsound 1 unhealthy, rotten. 2 **of unsound mind** mad. 3 (of arguments etc.) not based on fact or truth.

unsparing 1 giving generously. 2 showing no mercy.

unspeakable very bad, objectionable.

unstable not settled in mind, not having control of your emotions.

unstuck 1 no longer stuck to something else. 2 (of plans) that have come to grief, collapsed.

unsubstantiated not supported by evidence.

unthinkable not able to be considered.

untidy not tidy, not neat in appearance.

untie to loosen (a knot in string, for example).

untimely 1 (of death, for example) happening before it should, premature. 2 happening at an unsuitable time.

untold so large that it cannot be counted.

untoward unexpected and unlucky.

untruth a lie; something which is not true.

unusual not usual, strange.

unvarnished (of a statement etc.) plain and straightforward.

unveil show publicly, reveal.

unwarranted not authorised, unjustified.

unwell ill.

unwieldy awkward to carry or hold.

unwind 1 to loosen, unroll. 2 to relax.

unyielding not giving in, hard, firm.

up to a higher place.

upbraid to speak sternly to (someone) because of some fault.

uphill going up; difficult, hard to do.

uphold to support, defend; to keep (something) going.

upholstery soft coverings for chairs etc.; the fixing of these to the furniture.

upkeep the cost of keeping something in good condition.

upon on, on top of.

upper higher.

uppermost in the highest place.

upright 1 standing straight up. 2 honest and trustworthy.

uprising a rebellion, revolt.

uproar a lot of loud noise and excitement.

uproarious noisy, especially with laughter.

uproot 1 to pull up by the roots. 2 to move (people) from their homes.

upset 1 to make (others) unhappy. 2 to turn over, to knock down.

upshot the final result, the conclusion.

upside-down the wrong way up.

upstart someone who rises from a lowly position and then treats others badly.

upstream in the direction opposite to the one in which a river flows.

uptight anxious, worried.

upwards up to a higher place.

upwind in the direction opposite to the one in which the wind is blowing.

uranium a heavy metal used in producing nuclear energy.

urban living in or belonging to a city or town.

urbane elegant of mind and manner, courteous.

urchin a small boy, especially a ragged or badly-behaved one.

urge *verb* to try to get (somebody) to do a certain thing.
noun a strong need or desire to do something.

urgent of great importance so that it needs to be done at once.

urn 1 a container for making tea in large quantities. 2 a kind of ornamental vase, especially one for holding the ashes of a dead person.

usage 1 the manner of using or treating (something). 2 common practice, especially in a language.

use *verb* [yooz] 1 to do something with. 2 to consume part or the whole of (something).

use *noun* [yoos] 1 what you do with something. 2 the benefit, gain.

useful of some use, helpful.

useless of no use, not useful.

usher *noun* a person who shows you to your seat, for example at a wedding or in a theatre.
verb to bring in.

usual often done; happening often.

usurer someone who practises usury.

usurp to seize power illegally from someone else.

usury the practice of lending money at very high rates of interest.

utensil a useful tool or container, especially in the kitchen.

utility usefulness.

utilise to use, make use of.

utmost 1 the most that is possible. 2 the greatest.

utopian desirable but not able to be put into practice, unrealistic.

utter *verb* to speak.
adjective complete.

utterance something spoken.

utterly completely.

U-turn (of a car etc.) a turn right round to face the way it came.

V

vacancy 1 emptiness. 2 an unfilled job.
vacant empty.
vacation a time when you are on holiday from work.
vaccinate to inoculate (someone), especially against smallpox.
vacillate to hesitate, waver, change your mind too often.
vacuous empty-headed, stupid.
vacuum 1 a space with no air in it. 2 **vacuum cleaner** a machine for lifting dirt out of carpets, for example. 3 **vacuum flask** a container for keeping liquids hot, usually.
vagabond a person who has no fixed home and wanders from one part of the country to another.
vagrant a person who wanders about from place to place without any home or job.
vague not certain or clear.
vain 1 too proud, conceited. 2 **in vain** uselessly.
valiant brave.
valid sound, acceptable for a purpose.
valley low ground between two hills or mountains.
valour bravery.
valuable worth a lot.
value the importance you put on something, its price.
valve an instrument to control a flow of water, air or electricity.
vampire 1 a kind of bat. 2 a spirit who is supposed to suck people's blood.
van 1 a covered lorry. 2 a railway coach for luggage and parcels.
vandal a person who deliberately destroys or damages other people's property.
vandalism being a vandal.

vanguard 1 the advancing front line of an army or navy. 2 those who are ahead in ideas or actions.
vanilla a sweet flavouring used in ice-cream, for example.
vanish to go out of sight, to disappear.
vanity love and admiration of yourself.
vanquish to overcome, defeat.
vapid (of speech etc.) flat, uninteresting.
vaporise to turn into vapour.
vapour liquid in the form of mist, steam or cloud.
variable able to change or to be changed.
variant (something) differing in form or composition from something else which has been named.
variation 1 change. 2 something that is slightly different from its type or kind.
variegated marked with irregular patterns of different colours.
variety 1 many different things mixed together. 2 a kind.
various different.
varnish a substance painted on a surface to make it shiny.
vary to be or make different, to change.
vase a container for holding flowers.
vassal (long ago) a person who had the use of land belonging to someone else, in return for certain services.
vast very large, of great size.
vat a large barrel for storing wine, oil etc.
vault *verb* to jump over something. *noun* 1 a vaulting jump. 2 an arched ceiling. 3 an underground room.
VDU *see* **visual display unit.**
veal meat from a calf.
veer to turn aside, change direction.

vegan someone who does not eat meat, fish or any animal products such as eggs, milk etc., a strict vegetarian.

vegetable a plant grown for food, for example carrot or cabbage.

vegetarian a person who does not eat meat and fish.

vegetation plant life.

vehement showing strong feelings.

vehicle something such as a cart, car or van used for carrying people or goods.

veil a thin covering for the face or head, usually to hide it.

vein one of the thin tubes which carry blood round the body to the heart.

vellum 1 a very fine, smooth writing-paper. 2 a fine parchment.

velocity speed.

velvet a kind of cloth which is soft and smooth on one side.

vendetta a fight between people or families which goes on for a very long time.

vending machine a machine from which things can be bought by putting coins in.

veneer a thin layer put on the surface of wood etc. to make it look better; an outer appearance which makes something seem better.

venerate to respect very highly.

venereal disease a disease passed on by sexual intercourse.

vengeance punishment given for harm done to you.

vengeful seeking revenge, vindictive.

venison meat from deer.

venom 1 poison from a snake. 2 great hate.

venomous 1 poisonous. 2 showing great hate.

vent 1 a hole or opening. 2 a slit made in the lower back of a jacket or coat. 3 **give vent to** give free expression to (feelings etc.).

ventilate to let fresh air into (a room, for example).

ventilator a device which helps to keep the air in a room etc. fresh.

ventriloquist a person who is skilled at making his voice sound as if it is coming from somewhere else.

venture a (risky) business undertaking.

veranda an open but roofed-over area attached to a house.

verb a word which says what someone or something does or is.

verbal 1 of or concerned with words. 2 spoken, not written.

verbalise to put (something) into words.

verbatim word for word, exactly as it was said.

verdant (in poetry) green and leafy, fresh-looking.

verdict what is decided, especially in a law court.

verge the edge of a road or path.

verify to show or prove the truth of.

veritable real, rightly, so called.

vermillion a bright-red colour.

vermin small harmful animals or insects.

vernacular (of or in) the language of a particular group within the population, local speech.

verruca [ve**roo**ka] a wartlike growth on the sole of your foot.

versatile able to do or be used for many different things.

verse 1 poetry. 2 part of a poem. 3 a small section from the Bible.

version one person's description of what has happened.

versus against (another team, for example).

vertebra one of the bones which make up the backbone.

vertebrate an animal with a backbone.

vertical straight up, standing upright, at right angles to the horizon.

vertigo dizziness, especially if caused by being in a high place.

verve enthusiasm, energy.

vespers prayers said at evening, an evening service.

vessel 1 a container for liquids. 2 a ship.

vest a garment worn next to the skin on the top part of the body.

vestibule the small room just inside the outer door of a house from which doors lead to the other rooms, a hall.

vestige the slightest trace of something.

vestment an official or religious garment worn on special occasions.

vestry a room in a church where the clergyman and choir put on their robes.

vet (short for **veterinary surgeon**) an animal doctor.

veteran 1 someone who has a lot of experience in something, especially an old soldier. 2 **veteran car** a very old car.

veto to stop something happening by using your authority.

vex to annoy, make angry or troubled.

via by way of.

viable able to be put into operation, able to live or exist.

viaduct a kind of long bridge carrying a road or railway over a valley, river etc.

vibrant full of life, thrilling; (of colour) strong, bright.

vibrate to shake, throb.

vicar (in the Church of England) a priest who is in charge of a church or a parish.

vicarious done by someone else but experienced by you through imagination.

vice 1 evil, badness. 2 a fixed tool which grips things to stop them from moving.

viceroy an official who represents the authority of a king or queen in a colony, province etc.

vice versa the other way round

vicinity the neighbourhood, the area round about.

vicious very bad, very wicked, savage.

vicious circle a chain of events which affect one another, eventually bringing the first one back.

vicissitude changes of fortune, usually for the worse.

victim a person who has suffered because of what other people have done to him or because of illness or an accident.

victor the winner of a fight or contest.

victorious successful.

victory defeating an enemy in battle or an opponent in a competition.

victuals [vittles] (old-fashioned) food and drink.

video 1 a film for showing on a television set. 2 a machine which records and plays back films and television programmes.

view 1 what you can see. 2 what you think about something.

vie with compete against.

vigilance careful watchfulness.

vigilant showing vigilance.

vigilante a member of a self-appointed body who try to keep order in a poorly organised community.

vignette [vin**yet**] 1 a small drawing, especially one at the beginning of a chapter in a book. 2 a short description, a character sketch.

vigorous strong, active.

vigour strength, energy, liveliness.

vile very unpleasant, evil.

vilify — visual display unit

vilify to speak badly of (someone) to attack the character of (someone).

villa a house with a garden in the country or in the suburbs; a house you rent for holidays.

village a number of houses grouped together, a small town.

villain a wicked person, a rascal.

villainous evil, wicked.

vindicate to clear (someone) of suspicion, to prove the innocence of (someone).

vine a plant on which grapes grow.

vinegar a sour liquid used for flavouring and for preserving food.

vineyard a place where grapes are grown to make wine.

vintage 1 (of wine) of high quality and produced in a particular year. 2 (of a car) made between 1916 and 1930. 3 of high quality, coming from the best time for its kind.

viola a musical instrument like a violin but slightly larger and lower in pitch.

violate 1 to break (the law). 2 to cause injury to the person or the privacy of (another).

violence 1 great force. 2 wild, hurtful behaviour.

violent showing violence.

violet 1 a tiny bluish-purple flower. 2 a bluish-purple colour.

violin a stringed musical instrument held under the chin and played with a bow.

violoncello the full name for **cello**.

viper a kind of small poisonous snake, an adder.

virago a fierce, bad-tempered, loud-voiced woman.

virgin *noun* a person, especially a woman, who has had no sexual intercourse. *adjective* fresh, clean, untouched, unchanged.

virginal *adjective* of or like a virgin. *noun* (long ago) a kind of small keyboard musical instrument.

virile (of a man) having great strength or energy.

virtual as good as, being so in everything but name.

virtually as good as, nearly.

virtue goodness.

virtuoso a brilliant performer, especially in music.

virtuous very good.

virulent 1 poisonous, violent. 2 bitter, malignant.

virus a very small living thing in the blood that may cause illness.

visa a mark on your passport which allows you to enter, pass through or leave a foreign country.

visage the face, the countenance.

viscera the internal organs, especially those in the lower part of the body, the guts.

viscous sticky, thick-flowing, like heavy oil.

visibility being visible; how far or how well you can see things.

visible able to be seen.

vision 1 sight. 2 something seen (as if) in a dream.

visit to call to see (someone or something).

visor 1 the movable part of a helmet covering the face or eyes. 2 the shade at the top of a car's windscreen to shield the driver's eyes from the sun.

vista a long narrow view, for example between a line of trees or houses.

visual to do with seeing or what can be seen.

visual display unit (*often called* **VDU**) a device like a television screen on which you can see what a computer is doing while you control it from the keyboard.

visualise to imagine that you can see (something).
vital necessary for life, very important.
vitality liveliness, energy.
vitamin one of a group of substances in food which the body needs to stay healthy.
vitiate to spoil, to make useless.
vitriol 1 acid. 2 sarcastic or hurtful speech.
vitriolic of or like vitriol.
vivacious lively, bright.
vivid bright and clear.
vivisection cutting up living animals for the purpose of scientific research.
vixen a female fox.
vocabulary the words used in speaking and writing.
vocal of the voice; produced by the voice, spoken.
vocal cords thin bands of muscle at the top of the windpipe; air vibrating through them produces sound.
vocalist a singer.
vocation a job or profession, especially one you have a strong desire to belong to.
vocational of jobs or trades.
vociferous loud, noisy.
vogue the fashion, what is popular at the time.
voice the sound made by the mouth when speaking or singing.
void 1 empty, vacant. 2 invalid, not binding, having no effect.
volatile 1 very changeable in mood, quick tempered. 2 (of a liquid) changing into gas easily.
volcano a mountain which throws out melting rock, hot ashes, steam and flames.
vole a kind of small short-tailed rat-like animal.
volition what you want to do for yourself, your own choice.

volley 1 a number of gunshots fired at the same time. 2 the return of a tennis ball, for example, before it has struck the ground.
volleyball a game in which a ball is played back and forward over a net by hand without letting it touch the ground.
volt a unit of force in electricity.
voltage an electrical force measured in volts.
voluble very talkative, talking without stopping.
volume 1 the space something fills. 2 a book. 3 how loud a sound is.
voluminous 1 (of writing) in too great a quantity. 2 (of clothes) having many loose layers.
voluntary done freely and openly.
volunteer a person who offers to do something.
voluptuous tending to cause (sexual) excitement, giving a great deal of pleasure to the senses.
vomit to be sick.
voodoo use of or belief in black magic, especially as practised in the West Indies.
voracious very greedy, eating or consuming large quantities.
vortex a mass of swirling water or air, a whirlpool or whirlwind.
vote to make a choice, to choose at an election.
vouch to answer for (something), to say that something is true.
voucher a piece of paper that can be exchanged for goods or services.
vow a solemn promise.
vowel the letter **a**, **e**, **i**, **o**, or **u**.
voyage a long journey, usually by sea.
vulgar rude, not polite.
vulnerable likely to be hurt, physically or in feelings.
vulture a large powerful bird which feeds mainly on dead animals.

W

wad a pad of soft material pressed together tightly.

waddle to walk awkwardly, like a duck, for example.

wade to walk through water.

wader a kind of long-legged bird that wades.

wafer a thin biscuit often eaten with ice cream.

waffle *verb* to talk a lot without saying much of importance. *noun* a kind of light cake cooked in a special iron implement.

waft to (cause to) move lightly and easily through the air, like smoke for example.

wag to move (something) from side to side.

wage money given for work done, often paid weekly.

wager a bet.

waggle to wag (unsteadily).

wagon, waggon 1 a cart to carry heavy loads. 2 a railway truck.

wagtail a kind of small bird with a long tail which it wags when it walks.

waif 1 a homeless person, especially a child. 2 an ownerless animal.

wail to cry in sorrow.

waist the middle of the body, just above the hips.

waistcoat a short sleeveless garment, usually worn under a jacket.

wait to stay in a place for a reason.

waiter a man who serves food in a restaurant or café.

waitress a woman who serves food in a restaurant or café.

waive to give up your right to something.

wake *verb* to stop sleeping. *noun* the foam made in the water behind a ship etc.

walk to move on the feet.

wall a barrier or part of a building usually made of bricks or stones.

wallaby a kind of small kangaroo.

wallet a small flat folder for money and cards, usually carried in the pocket.

wallflower a kind of sweet-smelling spring flower which grows near walls.

wallop to hit hard, to beat.

wallow to roll about in mud or water.

walnut 1 a kind of nut. 2 the tree it grows on; the wood is used for making furniture.

walrus a water animal like a large seal with two long tusks.

waltz a graceful dance for two people.

wan pale and ill-looking.

wand a thin, straight stick used by magicians.

wander to roam about.

wane to sink down, to become smaller or weaker.

wangle to make something happen by some form of deceit or dishonesty.

want to wish to have.

wanton 1 irresponsible, wild. 2 serving no purpose, pointless.

war fighting between countries or large groups of people.

warble to sing softly, as some birds do.

ward a room at a hospital with, usually, a lot of beds.

warden a person who looks after a building where people live or a game reserve, for example.

warder a man who looks after prisoners in a jail.

wardrobe a cupboard for storing clothes.

warehouse a large building where goods are stored.

wares articles that a person has for sale.

warfare fighting in a war.

warily with great care.

warlock a male witch.

warm fairly hot.

warmth being warm.

warn to tell beforehand of difficulty or danger.

warp to twist, bend, because of damp, for example.

warrant *noun* written authority to do something.
verb 1 to make to appear justified. 2 to guarantee.

warrior a fighter, a soldier.

wart a small hard lump on the skin.

wary very careful, cautious.

wash to clean using water.

wasp a black-and-yellow striped insect with a painful sting.

waspish bad-tempered, irritable.

waste *noun* useless things.
verb to spoil or use up carelessly.

watch *noun* a small clock, usually worn on the wrist.
verb 1 to look at carefully. 2 to guard.

watchman a man who looks after a place.

water the liquid that is found in rivers and in the sea and falls as rain.

waterfall a stream or river falling from a height.

water lily a kind of plant with large flowers which float on the surface of water.

waterproof made of material through which water cannot go.

watershed 1 the line in the hills from which streams flow in both directions. 2 a turning point, for example in history.

watt a unit of electrical power.

wattle 1 the loose flesh on the head or throat of a turkey etc. 2 thin and thick sticks woven together, especially to make fences.

wave *noun* 1 a higher part of the moving surface of water. 2 a curl in your hair.
verb to move the hand and arm from side to side.

waver to hesitate, to be undecided or unsteady.

wax *noun* a substance which melts easily, used to make candles, for example.
verb to grow bigger.

waxwork a figure made of wax, usually for public display.

way 1 how you do something or go somewhere. 2 a road or path.

waylay to lie in wait for, to ambush.

weak not strong.

weakling a weak person.

weal a raised mark made on the skin by the blow of a whip or cane, for example.

wealthy having a lot of money.

weapon something you use to fight or hunt.

wear 1 to have (clothes) on. 2 to become damaged by a lot of use.

weary very tired.

weasel a small furry animal with a long body which hunts birds, mice etc.

weather the kind of day it is, for example sunny, cold or wet.

weather-beaten hardened or lined by being out in all weathers.

weave to make cloth by twisting threads over and under each other.

web the thin net made by a spider to catch flies.

webbing strong closely-woven fabric used to support upholstery, for belts etc.

wedding when two people get married.

wedge a piece of wood etc. which is thinner at one end than the other.

weed *noun* a wild plant which grows where it is not wanted.
verb to dig out weeds.

week seven days.

weep to have tears in your eyes, to cry.

weigh 1 to measure how heavy something is. 2 to be a certain weight.

weight how heavy something is.

weighty 1 weighing a lot. 2 important, worthy of consideration.

weird very strange.

welcome to show you are happy because someone has come.

weld to join together (especially two pieces of metal by heat or pressure).

welfare happiness, good health.

well *noun* a deep hole holding water or oil.
adjective in good health.
adverb in a good way.

wellingtons long rubber boots.

welter a confused mixture.

werewolf a human being who is supposed to turn into a wolf at the time of the full moon.

west the direction where the sun sets.

western of, in or facing the west.

wet having a lot of liquid in or on it.

whack a sharp blow or the noise made by such a blow.

whale the largest sea animal.

whaling the trade of hunting and killing whales.

wharf a kind of platform at the edge of the sea or a river where ships can load and unload.

wheat a plant producing grain which is used to make flour etc.

wheel *noun* a ring of metal, plastic etc. which turns on its centre, for example on a car or bicycle.
verb to push something that has wheels.

wheeze to breathe hoarsely with a whistling noise.

whelk a small snail-like shellfish.

whelp *noun* the young of certain animals, dogs, wolves for example.
verb (of these animals) to give birth to young.

wherewithal the means to do something.

whet to sharpen (a knife etc.) by rubbing it on a stone.

whey the clear liquid left when sour milk solidifies.

whiff a puff of air, smoke or smell.

whimper to cry softly.

whimsical (of humour) unusual, quirky.

whine *noun* a long sad cry like the cry of a dog.
verb to complain a lot without good reason.

whinny *noun* the noise made by a horse.
verb to make this noise.

whip *noun* a piece of thin leather or cord on a handle, used for hitting things.
verb to beat.

whiplash 1 a blow from a whip. 2 *also* **whiplash injury** when the head is thrown forward and then back, as in a car crash.

whippet a kind of dog like a small greyhound.

whirl to spin round quickly.

whirlpool a circular motion in water which pulls things down to its centre.

whirlwind a very strong spinning wind.

whisk 1 to beat (eggs, for example) into froth. 2 to move with a sweeping movement.

whiskers hair on the face, for example the long stiff hair at the side of a cat's mouth.

whisky a kind of very strong drink made from grain.

whisper to speak very quietly.

whist a kind of card game for four people.

whist drive a social gathering at which people play whist.

whistle 1 a high shrill note made by blowing through the lips and teeth. 2 an instrument for making a high note.

white 1 the colour of clean snow. 2 the part of an egg round the yolk.

whitewash 1 a substance used to whiten walls, fences etc. 2 (in politics etc.) a cover-up.

whiting a kind of small seafish used as food.

whittle to cut strips off (wood) with a knife.

whiz to move very quickly (with a hissing sound).

whole complete, with nothing missing.

wholesale buying and selling in large quantities, usually to shops.

wholesome healthy, good for your health.

wholly completely, totally.

whoop to make loud cries of excitement.

whooping cough a disease which gives you a cough with a long breath at the end.

whorl anything shaped like a coil, for example a human fingerprint.

wick the string which burns in candles and oil-lamps.

wicked very bad, evil.

wickerwork twigs, reeds etc. plaited into baskets, chairs etc.

wicket the three stumps at cricket.

wide not narrow, broad.

widow a woman whose husband is dead.

widower a man whose wife is dead.

width how wide something is.

wield to hold ready for use.

wife a married woman.

wig false hair to cover the head.

wiggle to move with jerky, movements from side to side.

wigwam a North American Indian tent.

wild 1 not tame, fierce. 2 not looked after by people. 3 out of control.

wilderness a wild place where few plants grow and no one lives.

wildfire: like wildfire spreading very rapidly, for example of a rumour.

wildfowl any bird that is hunted in the wild, for example duck, pigeon.

wiles tricks, especially used to deceive someone.

will 1 a written piece of paper saying who is to have a person's belongings when they are dead. 2 the power to choose what you want to do.

will o' the wisp a moving light sometimes seen on marshy ground.

willow a kind of tree with thin drooping branches.

wilt to droop, to become weaker.

wily crafty, cunning.

win to be first or do best in a competition, race or fight.

wince to show fear, pain etc. by giving a slight start.

winch a handle for turning a wheel; a device for pulling or lifting by a rope wound round a wheel.

wind [rhymes with 'pinned'] quickly-moving air.

wind [rhymes with 'mind'] to turn round and round.

windlass a machine for raising weights by using a rope or chain wound round a barrel or post.

windmill — wood

windmill a building with a machine which is turned by the wind.

window an opening in the wall of a building to let light in.

windowsill the flat piece of wood or stone on which a window frame rests.

windpipe the passage which carries air from the mouth and nose to the lungs.

windsock a stocking-like cone of material that fills with wind and shows the direction in which it is blowing.

windsurfing the sport of riding on sailboards.

wine a strong drink made from the juice of crushed fruit, usually grapes.

wing 1 one of the two parts of a bird or insect, used for flying. 2 a part of an aeroplane which keeps it in the air.

wink to shut and open one eye.

winsome charming, attractive.

winter the coldest season of the year, between autumn and spring.

wipe to dry or clean with a cloth.

wire thin metal thread.

wireless radio; a radio set.

wiry tough, strong.

wisdom being wise.

wise showing good sense, clever, understanding a lot.

wish 1 to want very much, especially something you are unlikely to get. 2 what you wish for.

wishbone the V-shaped bone above the breastbone in a chicken etc.

wisp a small twisted piece of hair, straw, smoke etc.

wispy (of hair) growing in wisps.

wit cleverness, quickness of mind.

witch a woman who is supposed to have magic powers.

witchcraft using magic for evil purposes.

withdraw 1 to go away (from), to leave. 2 to take back (something you have said or given).

wither especially of plants, to become smaller, drier and paler.

withers where a horse's neck joins the shoulder blades.

withhold to keep back.

withstand to oppose or endure successfully.

witness a person who sees something happen.

witness box the place in a law court where a witness stands to give evidence.

witticism a witty remark.

witty humorous, funny in a clever way.

wizard a man who is supposed to have magic powers.

wizened wrinkled, shrivelled.

wobble to move unsteadily from one side to the other.

woe misery, great sadness.

woebegone sorrowful or sad in appearance.

woeful 1 sad-looking. 2 terrible, pitiful.

wolf a kind of wild animal like a large dog.

woman an adult female person.

womb the part of a woman or female animal in which a baby grows before it is born.

wombat a kind of small bearlike Australian animal with a pouch for its young.

wonder 1 to be surprised at. 2 to want to know.

wonderful very good or pleasant, amazing.

wonderment great surprise, awe.

woo (*old-fashioned*) to seek as a wife.

wood 1 a lot of trees growing together. 2 the material which trees are made of.

woodpecker a bird which pecks holes in the bark of trees to find insects.

woodwind wind instruments in an orchestra which are, or were originally, made of wood.

wool 1 the short curly hair on the backs of sheep and lambs. 2 thread made from this, used in weaving, knitting etc.

woolgathering daydreaming.

woollen made of wool.

woolly 1 of or like wool. 2 (of ideas etc.) not clearly thought out.

word 1 letters together which mean something when spoken or read. 2 a solemn promise.

word processor a small computer on which you can type, and which can store and organise what is typed.

work something you do, especially for payment.

workload the amount of work set to be done in a specified period of time.

world the earth; all human beings together.

worm a long thin animal with a soft body that lives in soil.

worn when something has been used so much that it is of little further use.

worry to feel anxious or troubled.

worse not as good as, less well.

worship 1 respect paid to God, especially in a religious service. 2 **Your Worship** a title given out of respect to a lord mayor etc.

worsted a kind of fine woollen thread; cloth made from it.

worth value.

wound an injury where the skin is cut.

wrangle a noisy quarrel, a brawl.

wrap to put a covering closely round (something).

wrapper the cover, of paper or plastic usually, in which something is wrapped.

wrath anger, rage.

wreak to cause (great trouble in or to).

wreath a ring of leaves or flowers specially made.

wreathe to encircle, drift round (as smoke, for example).

wreck to smash up completely.

wren a kind of very small brown bird.

wrest to take by force.

wrestle to struggle with a person and try to throw him to the ground, sometimes as a sport.

wretch a miserable or unlikeable person.

wretched 1 very miserable and unhappy. 2 unlikeable, annoying.

wriggle to twist the body about.

wring to twist and squeeze (something) tightly to get water out.

wrinkle a line or crease on the skin or in material.

wrist the joint between the hand and the arm.

writ a legal document ordering a person to do or to stop doing something.

write to put words or letters on paper, for example, so that they can be read and understood.

writhe to roll or twist about, especially in pain.

wrong not right, not correct.

wry 1 (of a smile etc.) twisted or mocking. 2 drily humorous.

X

Xerox [**zee**rox] *noun* 1 trade name for a machine for making photocopies. 2 a photocopy.
verb to make a photocopy of.

X-ray a special photograph of the inside of something, for example your body.

xylophone [**zylo**-phone] a musical instrument played by hitting bars of wood with a small hammer.

Y

yacht a light sailing boat, often used for racing.

yak a kind of long-haired ox of Central Asia.

yam a potato-like vegetable of tropical countries.

yank to pull with a sudden jerk.

yap to bark like a small dog.

yard 1 a measure of length equal to just under a metre. 2 a piece of ground next to a building with a fence or wall around it.

yarn 1 thread, especially for weaving into cloth. 2 a story, especially a long or untrue one.

yawn to open the mouth and breathe in and out deeply, especially when tired.

year a period of time equal to twelve months; the time that the earth takes to go once round the sun.

yearling an animal, especially a horse, that is more than one year old and less than two.

yearn to long (for something).

yeast a substance used in baking bread to make the dough rise.

yell to shout very loudly.

yellow the colour of the yolk of an egg or a lemon.

yelp a sharp bark, a cry of pain.

yesterday the day before today.

yet 1 until now. 2 still.

yew an evergreen tree with red berries.

yield 1 to give way; to give in. 2 to produce fruit or crops.

yodel to sing with frequent changes of voice, heard especially in the Alps.

yoga an Eastern form of religious meditation, often using special exercises; these exercises.

yoghurt a sour food made from milk, often flavoured with fruit.

yoke a piece of wood put across the necks of cattle for pulling carts etc.

yolk the yellow centre part of an egg.

yonder over there, in the direction in which I am pointing.

young not old.

youth 1 the time when you are young. 2 a young man.

yucca a kind of American plant with tough pointed leaves, often used as a houseplant.

Yuletide Christmas time.

Z

zeal enthusiasm, keenness.

zealot a fanatic, a very enthusiastic follower of a religion for example.

zealous full of zeal.

zebra an African animal like a small horse with black and white stripes.

zenith the highest point, time or place of (something's) prosperity.

zephyr (in poetry) a soft gentle breeze.

zero the number 0, nothing.

zest eager enjoyment.

zigzag to move sharply to one side and then to the other.

zinc a whitish metal.

zip a sliding fastener used on clothes.

zither a flat many-stringed musical instrument, played with the fingers.

zodiac an imaginary section of the sky, divided into twelve parts, each with a special sign, used in astrology.

zone a district, an area.

zoo a place where wild animals are kept so that people can look at them.

zoology the study of animals.

Abbreviations

AA	Automobile Association; Alcoholics Anonymous.
AB	Able-Seaman.
a/c	account.
AC	alternating current.
ad (*informal*)	advertisement.
AD	Anno Domini, in the year of our Lord.
adj.	adjective.
Adm.	Admiral.
admin.	administration.
adv.	adverb.
AEU	Amalgamated Engineering Union.
AI	Artificial Insemination.
AID	Artificial Insemination by Donor.
AIDS	Acquired Immune Deficiency Syndrome.
a.m.	before noon, ante meridiem.
amp	ampere.
anon	anonymous.
appro	approval.
Apr.	April.
ASA	Amateur Swimming Association.
Asscn, Assoc.	Association.
Asst.	Assistant.
ATC	Air Training Corps.
Aug.	August.
AWOL	absent without leave.
b.	born; (in cricket) bowled by.
B & B or b. & b.	bed and breakfast.
BA	Bachelor of Arts; British Airways.
Bart.	Baronet.
BBC	British Broadcasting Corporation.
BC	before Christ; British Columbia.
BD	Bachelor of Divinity.
BDS	Bachelor of Dental Surgery.
B.Ed.	Bachelor of Education.
BEM	British Empire Medal.
b/f	(in book-keeping) brought forward.
BMA	British Medical Association.
B.Mus.	Bachelor of Music.
BO	body odour.
BP	British Petroleum; British Pharmacopoeia; Be Prepared.
Br.	Britain, British; Brother.
BR	British Rail.
Brig.	Brigadier.
Brit.	Britain, British.
Bros.	Brothers (especially in the title of a firm).
BS	British Standard(s).
B.Sc.	Bachelor of Science.
BSI	British Standards Institution.
BST	British Summer Time; British Standard Time.
Bt.	Baronet.
BT	British Telecom.
c	cent(s); (in cricket) caught; circa, about (used in front of a date, for example); century.
c or cu.	cubic.
C	(in temperature) Celsius, Centigrade.
©	symbol for copyright.
CAA	Civil Aviation Authority.
CAB	Citizen's Advice Bureau.
Cal	Calorie.
c & b	(in cricket) caught and bowled.
C & W	Country and Western.
cap.	capital; capital letter.
Capt.	Captain.
Card.	Cardinal (RC Church).
Cath.	cathedral; Catholic.
CB	citizen's band (radio); Companion of the Order of the Bath.
CBE	Commander of the British Empire.
CBI	Confederation of British Industry.
cc	cubic centimetre; carbon copy.
CC	County Council; City Council; Cricket Club.
CD	compact disk.
Cdr.	Commander.
CE	Church of England.
CET	Central European Time.
c/f	(in book-keeping) carried forward.
cg.	centigram(s).
ch.	chapter; (in chess) check; church.
CH	Companion of Honour.
chem	chemistry, chemical.
CIA	Central Intelligence Agency.
CID	Criminal Investigation Department.
CIGS	Chief of the Imperial General Staff.

C.-in-C.	Commander in Chief.	DSS	Department of Social Security.
cl., cl.	centilitre(s).	DTI	Department of Trade and Industry.
Cllr.	Councillor.	DV	Deo Volente, God willing.
cm.	centimetre(s).	E	East(ern).
Cmdr.	Commander.	ea.	each.
CND	Campaign for Nuclear Disarmament.	ed.	editor; edition; educated.
Co	company, business organisation; county.	EEC	European Economic Community.
CO	Commanding Officer.	ENE	East-North-East.
c/o	(in addresses) care of; (in book-keeping) carried over.	ER	Elizabetha Regina, Queen Elizabeth.
		ESE	East-South-East.
COD	Cash on Delivery.	esp.	especially.
C. of E.	Church of England.	ESP	extrasensory perception.
col.	column.	Esq.	Esquire (sometimes used in letters after a man's name).
Col.	Colonel.		
Con.	Conservative.	etc.	et cetera, and so forth.
conj.	conjunction.	Eur	Europe.
cons.	consonant.	f	female; feminine; (in music) forte, loud.
Cpl.	Corporal.		
CPO	Chief Petty Officer.	F	Fahrenheit.
CPU	(in computing) Central Processing Unit.	FA	Football Association.
		FBI	(in USA) Federal Bureau of Investigation.
cr.	credit; creditor.		
Cres.	Crescent.	FC	Football Club.
CSE	Certificate of Secondary Education.	FCO	Foreign and Commonwealth Office.
CSM	Company Sergeant-Major.	Feb.	February.
cu.	cubic.	fem.	feminine.
cwt.	hundredweight.	ff	(in music) fortissimo, very loud.
d.	died; daughter; depth.	FIFA	International Football Federation.
DC	direct current; (in USA) District of Columbia.	FM	Field Marshal; frequency modulation.
		FO	Foreign Office.
DCM	Distinguished Conduct Medal.	FP	former pupil; freezing point.
dd	delivered.	Fr.	Father; French.
DD	Doctor of Divinity.	Fri.	Friday.
Dec.	December.	ft.	foot, feet.
DES	Department of Education and Science.	Ft.	Fort.
DG	Deo Gratias, by the Grace of God.	g.	gram(s).
Dip.	Diploma.	gal.	gallon(s).
Dip.Ed.	Diploma in Education.	GB	Great Britain.
DIY	do-it-yourself.	GBH	grievous bodily harm.
DJ	disc jockey; dinner-jacket.	GC	George Cross.
D.Litt.	Doctor of Letters; Doctor of Literature.	GCSE	General Certificate of Secondary Education.
DMA	(in computing) Direct Memory Access.	Gdn(s)	(in street names) Garden(s).
D.Mus.	Doctor of Music.	GHQ	General Headquarters.
DOA	dead on arrival.	GI	US Private soldier.
DoE	Department of the Environment.	gm.	gram(s).
Dr	Doctor; (in street names) Drive.	GMT	Greenwich Mean Time.
D.Sc.	Doctor of Science.	GNP	Gross National Product.
DSM	Distinguished Service Medal.	Gov.	Governor; Government.

Govt.	Government.	Knt.	Knight.
GP	General Practitioner (doctor).	KO	knockout; kick-off.
GPO	General Post Office.	Kt.	Knight.
hf.	half.	kW	kilowatt(s).
HGV	Heavy Goods Vehicle.	ℓ	litre(s).
HM	Her Majesty('s).	l	litre(s); line; left; length.
HMG	Her Majesty's Government.	L	Lake.
HMI	Her Majesty's Inspector of Schools.	Lab.	Labour.
HMSO	Her Majesty's Stationery Office.	lat.	latitude.
HNC	Higher National Certificate.	lb.	pound(s).
Hon.	Honorary; Honourable.	l.b.w.	(in cricket) leg before wicket.
Hons.	Honours.	Ld.	Lord.
Hon. Sec.	Honorary Secretary.	LDS	Licentiate in Dental Surgery.
h.p.	horsepower.	LLB	Bachelor of Laws.
HP	hire purchase.	LLD	Doctor of Laws.
hr(s).	hour(s).	long.	longitude.
ht.	height.	Lt.	Lieutenant.
I(s)	Island(s), Isle(s).	LTA	Lawn Tennis Association.
IBA	Independent Broadcasting Authority.	Ltd.	Limited.
IBM	International Business Machines.	m	male; masculine; married; (in cricket) maiden (over); metre(s); minute(s); mile(s).
ICBM	intercontinental ballistic missile.		
ICI	Imperial Chemical Industries.		
ID	identification.	MA	Master of Arts.
IHS	Jesus.	Mar.	March.
IMF	International Monetary Fund.	masc.	masculine.
in.	inch(es).	max.	maximum.
IOU	I Owe You.	MB	Bachelor of Medicine; (in computing) megabyte.
IOW	Isle of Wight.		
IQ	Intelligence Quotient.	MBE	Member of the Order of the British Empire.
IRA	Irish Republic Army.		
i.t.a.	Initial Teaching Alphabet.	MC	Master of Ceremonies; Military Cross.
ITV	Independent Television.	MCC	Marylebone Cricket Club.
Jan.	January.	M.Ed.	Master of Education.
Jnr.	Junior.	memo	memorandum.
JP	Justice of the Peace.	MEP	Member of the European Parliament.
Jr.	Junior.	min.	minute(s); minimum.
jt.	joint.	mg.	milligram(s).
Jul.	July.	Mgr.	Monsignor; manager.
Jun.	June; Junior.	mℓ.	millilitre(s).
K	King('s); one thousand; (in computing) 1024 bytes or bits.	ml.	millilitre(s); mile(s).
		mm.	millimetre(s).
KG	Knight of the Order of the Garter.	MM	Military Medal.
KGB	USSR secret police.	MN	Merchant Navy.
kg.	kilogram(s).	MO	Medical Officer; money order.
KKK	(in USA) Ku-Klux-Klan.	Mon.	Monday.
kℓ., kl.	kilolitre(s).	MP	Member of Parliament; military police
km.	kilometre(s).	m.p.g.	miles per gallon.
		m.p.h.	miles per hour.
		Mr	mister, title of a man.

Mrs	title of married woman.	op. cit.	in the work already quoted.
Ms	title of woman either married or not.	OPEC	Organisation of Petroleum Exporting Countries.
MS	manuscript; multiple sclerosis.		
M.Sc.	Master of Science.	OS	Ordnance Survey; outside.
mt.	Mount(ain).	OT	Old Testament.
		OU	Open University; Oxford University.
n	name; noon; noun; neuter.	OUP	Oxford University Press.
N	North(ern).	oz	ounce(s).
n/a	not applicable; not available.		
NALGO	National and Local Government Officers' Association.	p	page; penny; (in music) piano, softly.
		P	parking.
NASA	(in USA) National Aeronautics and Space Administration.	p.a.	per annum.
		PA	Public Address (system); personal assistant.
Nat.	National; Nationalist.		
NATO	North Atlantic Treaty Organisation.	p. & p.	post and package.
NE	North-East(ern).	PAYE	pay-as-you-earn.
NF	National Front.	p.c.	per cent; postcard.
NFU	National Farmers' Union.	PC	Police Constable; Privy Counsellor; personal computer.
NHS	National Health Service.		
NI	National Insurance; Northern Ireland.	pd	paid.
NNE	North-North-East.	PE	Physical Education.
NNW	North-North-West.	Ph.D.	Doctor of Philosophy.
n.o.	(in cricket) not out.	pl.	plural.
No.	number; North.	PLO	Palestine Liberation Organisation.
Nov.	November.	p.m.	afternoon, post meridiem.
nr.	near.	PM	Prime Minister; post-mortem, examination after death.
NSPCC	National Society for the Prevention of Cruelty to Children.	POW	prisoner of war.
NT	New Testament.	pp	pages; (in music) pianissimo, very softly.
NUJ	National Union of Journalists.		
NUM	National Union of Mineworkers.	prep.	preposition.
NUPE	National Union of Public Employees.	Pres.	President.
NUR	National Union of Railwaymen.	Prof.	Professor.
NUS	National Union of Students; National Union of Seamen.	pron.	pronoun.
		PS	postscript, addition to letter.
NUT	National Union of Teachers.	pt.	pint(s).
NW	North-West(ern).	PT	physical training.
NY	New York.	PTA	parent-teacher association.
NZ	New Zealand.	Pte.	Private (soldier).
		QC	Queen's Counsel.
o	naught, nought, zero.	QED	Quod Erat Demonstrandum, which was to be demonstrated.
OAP	Old Age Pensioner.		
OB	Outside Broadcast.	QM	quartermaster.
OBE	Officer of the Order of the British Empire.	qt.	quart(s).
		q.t.	(on the) quiet.
OC	Officer Commanding.		
Oct.	October.	r	right.
OD	overdose.	RAC	Royal Automobile Club.
OED	Oxford English Dictionary.	RAF	Royal Air Force.
OK (*informal*)	all right.	R and A	Royal and Ancient (Golf Club).

RC	Roman Catholic.	TA	Territorial Army.
RCMP	Royal Canadian Mounted Police.	TB	tuberculosis.
RFC	Rugby Football Club.	tbsp.	(in cookery) tablespoon.
RIBA	Royal Institute of British Architects.	Ter.	Terrace.
RIP	rest in peace.	Thurs.	Thursday.
RL	Rugby League.	TU	Trade Union.
rm.	room.	TUC	Trades Union Congress.
RN	Royal Navy.	Tues.	Tuesday.
RNLI	Royal National Lifeboat Institution.		
r.p.m.	revolutions per minute.	UDA	Ulster Defence Association.
RSC	Royal Shakespeare Company.	UDR	Ulster Defence Regiment.
RSM	Regimental Sergeant-Major.	UFO	Unidentified Flying Object.
RSPCA	Royal Society for the Prevention of Cruelty to Animals.	UHF	ultra-high frequency.
		UK	United Kingdom.
RSVP	(on an invitation) please answer (répondez s'il vous plaît).	UN	United Nations.
		UNESCO	United Nations Educational, Scientific and Cultural Organisation.
rt.	right.		
RU	Rugby Union.	UNICEF	United Nations (International) Children's (Emergency) Fund.
RUC	Royal Ulster Constabulary.		
		UNO	United Nations Organisation.
s.	second(s); singular; son; shilling(s).	UNRWA	United Nations Relief and Works Agency.
S	South(ern); Saint.		
s.a.e.	stamped addressed envelope.	US, USA	United States (of America).
SALT	Strategic Arms Limitation Talks.	USSR	Union of Soviet Socialist Republics.
SAM	surface-to-air-missile.		
SAS	Special Air Services; Scandinavian Airlines System.	v	verse; very; volume; versus; verb.
		V and A	Victoria and Albert (Museum).
Sat.	Saturday.	VAT	value added tax.
SAYE	save-as-you-earn.	vb.	verb.
SE	South-East(ern).	VC	Victoria Cross.
sec.	second(s).	VD	venereal disease.
Sec.	Secretary.	VDU	(in computing) visual display unit.
Sept.	September.	VG	very good.
SF	science fiction.	VIP	Very Important Person.
SFA	Scottish Football Association.	viz.	namely, videlicet.
sgd.	signed.	vs.	versus.
Sgt.	Sergeant.	v.s.	vide supra, see above.
SJ	Society of Jesus, Jesuits.	VTOL	Vertical Take-off and Landing (vehicle).
SNP	Scottish National Party.		
SOS	save our souls, urgent appeal for help.		
SP	Starting Price.	w	weight; week; width; wife; (in cricket) wide, wicket.
sq.	square.		
SRN	State Registered Nurse.	W	West(ern).
SSE	South-South-East.	WASP	White Anglo-Saxon Protestant (of the group considered dominant in the United States).
SSW	South-South-West.		
st.	(in cricket) stumped; stone(s).		
St.	Saint; Street.	WC	water closet, toilet.
Sun.	Sunday.	WEA	Workers' Educational Association.
SW	South-West(ern).	Wed.	Wednesday.
		WHO	World Health Organisation.

wk.	week(s).	y	yard; year.
wkly	weekly.	yd.	yard(s).
WNW	West-North-West.	YMCA	Young Men's Christian Association.
WPC	woman police constable.	yr.	year(s); younger; your.
WRVS	Women's Royal Voluntary Service.	YWCA	Young Women's Christian Association.
WSW	West-South-West.	z	zero.

Measures

Metric

Length

10 millimetres (mm)	= 1 centimetre (cm)
100 centimetres	= 1 metre (m)
1000 metres	= 1 kilometre (km)
(1 metre	= 39.37 inches (in))

Mass and Weight

10 milligrams (mg)	= 1 centigram (cg)
100 centigrams	= 1 gram (g)
1000 grams	= 1 kilogram (kg)
1000 kilograms	= 1 tonne (t)
(1 kilogram	= 2.205 pounds (lb))

Capacity

10 millilitres (ml)	= 1 centilitre (cl)
100 centilitres	= 1 litre (l)
1000 litres	= 1 kilolitre (kl)
1000 millilitres	= 1 litre
(1 litre	= 1.7606 pints)

Volume

1000 cubic millimetres (mm^3)	= 1 cubic centimetre (cm^3)
1 000 000 cubic centimetres	= 1 cubic metre (m^3)
(1 cubic metre	= 1.308 cubic yards (yd^3))

Imperial

Length

12 inches (in)	= 1 foot (ft)
3 feet	= 1 yard (yd)
1760 yards	= 1 mile
(1 yard	= 0.9144 metres (m))

Mass and Weight

16 ounces (oz)	= 1 pound (lb)
14 pounds	= 1 stone (st)
8 stones	= 1 hundredweight (cwt)
20 hundredweight	= 1 long ton
2000 pounds	= 1 short ton
(1 pound	= 0.4536 kilograms (kg))

Capacity

4 gills	= 1 pint
8 pints	= 1 gallon (gal)
(1 pint	= 0.5683 litres (l))

Volume

1728 cubic inches (in^3)	= 1 cubic foot (ft^3)
27 cubic feet	= 1 cubic yard (yd^3)
(1 cubic yard	= 0.7646 cubic metres (m^3))